black

women

film and

video artists

edited by

jacqueline bobo

routledge
new york and london

Published in 1998 by

Routledge
29 West 35th Street
New York, NY 10001

Published in Great Britain by

Routledge
11 New Fetter Lane
London EC4P 4EE

Printed in the United States of America
Typography: Jack Donner

The author gratefully acknowledges the permission to reprint the following:
"The Ties That Bind: Cinematic Representations by Black Women Filmmakers," by Gloria J. Gibson-Hudson, *Quarterly Review of Film and Video*, Volume
15 #2 (1994), pp. 25–44. Reprinted by permission of the publisher.

Cover art "From the Story of MOM" (1986), by Camille Billops. Reprinted by
permission of the artist. Copyright by the artist.

Library of Congress Cataloging-in-Publication Data

Black women film and video artists / edited by Jacqueline Bobo.
  p.   cm. — (AFI film readers)
  ISBN 0–415–92041–8. — ISBN 0–415–92042–6 (pbk.)
    1. Afro-American women motion picture producers and directors.
I. Bobo, Jacqueline.   II. Series.
PN 1998.2.B57   1998
791.43'023'08996073—dc20
                                                    97–32062
                                                    CIP

contents

list of contributors   vii

preface   xi
Jacqueline Bobo

part one: critical perspectives

1. **Black Women's Films: Genesis of a Tradition**   3
   Jacqueline Bobo

2. **Women Directors of the Los Angeles School**   21
   Ntongela Masilela

3. **The Ties That Bind: Cinematic Representations by Black Women Filmmakers**   43
   Gloria J. Gibson-Hudson

4. **The Functional Family of Camille Billops**   67
   Monique Guillory

part two: critical practice

5. **Carol Munday Lawrence: Producer, Director, Writer**   93
   Carol Munday Lawrence

6. **How Deep, How Wide? Perspectives on the Making of *The Massachusetts 54th Colored Infantry***   109
   Jacqueline Shearer

7. **Fired-Up!**   125
   O. Funmilayo Makarah

8. **Love on My Mind: Creating Black Women's Love Stories**   139
   Carmen Coustaut

9. **Below the Line: (Re)Calibrating the Filmic Gaze**   153
   C. A. Griffith

part three: in their own words

10. Michelle Parkerson: A Visionary Risk Taker   177
     Gloria J. Gibson

11. An Intimate Talk with Ntozake Shange: An Interview   189
     P. Jane Splawn

     Suggested Course Design: 207
        Black Women Film and Video Artists

     Selected Video/Filmography: 217
        Black Women Video/Filmmakers

     Directory of Distributors   225

     Selected Bibliography   229

list of

contributors

Jacqueline Bobo is Associate Professor in the Women's Studies Program at the University of California, Santa Barbara, where she teaches courses on Black women filmmakers, women's film narratives, and representation and social activism. She is the author of *Black Women as Cultural Readers* (1995), and has published extensively in journals such as *Screen, Wide Angle, Callaloo, African American Review,* and chapters in the books *Female Spectators: Looking at Film and Television, Black Popular Culture,* and *Black American Cinema.*

Carmen Coustaut is Associate Professor in the Department of Theatre at the University of Maryland, College Park. She is also an independent filmmaker whose two short dramatic films, *Justifiable Homicide* and *Extra Change,* have won numerous awards. Her three feature-length screenplays focus on romantic love: *Harmonica Man, Round Table Discussion,* and *Listen to the Wind.* As a Fulbright Scholar, Carmen Coustaut conducted research in Mali and Senegal.

Gloria J. Gibson is Associate Professor of Afro-American Studies at Indiana University and Assistant Director of the Black Film Center/Archives and Director of the Archive of Traditional Black Music. She has published numerous articles about Black cinema and Black women's cinema. Gloria Gibson was the first African American elected to the Society for Cinema Studies Executive Council. Her forthcoming book, *Moving Tableaux of Consciousness: The Films and Videos of Black Women*, will examine the impact of Black women's cinema throughout the African Diaspora.

C. A. Grfffith is a film/videomaker and writer whose credits include *A Litany for Survival: The Life and Work of Audre Lorde, Juice, Eyes on the Prize*, and *The Angela Davis Project* (a work in progress). She is currently a Five Colleges Visiting Assistant Professor, where she teaches film and video production at Smith College and the University of Massachusetts, Amherst.

Monique Guillory received her Ph.D. in Comparative Literature from New York University and is currently a University of California President's Postdoctoral Fellow. She is coeditor of *Soul: Black Power, Politics and Pleasure* and is the author of "Under One Roof: The Sins and Sanctity of the Bourbon Orleans Hotel," in *Race Consciousness: African American Studies for the New Century*.

Carol Munday Lawrence has written and produced over twenty-five award-winning documentaries, dramas, animations, and variety specials. She became the first Black woman independent to produce a national television series when her program *Were You There* aired on public broadcasting. Her work in feature films includes Francis Coppola's *The Cotton Club* and Charles Burnett's *To Sleep with Anger*. She has received the CINE Golden Eagle and numerous festival awards. Carol Munday Lawrence serves on the boards of the Independent Feature Project and the International Documentary Association, and chairs the Committee of Black Writers of the Writers' Guild of America.

O.Funmilayo Makarah is a film/videomaker, installation artist, and educator from Los Angeles. Her award-winning work has been screened throughout the United States and in Canada and Europe. She holds a B.A. from Smith College, an M.F.A. in Film and Television Production from UCLA, and an M.A. in Visual and Cultural Studies from the University of Rochester.

Ntongela Masilela is Associate Professor of English and World Literature at Pitzer College in Claremont, California. He has previously published in *Black American Cinema* (edited by Manthia Diawara) and is the editor of the forthcoming volume *United States and South Africa: The Historical Field of Social and Cultural Interaction*.

Jacqueline Shearer produced and directed the 1977 landmark film *A Minor Altercation*, one of the first to be directed by a Black woman. She produced/directed "The Promised Land" and "The Keys to the Kingdom" for the PBS series *Eyes on the Prize II*, and produced, directed, and cowrote *The Massachusetts 54th Colored Infantry*, a segment of the PBS series *The American Experience*. Shearer was also past president and board chairperson of ITVS (Independent Television Service), an organization that awards grants to independent television producers. Jacqueline Shearer died on November 26, 1993.

P. Jane Splawn is currently a Fellow at the Center for Afro-American and African Studies at the University of Michigan. She has taught at Purdue University and Indiana University and has published articles on African American drama and literature in *Modern Drama, Modern Fiction Studies,* and *CLA Journal*. Currently, she is completing a book on contemporary Black women's drama and ritual.

preface

This collection of original essays (and one reprinted article) about Black women film and video artists was initially started in 1991 on a broader topic—Black feminist cultural criticism—with different contributors than presently make up the volume. Over time, withstanding a confluence of circumstances, the project continued in development with its current publisher, with the content devoted exclusively to Black women film videomakers. A significant element is that the makers form a valuable component of the volume. In addition to the critical and historical articles, Black women film and video artists discuss their works, providing indispensable information about their production backgrounds, and media training.

Information about Black women's formal training is important because their works are, many times, perceived as small, anomalous works of interest to a small circle of intimate friends. On the contrary, Black women have earned Master of Fine Arts degrees from prestigious graduate film and television programs—such as Columbia, UCLA, USC, Chicago Institute of the Arts, Northwestern—and many have undergraduate degrees from NYU, Howard, Temple, and San Francisco State University. Thus, Black women's works demonstrate the makers' thorough understanding of cinema and media history, theory, and criticism, which is reflected in the exemplary quality of their films and videos. The women have produced long-form narratives as well as complex innovations with a variety of forms. The subject matter is also diverse and significant and is concerned with such vital issues as cultural politics, domestic relations, sexuality, Black women's relationship to concepts of physical beauty (including hairstyles and color consciousness) and portraits of cultural, social, and political activists, among other topics.

The book is divided into three sections: "Critical Perspectives," "Critical Practice," and "In Their Own Words." The first section presents a historical overview of the early works of Black women filmmakers. In the first article, "Black Women's Films: Genesis of a Tradition," I situate the films of the 1970s and the early 1980s, in conjunction with those from the first decades of the century, as forming a foundation of socially conscious content that was taken up by later filmmakers. Using the archival research of Pearl Bowser and Gloria J. Gibson-Hudson on women at the turn of the century who were involved in filmmaking, I establish that Black women filmmakers have been productive throughout the twentieth-century. Contemporary films that are more accessible and thus have more of an impact, which are examined in the article, include those directed by Madeline Anderson, Monica Freeman, Kathleen Collins, Joanne Grant, and Michelle Parkerson.

Ntongela Masilela, in "Women Directors of the Los Angeles School," contrasts these artists with the Black male filmmakers who were mainly concerned with documentary production on the East Coast in the 1960s, 1970s, and early 1980s. According to Masilela, the West Coast women were in the vanguard of production, using innovative techniques and concepts to move beyond documentary toward the far-reaching potential of narrative and experimental film and video production. He analyzes in depth the works of Julie Dash, Alile Sharon Larkin, Barbara McCullough, and Carroll Parrott Blue. Even though Blue works mainly in documentary, Masilela views her works as advancing the form of the genre through the subjects she selects and the complementary production techniques. Blue's portraits of artist Varnette Honeywood, photographer Roy DeCarava, and insightful exploration of Nigerian Art for the PBS series *Smithsonian World,* connect the artists with historical representations of history, memory, and tradition. Masilela also investigates the ways in which the works of Dash, Larkin, McCullough, and Blue exemplify the concept of American Africanism, which he perceives as a form of pan-Africanism as reconstituted by Toni Morrison in her book *Playing in the Dark: Whiteness and the Literary Imagination* (1992). In Masilela's view, this paradigm defines Africanism as the denotative and connotative Blackness that African people signify. Knowledge becomes, in this construction, revelation and choice, rather than invasion and conquest as the theory has been appropriated by other proponents of African influences.

In "The Ties that Bind: Cinematic Representations by Black Women Filmmakers," Gloria J. Gibson-Hudson develops a framework for analyzing the films of Black women filmmakers. Although it would be premature to assign an overarching theme to these films, Gibson-Hudson submits that commonalities should be considered. The films evolve from similar social and historical circumstances and have clear goals of promoting survival strategies for Black women and transforming them into socially committed viewers. Gibson-Hudson sees a corollary in the resistance to oppression by Black women in their daily lives and the oppositional structure of many of Black women's films. She insists, further, that Black women cultural scholars need to resist irrelevant hegemonic analytical frameworks. For this reason, there is an urgent need for Black women to use analytical tools that are in line with the aims and goals of the filmmakers. As the films are not "art" for art's sake, neither should Black women's critical practice become mere "theory" for theory's sake.

Gibson-Hudson has chosen specific films from different geographical regions—the United States, Ethiopia, Britain, and Canada—which are developed in a variety of forms: narrative, documentary, experimental documentary, and a mixture of narrative/documentary. The films are *Daughters of the Dust* (1991), by Julie Dash; *Sidet: Forced Exile* (1991), by Salem Mekuria; *And Still I Rise* (1991), by Ngozi Onwurah; and *Sisters in the Struggle* (1991), by Dionne Brand and Ginny Strikeman.

Following Gibson-Hudson's analysis of selected films by Black women filmmakers, the article on Camille Billops offers specific explication of the works of a significant and award-winning filmmaker, whose *Finding Christa* (1991) won the Grand Jury Award in the documentary category at the 1992 Sundance Film Festival. From their first film, *Suzanne, Suzanne* (1982), through the latest, *The KKK Boutique Ain't Just Rednecks* (1994), Billops and her husband James Hatch have confounded audiences' prior conceptions of family ties, the mother/daughter bond, older women's sexual desires, and the ever-changing faces of racism. In "The Functional Family of Camille Billops," Monique Guillory interrogates the manner in which Billops's family is present in all of her works, yet the films transcend simply the personal. Paradoxically, by focusing so specifically on her family, Billops is able to present a much larger political agenda. Guillory suggests that Billops constantly intermingles the various facets of private life and public domain to provoke reconsiderations of prescribed social and cultural tenets. *Finding Christa,* for example, records the reunion of Camille and her daughter Christa, whom Camille left in the care of the Children's Home Society when the child was four years old. The surface story and the title both belie the subterranean issues of gender expectations and women's societal roles attendant to a mother who gives up a child then pursues her artistic career. As Guillory demonstrates, Billops is unafraid to brave these social tracts, broaching the sacred to yield clarity and insight.

The next section of *Black Women Film and Video Artists* contains articles written by the makers themselves about their works. The women selected for inclusion have made distinctive marks in the areas of production, distribution, research, and media activism. Carol Munday Lawrence created an innovative television series that was shown to a nationwide audience, the first initiated by a Black woman to gain that level of exposure. Jacqueline Shearer, continuing a life-time commitment to social and political issues, campaigned diligently for increased government funding for independent video artists and in 1992 was elected president and Board Chair of the Independent Television Service (ITVS). O.Funmilayo Makarah is a film and videomaker, curator, teacher, and installation artist who not only distributes her own work but those of other independent makers as well. Makarah is founder of the Los Angeles media arts organization IN VISIBLE COLORS and an organizer of the independent video festival LA Freewaves.

Combining research and teaching with film production and screenplay writing, Carmen Coustaut has received a number of national and international awards, including a Fulbright Fellowship, National Endowment for the Humanities Grant, National Endowment for the Arts–sponsored American Film Institute grant; and, through the assistance of a Rockefeller Foundation grant, has conducted interviews with thirty Black women filmmakers. These forthcoming interviews will add depth to an understanding of Black women's media history. Carmen Coustaut holds an M.F.A. in Cinema Production from the University of Southern California, an M.A. in Education from Harvard University, and is one of the few Black female filmmakers in a tenured position at a major university (along with Zeinabu irene Davis at Northwestern, Carroll Parrott Blue at San Diego State University, and Ayoka Chenzira at the City College of New York).

The opportunity to become a union camera operator has been a hard-fought battle for Black women. The first to win was Jessie Maple in 1974. Her successful fight is chronicled in her book *How to Become a Union Camerawoman: Film-Videotape* (1977). Several other Black women have since earned that status, including Michelle Crenshaw, Jean Young, and C. A. Griffith, who writes about her experiences behind the camera in this volume.

In the first article in this section, "Carol Munday Lawrence: Producer, Director, Writer," the author observes that her training for a career in television and film production was predicated on the political imperative to advance the cause of Black people. Lawrence started off in 1968 as the director of operations for a fledgling organization, Blackside, Inc., now famous for its two series on civil rights activism, *Eyes on the Prize I* and *II*. She next worked as an associate producer for a landmark Black program, *"Say Brother,"* produced at public television station WGBH-TV in Boston. In the company of others who are now seasoned veterans in film and television production—people such as Stan Lathan, Madeline Anderson, and Henry Johnson Lawrence—refined her skills working on the program. She later moved to San Francisco and founded Nguzo Saba Films, Inc., and through this organization produced the well-known series, the *Nguzo Saba Folklore Series of Animated Films,* which depicted Nguzo Saba (the "Seven Principles" in the Kiswahili language) derived from the teachings of Julius Nyerere, former president of Tanzania. Lawrence's production company also produced the series *Were You There* for broadcast on public broadcasting stations, an achievement that distinguished Lawrence as the first Black woman independent to write and produce a national television series. Carol Lawrence is currently the chair of the Black writers committee of the Writers Guild of America, West.

That there were free Black people before the Civil War and scores of Black abolitionists in staunch opposition to slavery are little-known facts that are highlighted in Jacqueline Shearer's *The Massachusetts 54th Colored Infantry* (1991). The television documentary tells the story of the first company of Black soldiers in the Union army, assembled because of agitation from the Black abolitionist community in Boston in the nineteenth century. The documentary is as much the chronicle of the lives of free Black people in Boston as it is the story of the founding of the Massachusetts 54th.

Shearer, writing from her long experience as a filmmaker, notes in her essay, "How Deep, How Wide? Perspectives on the Making of *The Massachusetts 54th Colored* Infantry," that creating a film where men were the center of the story was a unique challenge for her. She observes that usually men *look* and women are *looked at*; in this case there was the opportunity to reverse the gaze. It was also a chance to portray a different aspect of the relationship between Black women and Black men: "something other than the posturing and sniping that too often wins the headlines."

It is perhaps erroneously thought that Black women can only write about "soft" subjects, not those that have a wider impact and affect large numbers of people of color. In a radical reversal to that sentiment, the next article by O.Funmilayo Makarah provides stringent, pointed commentary and analysis on a topic that has ramifications beyond the events chronicled in her article. Makarah describes her outrage at the actions of the police in Los Angeles during the spring of 1992. She relates how her training in film and video allowed her to turn that rage into a video installation titled *Fired-Up*, the same title given to her article in this volume. Video installations are created through working with environment and experience to transform the installation space. In her installation Makarah worked with a space at the California Afro-American Museum in Los Angeles. Part of the design consisted of replaying videotaped interviews of various people around the country talking about their reactions to the events in Los Angeles over the course of two years: First, during 1991, when the videotape of the police beating Rodney King was shown, and then in 1992, when the police officers were found innocent.

Makarah also converted her space by the strategic placement of articles clipped from newspapers and magazines that reported on the beating, the investigation of the Los Angeles police department, and the trial of the police accused of beating King. Bits of modern-day paraphernalia related to what she labels the LA Rebellion were added. Examples included T-shirts with sayings such as "Justice or Just-Us" and "White Men Can't Judge, Either." Also included were bumper stickers, declaring "Jail to the Chief" and "Silence Equals Death." Other elements in the installation are consumer items with price tags. These symbolize, for Makarah, the rampant overpricing of consumer items in Black communities and underscore the inequalities of this society. As she writes: "For me the LA Rebellion was no real surprise; it was yet another indicator of the differences that continue to stress tensions in this country around race and culture."

"Love on My Mind: Creating Black Women's Love Stories," by Carmen Coustaut, introduces a novel concept, that Black women's interest in romantic love is a viable and interesting subject for cinematic representation. Coustaut provides insight into her prospective feature films on the subject, *Harmonica Man, Listen to the Wind*, and *Roundtable Discussion*. In a humorous manner, Coustaut offers a wry assessment of Black women's experiences in the area of romantic attachments. Affectionately, Coustaut also reminds us of the examples presented by our mothers, aunts, and grandmothers in their relationships with the men in their lives. In her finished film, *Extra Change* (1987), Coustaut reviews the process of writing the screenplay and constructing the film. A vivid moment concerns the central character, the young twelve-year-old Rita, who incurs her mother's ire as she pursues her quest for the affections of her schoolmate, Rodney. Coustaut explains that in the making of the film, she sought to use film language to reflect a sense of Black culture. As she describes the scene, "We all know that 'you really in trouble' when Mama puts her hands on her hips. When Rita's mother discovers her activities and begins to scold her, I frame a close shot of the defenseless, guilty Rita framed through her mother's hand/arm on her hip." It is a poignant interlude in a charming film that, as Coustaut contends, makes a strong political statement in its faithful representation of a slice of Black life.

C. A. Griffith, cinematographer, filmmaker, writer, and poet, suggests that critics and scholars need to analyze further the dynamics of film construction that occurs separate from the existence of the finished film itself. In "Below the Line: (Re)Calibrating the Filmic Gaze," Griffith argues that much of the meaning of a film can be extracted from the input of those who are little acknowledged—the production and camera assistants, lighting and sound technicians, among others, who are a vital part of film production. From her experiences as camera assistant working on music videos and feature films such as *Juice,* through being the director of photography for independents Ada Gay Griffin and Michelle Parkerson and their documentary, *A Litany for Survival: The Life and Work of Audre Lorde* (1995), followed by creating her own video *Border Line ... Family Pictures* (1996), Griffith sees a need for a clearer vision in film analysis. Much more careful attention should be given to every stage of production, both above and below the line. Scholarship would benefit by providing more knowledgeable information about the entirety of film production.

The final section of the book features interviews with experienced Black women creative artists. In "Michelle Parkerson: A Visionary Risk Taker," Gloria J. Gibson talks with Parkerson about the extensive range and multi-faceted nature of her works. Parkerson's first film was created while she was a student at Temple University in the mid-1970s. She has since directed an intriguing array of films, from *Storme: The Lady of the Jewel Box* (1987), about a Black woman who performed as a male impersonator in a traveling entertainment show, to her directing project, *Odds and Ends* (1993), a Black Amazon science fiction set in the year 2086, undertaken while she was in residence at the American Film Institute in its Directing Workshop for Women program. Parkerson imparts necessary background on the eight-year endeavor by her and producer and codirector Ada Gay Griffin to acquire funding for the production of the documentary on the life and work of poet, writer, and lesbian activist Audre Lorde, *A Litany for Survival.* In a very insightful segment, Parkerson talks candidly about homophobia in Black communities, the conflicts within gay and lesbian communities, both racial schisms and contretemps between men and women, and the emerging homoerotic cinematic aesthetic.

In 1982, Ntozake Shange brought her provocative choreopoem, *for colored girls who have considered suicide/when the rainbow is enuf,* to public broadcasting. She served as writer and assistant to the director, Oz Scott. Featured in the television adaptation of the 1976 off-Broadway play are now-well-known actresses Alfre Woodard and Lynn Whitfield. A critical difference between the stage version and the televised play was the on-camera presence of the men who were discussed in the play. For this book, P. Jane Splawn interviews poet, playwright, and novelist Ntozake Shange. Shange was thrust into public prominence through the controversy surrounding *for colored girls*. Following the heated debates emanating from the film version of Alice Walker's novel, *The Color Purple* (1985), *colored girls* was itself foisted, once again, into the public spotlight. It became a part of the public dialogue concerning Black women's right to depict Black life in whatever manner they chose. Splawn's interview with Shange takes us beyond the constructed controversy to Shange's views on Black women's creative process; feminism and the question of whether women of color need a separate movement; women's fight against pornography; and the problematic African ritual of clitorectomy, among other topics.

The articles presented in this collection represent a pivotal moment within the continuum of Black women's cultural history. Through the recounting of the contributions of Black women film and videomakers, the women are situated within a creative lineage that extends as far back as the seventeenth century. They are thus an integral component of an activist tradition that re-affirms the value of Black women's lives and experiences and works to reclaim a history that has been either ignored or distorted. This work of reclamation can have an effect on the consciousness of Black women themselves, and it can also alter the perception of Black women in the larger world.

—Jacqueline Bobo

critical

perspectives

black

women's

films

genesis

of a tradition

j a c q u e l i n e   b o b o

My earliest introduction to the work of Black women makers occurred at several venues—an insightful paper given by Gloria Gibson at the 1989 Society for Cinema Studies Conference and, next, during Zeinabu irene Davis's challenging advocacy at the Twelfth Annual Ohio University Film Conference in 1990. These presentations stimulated my interest in and confirmed the need for more information about this vital aspect of Black women's creative contributions. Not only had these papers whetted the research appetite of those at the conferences, but also Gloria and Zeinabu had continued a tradition of insuring that the work of Black women makers would be given their deserved critical attention.[1] Archivist and programmer Pearl Bowser had previously presented the work of Black women in a retrospective of Black American Independent Cinema 1920–1980 at a festival in Paris in 1980. Fortuitously, the event was preserved through the publication of a very useful document of the same title which is available through Third World Newsreel.[2]

Other events showcasing the films and videos of Black women kept the work in public view. Pearl Bowser was involved in yet another research endeavor critical for outlining the history of not only Black women makers, but, as the title confers, *In Color: Sixty Years of Images of Minority Women in the Media.*[3] Groundbreaking essays included in the publication were written by Kathleen Collins, Christine Choy, Renee Tajima, Ada Gay Griffin, and Toni Cade Bambara, among others. Throughout the early 1980s, articles were written about Black women filmmakers in publications such as *Heresies, Jump Cut, Black Film Review,* and elsewhere.[4] In 1987, Valerie Smith curated a showing of Black women's films, "The Black Woman Independent: Representing Race and Gender," at the Whitney Museum of American Art in New York City. Later, Smith published an overview and analysis of Black women's work in *Callaloo.*[5]

I was fortunate to meet several of the makers in the summer of 1992 at a conference exploring ways to effectively distribute the product of Black independent film/videomakers.[6] I made contact with O.Funmilayo Makarah, Linda Gibson, Cheryl Fabio Bradford, and Jacqueline Shearer, and reconnected with Pearl Bowser and Zeinabu irene Davis. An earlier chance encounter with filmmaker, programmer, and later marketer Michelle Materre proved to be a godsend for my research on *Daughters of the Dust* (1991). I was a participant in the Black Popular Culture Conference[7] in New York City in December 1991 and decided to take advantage of the time there to preview Black women's films at the independent distribution organization Women Make Movies. Fortunately, Michelle, who worked there at the time, approached me about having a look at a video copy of *Daughters of the Dust.* I was impressed with the sheer power of Julie Dash's film. From Michelle I obtained a preview videotape copy of the film to show to groups of Black women I was interviewing for my book *Black Women as Cultural Readers* (1995). The women in my research group were even more taken with the film than I, incredible as that may have seemed at the time, for the earliest reviews posited that *Daughters of the Dust* would test the patience and comprehension of untutored audiences. Michelle also introduced me to Julie Dash, setting up an interview in Los Angeles that proved pivotal in my analysis of the film.

By this time Black women scholars and artists were teaching courses about Black female makers at several universities in the country: Claire Andrade Watkins at Wellesley College, Carmen Coustaut at Howard University and later at the University of Maryland, College Park; Gloria Gibson at Indiana University, and Michelle Parkerson was keeping the topic vibrant at Temple, Northwestern, Howard, and in early articles detailing the artists' history and significance.[8]

I started teaching courses on Black women filmmakers about five years ago, and have continued to do so at three universities: the University of California, Santa Cruz; the University of North Carolina at Chapel Hill; and at my present location, the University of California, Santa Barbara. I encountered the same impediments that others faced, regardless of whether they taught courses devoted exclusively to the topic or incorporated the films with complementary subject matter within other courses. I considered these obstacles to be challenges rather than problems, but I also understood how those less involved in the subject would be intimidated by the lack of accessible background information about the films' production history and the relative absence of material about the filmmakers themselves. Also, many of the later films, and especially the videos and interactive media, were experimental works, in which some form of background material would enhance students' understanding.

To redress the issue in my courses, I began to invite many of the makers—Cheryl Fabio Bradford, Cauleen Smith, Aarin Burch, Linda Gibson, O.Funmilayo Makarah, Yvonne Welbon, Crystal Griffith, and programmer Margaret Daniel—to speak about their works in my classes. The students were enormously impressed with the women's knowledge, skill, and training. The women not only provided astute analyses of Black women's films and videos but also contextualized the works within the broader spectrum of film and video production and criticism. I was reminded of the three days at the independent distribution conference, when, even in a casual setting, O.Funmilayo Makarah and Zeinabu Davis expertly explicated the works shown to the participants.

These events made me acutely aware that further information about the history of Black women film and videomakers would fill an egregious void within cinema scholarship. This was reaffirmed in Jacqueline Shearer's keynote address at the independent distributor's conference. Shearer's documentary *The Massachusetts 54th Colored Infantry* (1991) had just recently aired on public broadcasting as part of the prestigious *American Experience* series. Although she recognized the valuable opportunity for such a national presentation, Shearer reminded us that more work needed to be done to insure greater opportunities for more exhibition of the works of Black independent makers. She detailed her experiences with distribution, including her first production, *A Minor Altercation* (1977). Shearer was at that time a founding member of the Boston Newsreel Collective, which operated with a political intent: that media could augment people's understanding of the social matrices in which they were involved. The collective held community screenings, which led to discussions and interactions with audiences, and brought the images that people viewed into perspective with their daily lives. Shearer related that it became clear to me that a film had no political merit gathering dust on the shelf. It was only in interaction with an audience that it had power. This is a very simpleminded truth but one that is still stunning to me in its significance and consequences. So a longstanding cornerstone of my understanding about media is that the production of a piece is not finished until and unless it plays to its audience.[9]

Despite the tremendous success of *A Minor Altercation* (which dealt with the desegregation conflicts in Boston in the early 1970s) through the grassroots efforts of the Boston Collective, the film was rejected by distributors. The early incarnation of Women Make Movies dismissed the film as not being feminist, even though the makers were women and the protagonists in the story were two teenage girls and their working-class mothers. Other organizations considered the film not polished enough, asserting that it lacked sophisticated production aesthetics. *A Minor Altercation* has since gone on to be distributed by the present Women Make Movies and is regarded as a classic early Black feminist work.

There is a substantial body of work created by Black women film/videomakers, extending back to the early part of this century. Unfortunately, the work is overlooked not only by many distributors, but also by critical reviews and scholarly analyses, with the notable exception of those by Black women scholars, have been few and far between. The recent success of filmmaker Julie Dash's *Daughters of the Dust* (1991), due in large measure to the fervent support of Black female audiences, underscores the critical role of Black women's films within this far-reaching creative tradition. Through the aid of other women filmmakers and an independent publicity campaign, *Daughters of the Dust* circumvented traditional venues to be placed before receptive audiences hungry for depictions of their history long missing from mainstream white productions. The film chronicles a loving, though complicated, multigenerational Black family at the turn of the century. They struggle, yet eventually triumph over the oppressive legacies of forced removal from their homeland and the tortuous regimens of enslavement. Dash's piece is historic; it proved, yet again, that there was a large untapped market for creative work that seriously examined Black women's experiences.

The demonstrated interest in *Daughters of the Dust* notwithstanding, widespread recognition of Black women film and video artists lags behind their extensive history. Documentation exists of Black women producing and directing films during the prolific interim of Black film production from 1910 through the 1920s. Archivist and film scholar Pearl Bowser notes that Black women worked behind the camera on numerous films during this time on what were known as "race" films, that is, independent films produced by Black filmmakers, rather than white-controlled films about Black life.[10]

Historical records show that two women were especially noteworthy in filmmaking during this period. Madame C. J. Walker, one of the first Black millionaires, made her fortune manufacturing and distributing cosmetics and hair-care products for Black women. In addition to her retail business, Walker owned the Walker Theater in Indianapolis, and produced training and promotional films about her cosmetics factory. These films, Bowser declares, "offered a visual record of women's work history" and the "development of cottage industries."[11] Bowser also points to the importance of Madam Toussaint Welcome, Booker T. Washington's personal photographer, who produced at least one film about Black soldiers who fought in World War I.

Film scholar Gloria J. Gibson-Hudson provides further evidence of Black women's production background. Gibson-Hudson's research fills out important details on earlier Black women filmmakers, but she also works to restore, in conjunction with the Library of Congress, the films of Eloyce Gist. Gist was a traveling evangelist, who toured the country in the 1920s with her religious folk dramas, exhibiting them in churches to Black audiences.[12] Her two known films, *Hell Bound Train* and *Verdict Not Guilty* are considered to be as rich and provocative as those of her more studied contemporaries such as Oscar Micheaux and the brothers Noble and George Johnson.

Other pioneer Black female filmmakers examined in Gibson-Hudson's study include folklorist Zora Neale Hurston, who made ethnographic films in the 1930s. Hurston earned an MA in Cultural Anthropology, working with Franz Boas at Columbia University. Currently, several reels of Hurston's film footage are available for viewing at the Library of Congress. Similarly, footage exists of the films shot by Eslanda Goode Robeson (whose husband was Paul Robeson), but its fragile condition renders it inaccessible for public screening. Robeson, who held a Ph.D. in Anthropology, made ethnographic films in the 1940s. Alice B. Russell, another key person, worked with and was perhaps the driving force behind many of the films of Oscar Micheaux.[13]

Confronted with the dearth of scholarship about early Black female filmmakers, these activist researchers—Bowser, Gibson-Hudson, and others—retrieved the history of a long-neglected body of films that dealt substantively with important issues. The works addressed an array of matters crucial to understanding various facets of Black life and culture, including the role of religion in Black people's lives, the contributions of Black soldiers fighting for a country that afforded them little honor, and Black women's work and business history. Certainly, an even more bountiful cache will surface once scholars begin to uncover the largely obscured output of Black women filmmakers from the 1950s and early 1960s. Pearl Bowser is currently compiling information about Black female photographers who were involved in filmmaking at that time.

That Black women filmmakers were active in every decade of this century is not insignificant. The newly discovered films increase the opportunities to advance an understanding of Black women's cultural history and the social determinants molding Black women's lives. Furthermore, these texts demonstrate the ways in which filmmakers within the social group present stories that have an effect on altering these conditions for the better.

Concomitantly, exposure of their existence links the present to the past, outlining the expansive contours of a fertile lineage of creativity. We can now enlarge the process of assessing commonalities, pervasive themes, and preoccupations, as well as dissimilarities, discontinuities, and interruptions.

Such prominent patterns are recognizable in recent films and offer insight into Black women's perspectives on their ongoing efforts to better their lives. The contemporary film that is generally singled out as the first created by a Black woman is *I am Somebody* (1970), directed by Madeline Anderson. It records the successful 113-day strike in 1969 by hospital workers in Charleston, South Carolina. Anderson's documentary is an empathetic portrait of Black women and their supporters, including the Southern Christian Leadership Conference in its first mass demonstration after the death of Martin Luther King Jr. Also involved were the labor union organizations UAW and the AFL-CIO, along with white women who were members of the Spartanburg, South Carolina, chapter of ILGWU.[14] The importance of the strike (initiated by what later became local 1199B of the national union of hospital workers) was that lowly regarded women persevered in their struggle to demand what was their right—"recognition as human beings," as one striker stated at the end of the film.

Centering Black women as subjects recognizable as human beings is paramount in Black women's films. Starting with *I am Somebody*, the following works form a nucleus that shapes and gives definition to a comprehensive movement of Black women film and video artists: *Valerie: A Woman, an Artist, a Philosophy of Life* (1975), directed by Monica Freeman, is a documentary about sculptor Valerie Maynard, who considers her art a vital part of her political impulse. Jacqueline Shearer's *A Minor Altercation* (1977) dramatizes the activities in Boston in the early 1970s surrounding the conflicts over busing. The film is based on interviews with participants and community members, but is a dramatic depiction of events. It is different from the other works created by Black women during this period in that it is not a documentary, it is a narrative reconstruction.

Kathleen Collins, with her two feature narratives *The Cruz Brothers and*

Miss Malloy (1980) and *Losing Ground* (1982), further extended the range of Black women's films. Although *Losing Ground* was denied large-scale exhibition, it was among the first films created by a Black woman deliberately designed to tell a story intended for popular consumption, with a feature-length narrative structure. Collins's film thus paved the way for *Daughters of the Dust* to become the first feature-length narrative film created by a Black woman to be placed in commercial distribution. Finally, *Fundi: The Story of Ella Baker* (1981), directed by Joanne Grant, powerfully restores Ella Baker to the pantheon of civil rights organizers and thinkers. In conjunction with Michelle Parkerson's *Gotta Make This Journey: Sweet Honey in the Rock* (1983), the films are compelling examples of art transforming people's consciousness, facilely intertwining cultural expression with cogent political analysis.

These early makers successfully battled debilitating societal restraints of scarce resources and blocked access to production facilities to redress significant omissions within Black women's history. Even in the face of continual rejection from established funding sources, and despite their films being refused exhibition by festival committees and alternative distribution centers, the women stayed true to their belief that stories about Black women's lives merited creative representation. Their portfolios included, for example, films about overlooked cultural and political activists and social documentaries charting Black women's essential contributions at pivotal historical moments. The filmmakers maintained contact with Black audiences by personally carrying their films wherever people desired to see them. And they conscientiously tailored their works to match the requisites of audience understanding, traversing the spectrum of filmmaking, from documentary to fictional re-creation, and moving onward toward the subversive potential of narrative cinema. This legacy was passed on to present-day filmmakers. Thus, the innovative forms and impressive content of the early films, the stories the makers selected to tell, combined with the social context governing the works' production and their eventual favorable reception over time, established a germinative foundation for Black women film and videomakers who followed.

documenting black lives

Congruence between the personal histories of filmmaker and subject is a predominant feature of Black women's biographical documentaries. The works are more than a distanced, voyeuristic examination of an isolated artist, but rather illustrate how both filmmaker and artist have overcome obstacles to create art that is meaningful for Black audiences. Monica Freeman's *Valerie* was among the first of this kind. Other examples include Ayoka Chenzira's *Syvilla: They Dance to Her Drum* (1979); ... *But Then,*

She's Betty Carter (1980); and *Storme: The Lady of the Jewel Box* (1987) by Michelle Parkerson, as well as her later film codirected with Ada Gay Griffin *A Litany for Survival: The Life and Work of Audre Lorde* (1995); Carroll Parrott Blue's *Varnette's World: A Study of a Young Artist* (1979); *Miss Fluci Moses: A Video Documentary* (1987) by Alile Sharon Larkin; and Kathe Sandler's *Remembering Thelma* (1981).

Evident in Freeman's film about Valerie Maynard are the two women's affinities as Black women and as artists. *Valerie* is a sensory, evocative examination of a printmaker and sculptor who is inspired by the people and the rhythms of her native Harlem. For her, Harlem is "continual conversation, continual change, continual movement." This sentiment emerges in the tightly structured film; it is dynamic and fluid, emulating Maynard's art and life as she works in her studio, interacts with the residents of her neighborhood, arranges an exhibit at the University of Massachusetts. As the documentary begins, the filmmaker draws the viewer into the artist's environment. There are lingering shots of Maynard's larger-than-life figures followed by slow camera movement along the length of a female form with its upraised arm and open palm. Accompanying the visuals are sounds of the artist using the tools of her craft: sanding, carving, pounding a mallet against a chisel. The voice-over consists entirely of Maynard speaking about her life and philosophy of art, and of her desire to display her work to as broad an audience as possible, including the conventional circles of galleries and university lectures, along with the less familiar turf of jails and people's homes. As much as Maynard's aesthetic draws from other's experiences, so does she seek to share her work with a vast and diverse audience.

Harlem forms the backdrop for Freeman's other two works as well: *A Sense of Pride: Hamilton Heights in Harlem* (1977) and *Learning Through the Arts: The Children's Art Carnival* (1979). Each documentary clearly functions to identify and preserve essential elements of Black culture. Hamilton Heights is a neighborhood in New York City that has been recognized as a historic landmark. Acknowledgment of that designation is evidenced by several longtime residents, who validate the significance of the community. Roy Thomas, born in 1906, states that he was probably one of the first Black people born in Harlem. He talks about Black people needing collective memories of their heritage, housed in communities such as his. In the film, Thomas displays copies of family mementos, one being the receipt given to his great-great-grandfather as proof that he had bought his freedom from enslavement.

Another resident, Alston Harris, noticing the onset of deterioration in his neighborhood, began planting ferns, flowers, trees, and other vegetation throughout the area as a "garden of pleasure for people." He states that people live better if they take pride in their surroundings: "the air here smells different than from a block away." Harris's neighbors soon began to follow his example, keeping the area clean, guarding against litter and vandalism, and tending the community gardens.

Pride in Harlem's legendary status is demonstrated by other inhabitants who moved to the neighborhood's grand brownstones. At the time of the film's production, Eleanor Holmes Norton was New York City's Human Rights Commissioner and a longtime resident of Harlem Heights. She explains that, for her, the best way to protect the area was to live there and serve as an example to lure other potential residents. She felt that there was a feeling of cohesion as the communities pulled together to maintain what had been designated a valuable component of Black people's past.

Harlem Heights was also the location of the Children's Art Carnival, a community-based arts school for children aged 4–18. The organization began as a summer program by the Museum of Modern Art in 1968 and later moved to Harlem. The film *Learning Through the Arts: The Children's Art Carnival* is an inspirational look at young people developing a variety of artistic skills: printmaking, silkscreen, animation, filmmaking, sewing and design, collage, and 3-D construction, among other disciplines. The narrator and director of the program, Betty Blayton Taylor, asserts that art is everywhere in people's lives and that an understanding of the arts motivates children in other aspects of their lives. One of the Carnival's programs, "Creative Reading Through the Arts," was used to stimulate children's curiosty about communication and used art as a bridge for verbal and written breakthroughs. The documentary illustrates how children, once they become curious, motivate themselves by wanting to read and communicate effectively. Because of their success, the Children's Art Carnival was cited as a model of arts education by the National Endowment for the Arts.

Monica Freeman's three 1970s documentaries all exemplify the skill and training of a committed cultural activist. Freeman studied with Madeline Anderson at Columbia University, earning an MFA in Film Production in 1977. She later served as mentor to other emerging filmmakers. Her film *A Sense of Pride* featured an all-woman crew who are now established makers in their own right with noteworthy production credits. The women included Ayoka Chenzira, whose landmark film *Hair Piece: A Film for Nappyheaded People* (1984) is an animated satire that is shown frequently at colleges and festivals. Chenzira recently directed *Alma's Rainbow* (1993), an ambitious and remarkably achieved 35mm feature-length narrative. Debra Robinson was also a member of Freeman's crew. She would later direct the well-known documentary about Black female comedians, *I Be Done Been Was Is* (1984), and a fictional feature story of a young Black girl's turmoil, *Kiss Grandmama Goodbye* (1992).

black women's narratives

Exploration of social conditions through documentary is a first step for many beginning filmmakers. This is also true of Black women filmmakers, but as their skills matured, the necessity for matching the format of their works with the theater-going experiences of specific audiences became a prime consideration. Even though the women were virtually shut out of the established film industry, the need to reach Black people with responsible depictions of Black life was imperative. One of the first to successfully achieve this goal was Kathleen Collins.

Collins understood that the effective use of cinema had the potential to evoke in the viewer a certain depth of response, similar to that experienced by other forms of art. In her films she was concerned with utilizing the grammar of film to resolve the structural and formal questions unique to film as a specific discipline. For independent makers, especially, this was necessary if audiences were to gain an appreciation of cinema as more than a commercial vehicle.[15]

Kathleen Collins embraced the principle that cinema has a literary parallel. Not in any direct way, but in the sense that every element of composition is a specific convention that makes up a film language. Collins's first film conscientiously employed cinematic techniques in translating a literary story to film. *The Cruz Brothers and Miss Malloy* is based on one of a series of episodes in a longer literary work, *The Cruz Chronicle: A Novel of Adventure and Close Calls* (1989), by Henry H. Roth.[16] The film tells the story of three Puerto Rican brothers, orphaned after their father is killed by guards while attempting to rob a bank, who live as exiles in a small isolated town in upstate New York. They are hired by an elderly Irish widow, Edna Malloy, a longtime resident of the town, to restore her home to its former grandeur as she prepares to give one last party.

The film is coherent, with a consistent tone and style. The brothers have survived unfortunate circumstances, from living in an orphanage to existing by their wiles in a potentially hostile environment. In spite of the element of danger in their lives, there is a whimsical, fanciful ambience to the film. This is apparent from the outset as the dead father appears as a ghost at the beginning of the film, giving it a surreal dimension. The father's presence is shown through the perspective of a hand-held camera, with his voice heard off-camera as a disembodied voice-over. The story is told alternately by the father and by the oldest son, Victor, who provides background information on the family as he constructs their history by talking into an audiotape recorder. Victor is the only one of the brothers who is able to converse with the dead father.

The suspense of the film builds as it becomes obvious that someone, not shown on camera, is spying on the brothers as they go about their business in the town. From the unseen voyeur's point of view, the brothers are presented, in one scene, playfully making their way along an extremely high narrow crossing spanning an enormous chasm. The inference is that the brothers lead risky lives with vastly different experiences from their observer. The brothers soon become aware that the elderly woman is following them, but they do not know her intentions. The viewer is also kept wondering. That the brothers' future is uncertain and in possible jeopardy is maintained throughout Edna Malloy's first appearance in the film. The fender of her classic automobile slowly enters the frame, as the brothers are seen walking off down the road. The car door swings open; Miss Malloy steps out, filling up the frame with her back to the camera, as the boys are shown much smaller and vulnerable in the distance. The brothers' apprehension increases when she eventually approaches them. A canted camera angle indicates that the boys perceive her to be odd and unusual. This is reinforced by her statement about their passage across the bridge: "I saw your act a few times previously. And I caught it again today. Each time you cross that bridge you tempt fate. You're tempted to jump. But I think you are definitely survivors. I have been one for many years, but now I'm going to die."

The technical properties of *The Cruz Brothers and Miss Malloy* were overlooked at the time of its debut because more attention was given to the absence of Black people in the film. However, Collins felt that any subject was open to Black artists.[17] Thematically, in *The Cruz Brothers* she was dealing with the notion of happiness and whether a person has lived a full life or, as Edna Malloy relates to the brothers, whether she has traded the security of living her entire life in the town in which she was born, married to a man with whom she was unhappy, for taking risks with her fate in unknown circumstances.

Amplifying the potential of the medium was a prime consideration in Collins's work. She was trained in France in the mid-1960s, earning an MA in film theory and production from the Middlebury Graduate School. She was a faculty member at the City College of New York from 1974 to 1988, teaching courses on directing for film, scriptwriting, theory and aesthetics of cinema, and editing. Collins was considered by many filmmakers the finest film editor of her era. She learned her craft by working with John Carter, one of the first Black union editors. Collins worked as an editor from 1967 to 1974 at WNET-NY.

The influence of Collins as one of the first contemporary Black women working within the genre of narrative cinema is seen in subsequent films directed by Black women. Commercially distributed films include *Daughters of the Dust*, Leslie Harris's *Just Another Girl on the IRT* (1992), and *I Like it Like That* (1994), by Darnell Martin.

Command of the fictional form raises Black women makers to another level of visibility. Within the genre of dramatic narratives, a variety of films are represented: *A Minor Altercation* (1977) directed by Jacqueline Shearer; *A Powerful Thang* (1991) and *Mother of the River* (1995) by Zeinabu irene Davis; *Your Children Come Back to You* (1979) and *A Different Image* (1982), directed by Alile Sharon Larkin; Carmen Coustaut's *Extra Change* (1987); *Twice as Nice* (1989) by Jessie Maple; Daresha Kyi's *Land Where My Fathers Died* (1991); and *Rags and Old Love* (1986) by Ellen Sumter, among others.

There are also feature-length narratives, though not in wide-scale distribution, that have been directed by Black women: Jessie Maple's *Will* (1981); *Love Your Mama* (1989) by Ruby Oliver; *Alma's Rainbow* (1993), directed by Ayoka Chenzira; *Naked Acts* (1995) by Bridgett Davis; *The Promised Land* (1995) by Monika Harris; *Medipaid Queens* (1995) by Karen Stone; and, *Watermelon Woman* (1996), directed by Cheryl Dunye.

Although only three dramatic films created by Black women—*Daughters of the Dust, I Like It Like That, Just Another Girl on the IRT*—have been exhibited theatrically, several others have been presented nationally. Helaine Head directed a CBS Schoolbreak Special, starring Whoopi Goldberg, that examined Black students' participation in the sit-ins of the 1960s, *My Past is My Own* (1989). Mary Neema Barnette, who has directed many network television programs including episodes of *The Cosby Show, Frank's Place, China Beach, A Different World*, among others, and one of the few Black women to receive an Emmy Award in a nonacting category, directed Ruby Dee's play *Zora is My Name* (1989), broadcast nationally on PBS. Finally, Dianne Houston's *Tuesday Morning Ride* (1995), produced as part of Showtime's short film series, was the first film directed by a Black woman to be nominated for an Academy Award.

social movements, cultural movements

In the construction of narrative films or creating social documentaries, Black women filmmakers have engaged questions of resistance and social oppression as a vital part of their work. Anderson's *I Am Somebody* led the way for examinations of Black women's roles in major political movements, followed by Joanne Grant's *Fundi: The Story of Ella Baker* (1981) and Michelle Parkerson's *Gotta Make This Journey: Sweet Honey in the Rock* (1983). The films focus on the lives of extraordinary women, but the central issues they raise concern the political activities of these women as they sparked catalytic events within historic moments. Each film superbly achieves the desired effect of political films: they contain mutually reinforcing components of historical exegesis, inspiration, and a call to action.

Although her name may not be as readily recognized as some of the more visible activists, Ella Baker (1903–1986) influenced several generations of civil rights workers. In the 1940s she was a field organizer for the NAACP, traveling throughout the South six months of the year organizing membership drives and working with communities to help them recognize their potential for collective action. She was born in the South, graduated from Shaw University in Raleigh, North Carolina, and eventually moved to New York right before the Depression. Baker's participation in radical organizations in New York, along with her work with Black groups in the South, nurtured her progressive ideas about social change.

Despite her impressive record of involvement and progressive initiatives in movement activities, Baker shunned being elevated to the status of a leader. She cautioned repeatedly against relying on a "charismatic leader," formulating instead the principle of participatory democracy: those involved in social movement organizations can be empowered to act on their own behalf if they participate in the decision-making process. It was Baker, rather than the white student leaders of the Students for a Democratic Society (as has been widely written about), who originated the underlying framework of participatory democracy. Movement scholar Carol Mueller insists that Baker was the primary impetus behind this powerful set of ideas that guided the organization she helped to found, the Student Nonviolent Coordinating Committee.[18]

Fundi: The Story of Ella Baker, skillfully blends archival footage of Baker's public life promoting group-centered leadership, with one-on-one interviews Baker gives in numerous settings: among her colleagues in the movement, including E. D. Nixon, the organizer of the 1955 Montgomery Bus Boycott; and Amzie Moore, who initiated the voter registration project in Mississippi in the 1960s. She is tenderly shown in the company of her extended family and friends and at a tribute arranged in her honor by those she inspired. These include activists such as Bob Moses, who heeded Baker's call for working and living in the communities where voter registration drives were conducted. Moses categorized Baker as the embodiment of Fundi: a designation of honor originating from Swahili, which refers to someone in a community who masters a craft, then passes on what they have learned by sharing it with others. Many renowned civil rights activists articulate their debt to Baker in the film, including Julian Bond, Ralph David Abernathy, Septima Clark, Bernice Johnson Reagon, Vincent Harding, and others who were politically active during the span of Baker's life.

One of the strengths of Grant's film is that it showcases Baker's speeches in such a powerful manner. She was a forceful, courageous person, tackling difficult issues forthrightly and honestly. A fundamental tenet of her life's work was that "no one will do for you that which you've had the power to do for yourself and did not." Ella Baker was also the organizer for the challenge mounted by the Mississippi Freedom Democratic Party in their bid to be seated at the 1964 Democratic National Convention in Atlantic City, New Jersey. During her keynote address to the delegation she referred to the sustained public outrage in the wake of the murders of the civil rights workers in Mississippi in 1964, two of whom were white workers from the North. Many Black people were aware that as the authorities searched for the missing workers, they found bodies of murdered Black men in the rivers of Mississippi that no one had previously investigated because they had not been killed along with white men. Baker expressed her anger with the following resolution: "Until the killing of Black men, Black mothers' sons, becomes as important to the rest of the country as a white mother's son, we who believe in freedom will not rest until it comes."

This declaration was responded to in a song by Bernice Johnson Reagon, "We Who Believe in Freedom" (also known as "Ella's Song") that is a part of the soundtrack sung by Reagon and Sweet Honey in the Rock for *Fundi*. Reagon had known and worked with Ella Baker since the beginnings of her own political transformation in Albany, Georgia, in the early 1960s. In her book, *We Who Believe in Freedom: Sweet Honey in the Rock . . . Still On the Journey* (1993), Reagon emphasizes the importance of Baker and her overriding philosophy that citizens are empowered through direct participation in social change.[19] It was this political privileging of "rank and file" members rather than the authoritarian head of an organization which placed Baker in conflict with the directors of the NAACP and, later, the group for which she was the first organizer, the Southern Christian Leadership Conference. With admirable foresight, Baker felt that the development of leadership capabilities within individuals would enhance their ability for long-term political action.

In yet another prescient endeavor that would accrue benefits in the years to come, Baker led the drive to recruit more women and young people into the SCLC. This constituency would ignite the push for a broader range of rights for a variety of social groups. Baker also initiated, in the late 1950s, the Crusade for Citizenship, composed of voter clinics, social action committees, and classes to teach basic reading and writing skills that would qualify Black citizens to vote. Ella Baker understood the power of targeted, large-scale demonstrations and knew that, by utilizing the strategy of mass, direct action, combined with the power of the vote, the collective will of the group would exert considerable influence.[20]

In the film *Gotta Make This Journey: Sweet Honey in the Rock*, Bernice Johnson Reagon discusses the tremendous courage of those who participated in the voter registration drives. The American public was aware of the large protest marches because these were the events attracting national media coverage, but the local campaigns for the right to vote cost Black people their lives. As a consequence, Reagon's first singing group, the SNCC Freedom Singers, became a "singing newspaper," keeping people at the grassroots level informed of the activities in the small cities and towns where Black people were fighting for their constitutional rights.

Reagon refers to Ella Baker as her "political mother" and uses her example of recognizing the potential for resistance to oppression in every individual. Her goal, in the formation of the singing group Sweet Honey in the Rock, was to provide the inspiration that motivated people toward collective action for social change. It was her participation in the freedom movement, Reagon states, that made her realize that songs can do more than make people feel good; they have the power to mobilize concentrated, large-scale opposition to varied manifestations of injustice.

Gotta Make This Journey: Sweet Honey in the Rock, produced by Michelle Parkerson, is a broadcast videotape of Sweet Honey's ninth anniversary concert held in 1982 at Gallaudet College in Washington, DC.[21] It is a thoughtful documentary and much more than a typical concert tape. There is a compatibility between the programming of the concert and the structure of the videotape, so that the force of Sweet Honey builds throughout, not overwhelming the viewer. Careful attention is given to the rhythm and pacing of the video, matching the content of the songs with the narrative provided by the individual women as they are interviewed in the field segments of the documentary.

Each section of *Gotta Make This Journey* is intersected by quick fades to black, followed by a song from the concert. These musical bridges further articulate the ideas and sentiments expressed in interviews and commentary. Several narrative lines evolve: the origin of the group, its overall philosophy, and how each member's personal history contributes to the collective. As an example, the six then-current members of Sweet Honey—Yasmeen Williams, Evelyn Harris, Aisha Kahlil, Ysaye Barnwell, Shirley Johnson (the sign language interpreter), and the group's founder and leader, Bernice Johnson Reagon—are all committed to Sweet Honey's political mission of creating awareness of specific human rights issues. When Evelyn Harris conveys that singing with Sweet Honey allows her to work for Black people through song, there is a juxtaposition with a clip of the Reverend Ben Chavis, who had been imprisoned as a member of the Wilmington Ten. Chavis speaks of his love for the group, and his gratitude to them for volunteering to provide the musical soundtrack for the film *The Wilmington Ten—U.S.A. Ten Thousand* (1978), created by director Haile Gerima. The song "You can break one human body, I see ten thousand Bikos" is then featured in the next segment of the anniversary concert. The song was composed by Bernice Johnson Reagon specifically for Gerima's documentary. In the film, the song accompanies a series of photographs of anti-apartheid marches in South Africa. The comparison likens the repression in South Africa with the condition of those imprisoned in Wilmington, North Carolina, and, in turn, draws a parallel to acts of social injustice as they occur throughout the world.

After the forceful and impassioned rendition of "I see ten thousand

Bikos," Bernice Johnson Reagon sets up a change of pace and introduces the title song inspired by the words of Ella Baker, "We Who Believe in Freedom." It imparts a quiet, understated resolve, matched in the next segment with comments from Angela Davis, speaking of the importance of the younger generation remembering the contributions of civil rights pioneers Fannie Lou Hamer and Ella Baker.

A comparison can be made between those who devoted their lives to the struggle for social equality and similarly dedicated Black women filmmakers. Ella Baker presents a formidable, yet attainable example. Her life's work corresponds to the filmmakers' creative commitment. Baker believed that political action should empower people to solve their own problems and that social change is finally achieved through enabling people to act on their own convictions. As she states in Grant's film *Fundi*: "The natural [impulse toward] resistance is there already. No human being, I don't care how undeveloped he is, relishes being sat upon and beaten as if he were an animal without any resistance."

Mainstream cultural forms are replete with devastating representations of Black women as victims, as pawns of systemic oppressive forces, lacking the will or agency to resist. Both *Fundi: The Story of Ella Baker* and *Gotta Make This Journey* present vastly different interpretations of Black women as social agents within historic political periods. The films are instrumental in the effort by Black women filmmakers to erase destructive ideologies affecting Black women. With their body of socially conscious work, the filmmakers form an integral component of a cultural movement, a configuration of activists that seeks to transform the status of Black women in popular imagination and in the minds of Black women themselves. Through meticulous concentration on Black women's history, faithfully representing their lives, Black women's films magnify female viewers' perception of their material circumstances, motivating them toward activism, thereby strengthening their viability as a potent social force.

notes

1. Gloria Gibson, Zeinabu Davis, and I also presented a panel on "Black Women's Films" at the Modern Language Association Annual Convention in Toronto, Ontario in December 1993; and we were part of a panel on the same topic with Mable Haddock, Kathe Sandler, Lisa Kennedy, and Kass Banning at the Black Cinema: An International Celebration of Pan-African Film Conference, at the New York University Tisch School of the Arts, in March 1994.

2. Pearl Bowser and Valerie Harris, eds., *Independent Black American Cinema* (New York: Third World Newsreel, 1981).

3. Pearl Bowser and Ada Gay Griffin, eds., *In Color: Sixty Years of Images of Minority Women in Film* (New York: Third World Newsreel, 1984).

4. See Loretta Campbell, "Reinventing Our Image: Eleven Black Women Filmmakers," *Heresies* 4: 4 (1983): 58–62; Claudia Springer, "Black Women Film-

makers," *Jump Cut 29* (1984): 34–37; and "The Special Section: Black Women Filmmakers Break the Silence," *Black Film Review* 2: 3 (Summer 1986).

5. Valerie Smith, "Reconstituting the Image: The Emergent Black Woman Director," *Callaloo; A Journal of Afro-American and African Arts and Letters* 11: 4 (Fall 1988): 710–19.

6. See the report of the conference in Jacqueline Bobo, ed., *Available Visions: Improving Distribution of African American Independent Film and Video Conference Proceedings* (San Francisco: California Newsreel, 1993).

7. For an overview of the conference see Gina Dent, ed. *Black Popular Culture: A Project by Michele Wallace* (Seattle, WA: Bay Press, 1992).

8. See her articles, "Did You Say the Mirror Talks?" in Lisa Albrecht and Rose M. Brewer, eds., *Bridges of Power: Women's Multicultural Alliances* (Santa Cruz, CA: New Society Publishers, 1990): 108–117; and "Women Throughout the Diaspora Tackle Their Firsts," *Black Film Review* 6: 1: 10–11.

9. Jacqueline Shearer, "Random Notes of a Homeless Filmmaker," in Bobo, *Available Visions*.

10. Pearl Bowser, "The Existence of Black Theatres," *Take Two Quarterly* (Columbus, Ohio: National Black Programming Consortium), 1.

11. Bowser, "The Existence of Black Theatres," 19.

12. Gloria J. Gibson-Hudson, "Recall and Recollect: Excavating the Life History of Eloyce King Patrick Gist," *Black Film Review* 8: 2 (1995): 20–21.

13. Gibson-Hudson, "Recall and Recollect," 20.

14. Philip Foner, *Women and the American Labor Movement* (New York: The Free Press, 1980), 443.

15. See her comments in the following interviews: Oliver Franklin, "An Interview: Kathleen Collins," *Independent Black American Cinema* (conference program brochure published by Third World Newsreel, February 1981): 22–24; David Nicholson, "Conflict and Complexity: Filmmaker Kathleen Collins," *Black Film Review* 2: 3 (Summer 1986): 16–17; and David Nicholson, "A Commitment to Writing: A Conversation with Kathleen Collins Prettyman," *Black Film Review* 5: 1 (Winter 1988/1989): 6–15.

16. Collins was working from Roth's book in manuscript form before it was eventually published.

17. Nicholson, "A Commitment to Writing," 8.

18. Carol Mueller, "Ella Baker and the Origins of 'Participatory Democracy'," in Vicki L. Crawford et al., eds., *Women in the Civil Rights Movement: Trailblazers and Torchbearers, 1941–1965* (Bloomington: Indiana University Press, 1993), 53.

19. Bernice Johnson Reagon et al., eds., *We Who Believe in Freedom: Sweet Honey in the Rock . . . Still On the Journey* (New York: Anchor Books, 1993), 20.

20. Mueller, "Ella Baker and the Origins of 'Participatory Democracy'," 65.

21. Sweet Honey in the Rock was formed in 1973, taking its name from a parable of religious origin, though not found in the Bible. According to the parable, there was a land that was so rich that when you cracked the rocks, honey would flow from them. Over the course of the group's twenty-plus years of existence, twenty women have at various times been a member.

women

directors

of the

los angeles

school

ntongela masilela

The Los Angeles School, whose historical moment extends from 1967 to 1982, represents a cultural movement in Black independent filmmaking and constitutes part of the avant-garde of African American culture.[1] Inasmuch as the Harlem Renaissance was the literary avant-garde of the 1920s and the Black Arts Movement was the poetic avant-garde of the 1960s, the Los Angeles School could be viewed as the filmic avant-garde of the 1970s.[2] Among its most renowned disciples are Ben Caldwell, Charles Burnett, Larry Clark, Abdosh Abdulhafiz, Jamaa Fanaka, Billy Woodberry, Haile Gerima, Alile Sharon Larkin, Bernard Nicolas, Julie Dash, Barbara McCullough, Carroll Parrott Blue, Melvonna Ballenger, O.Funmilayo Makarah, Teshome Gabriel, and Zeinabu irene Davis. These artists inherited a cultural legacy stretching from writers of the Harlem Renaissance to poet Sonia Sanchez, for by the late 1960s, UCLA, as a historical, cultural and intellectual repository, marked a critical crossroads for some of the most contested political and cultural forces in Black America at that time. In this paper, I will analyze the works of four significant women directors of the Los Angeles School: Julie Dash, Alile Sharon Larkin, Carroll Parrott Blue, and Barbara McCullough.

In the early 1960s, UCLA was the culminating point of a cultural movement and the site of new grounds in political engagement. The Watts Rebellion of 1965 compelled UCLA to open its doors not only to minority students but also to foreign students as varied and diverse as had not been seen before. This logistical reality prompted the university to make changes in the curricula, especially as it affected students of color. In a more consequential and direct way, the Watts Rebellion dramatized the historical context in which contradictory cultural politics of the nation would explosively culminate. The deaths of political activists Bunchy Carter and John Huggins at UCLA in 1969 marked the climax of confrontation between the cultural nationalism of the US (United Students) organization and the revolutionary nationalism of the Black Panther Party. In *The Autobiography of Leroi Jones*, Amiri Baraka marks this event as precipitating his shift from cultural nationalism of the late 1960s to the cultural politics of Maoism in the 1970s.[3] Angela Davis presents a slightly different interpretation of this pivotal tragedy. As she discusses in *An Autobiography*, the deaths of Carter and Huggins propelled a conscientious inquiry into the possible connections between Black American revolutionary nationalism and the internationalism of the International Workers' Movement.[4]

One of the most significant consequences of the 1969 UCLA tragedy was scholar Molefi Kete Asante's dramatic turn to Black cultural nationalism at the Center for Afro-American Studies. As director of the center, Asante's foundation for Afrocentrism circulated at the same time as the gestation of the Los Angeles School at UCLA. Although there was no direct connection or causal relationship between the cultural collective of the film movement and the intellectual formation of Afrocentricity, it is remarkable to observe how the women of the Los Angeles School extensively address and challenge the historical and political precepts espoused by Afrocentrism. Julie Dash's *Diary of An African Nun* (1977) and *The Legend of Carl Lee Duvall* (1973), along with Alile Sharon Larkin's *A Different Image* (1982), all re-evaluate the cultural merits and recuperation that Afrocentricism has historically claimed.

Only recently with Haile Gerima's widely acclaimed *Sankofa* (1993) has there been a male representative of the Los Angeles School who engages the question of philosophical and political unity within the Black world, even though the women's work from this group has explored this issue for years. This is not to suggest that prior to *Sankofa* no men from the Los Angeles School explored the significance of Africa to Black American artistic expression. Haile Gerima's *Bush Mama* (1976) and Larry Clark's *Passing Through* (1977) directly allude to the political and philosophical legacies inspired by revolutions that were then unfolding in Ethiopia, Angola, Mozambique, and Guinea-Bissau. In the films of Julie Dash and Alile Sharon Larkin, however, Africa is not only a historical construct for political reference and import but also a metaphorical construct of ontological inquiry and cultural identification. It is because of this investigation on the ontological and cultural planes that some women of the Los Angeles School are much closer to a whole series of issues raised by Afrocentricity: namely, the concerns of cultural and national identification. This is not to say that Dash and Larkin subscribe to the ideological conceptualization of Afrocentricity as articulated by Asante. We shall come back to these matters in a moment. But by drawing these parallels between the foundations of Afrocentrism and the cultural and political identification with Africa within the Los Angeles School, it becomes apparent that in the late 1960s and the early 1970s, UCLA nurtured a Black intellectual vitality that the Watts Rebellion of 1965 dramatically ignited.

The notion of pan-Africanism as delineated by the women from the Los Angeles School does not directly correspond to pan-Africanism in the classical sense as espoused by C.L.R. James, Du Bois and others. Contrary to these polemical treatises of African unity, the women of the Los Angeles School embraced a type of Pan-Africanism as reconstituted by Toni Morrison as American Africanism. Morrison, in her recent book of critical essays, *Playing in the Dark: Whiteness and the Literary Imagination* (1992), defines Africanism as the denotative and connotative Blackness that African people signify. This historically constructed Africanism, which is sometimes appropriated by Europeans in the interests of Eurocentricity to designate negativism, is re-appropriated by Blacks to reconstitute knowledge as revelation and choice rather than as invasion and conquest. Morrison makes clear that her revision of Africanism diametrically opposes conventional Afrocentricity, which often replicates the imperialistic tendencies of Eurocentric scholarship.[5]

Morrison's critique of Afrocentric scholarship is absolutely correct, particularly in light of recent dialogues between Asante, Henry Louis Gates Jr., and Manning Marable in a special issue of *Black Scholar* that in effect, articulated Afrocentrism as an imperializing process, in that it makes territorial claims on any knowledge emanating from Black scholars, even that which contradicts its fundamental premises and arguments.[6] *A Different Image* and *Diary of an African Nun* are eloquent and trenchant exemplifications of this Morrisonian Africanism.

Dash's *Diary of An African Nun* is the filmic rendition of a short story by Alice Walker that chronicles a young African woman's transformation from "primitive" to "civilized." Through her personal and spiritual evolution, the native woman's "primitive art" and "magical color" yield to Christianity as "the incarnation of civilization" and "the triumphing idea." Walker examines the role of religion, specifically the Catholic Church, in its complicity with colonialism and imperialism. This fictional piece engages one of the most pressing concerns in African history: the imposition of European history on African cosmology and the tragic consequences that resulted from this process of domination.[7] However, Walker abandons the reductive dichotomy of native culture poised against encroaching colonial forces. Rather, these sites remain in a state of unresolved tension, leaving Africa to wrestle with its own fate rather than the imperial presence of Europe.

Dash generally maintains the narrative structure of Walker's story but draws the tale deeper into the psyche of the title character. In the film, the narrative unfolds as an interior monologue of the African nun as she develops her personal and political consciousness and tries to make sense of the two colliding and irreconcilable perspectives of the world: the African and the European. Dash alters the narrative thereby, making it even more disjunctive and convoluted than it originally appeared in Alice Walker's story. In the film, the conflict of the European and African world views becomes a process through which the African nun gains self-knowledge as to her location in this momentous struggle—a struggle she perceives as being determined by deliberate choices and interventions. The film, a more elaborate and complex project than the short story, features a series of dialectical oppositions: the sensual polyrhythms of African music contrasted with the austerity of Catholic prayer and order; the expansive and unlimited horizon of the African landscape juxtaposed with the confinement and the claustrophobic atmosphere of the convent. *Diary of an African Nun* clearly indicates that Dash, from early on, had already mastered the fundamental grammar of film language. Both this film and Charles Burnett's *Killer of Sheep* (1977) mark the high points of the poetic lyricism that characterized the early period of the Los Angeles School.

Dash's adaptation of Walker's short story illuminates the interdependence between the Los Angeles School and African American women writers; a relationship emerging from their common roots in the fits and starts of the Second Reconstruction and the transformation of the Civil Rights Movement into the Black Liberation Movement. Dash's cultural ideology was undoubtedly shaped by the poetics and the nationalist agenda of women writers within the Black Arts Movement including Sonia Sanchez and Toni Cade Bambara. Sanchez's poetic manifesto of this movement, *Homecoming* (1969), had a lasting impact on Dash's philosophical outlook and aesthetic framework. Similarly, elements of Bambara's short stories from *Gorilla, My Love* (1972), correlate to images and themes that Dash expresses in her own work.[8] But Dash is not alone in drawing cinematic inspiration from literary works. Larkin has also discussed how Morrison's *The Bluest Eye* (1970) constantly informs her configurations of Black creativity. In addition to the bond between film and literature grounded at the Los Angeles School, artists there drew inspiration from other female artists; for instance, Barbara McCullough speaks of how moved she has been by the art work of Bettye Saar.

In addition to Dash's early work, several other women from the Los Angeles School exemplify what could be designated as Morrisonian Africanism. Larkin's *A Different Image* is poised as a foil to patriarchal domination in much the same way as *Diary of an African Nun*. In the former film, Africanism is articulated in the context of sexual politics within a patriarchal order. In the latter film, it is invoked in the context of colonial politics within an imperial order. Again, in both films, Africanism is a driving ideological force through which crucial aspects of personal identity crystallize: an awakening social and cultural consciousness of an African nun as an African, and, in the other film, an awakened social and historical consciousness of an African American woman as a woman. In one film, Africanism is a praxis philosophy against racism and religious prejudice, while the other presents Africanism as a means of resistance against sexism.

In Larkin's *A Different Image*, the woman, Alana, has surrounded herself in her private sphere with images of Africa and African American women who embody African sensibilities through their personal styles and physical traits. They attire themselves in traditional African dress and adhere to an Afrocentric world view. Alana has saturated her private sphere with African cultural symbols as a means of keeping her heightened state of consciousness in combativeness above the sexism and the cultural Eurocentrism that dominates the American public sphere. This sensitivity to the cultural symbolism of Africa has invariably led to charges that Larkin romanticizes Africa. She responded trenchantly to this challenge in a joint interview with Dash in the *Independent*:

> That's a question that often comes up with *A Different Image*. The film has been criticized negatively by women who consider themselves radical feminists, who say I romanticize Africa. I think that comes from lack of knowledge of African societies. I think that they should do some research and understand the roles of Black women in society from antiquity to colonization and European contact.[9]

A Different Image attempts to reconstitute knowledge as choice in order to decolonize the mind, as Ngugi wa Thiong'o would say, and the soul. The strength of the film comes from the tension it creates between a free private domain and a hegemonized public sphere.

cultural and creative processes

Along with the question of Africanism, the women of the Los Angeles School have also fundamentally examined the nature of culture and the creative process that culture itself entails. This is one of the richest branches of the School, with a number of films encompassing this motif including Carroll Parrott Blue's *Conversations with Roy DeCarava* (1983), *Varnette's World: A Study of a Young Artist* (1979); and *Nigerian Art: Kindred Spirits* (1990); through Barbara McCullough's documentary video *Shopping Bag Spirits and Freeway Fetishes: Reflections on Ritual Space* (1979) and the other documentary videos in progress, *The World of Saxophone Quartet*, and *Horace Tapscott: Musical Griot* (1991); and Julie Dash's *Four Women* (1975).[10]

Although the Los Angeles School has largely been associated with works of fiction, documentary form has also been one of its strongest achievements. Though Gerima has often been aligned with *Bush Mama* or *Sankofa*, among his earliest accomplishments were several documentaries including *After Winter: Sterling Brown* (1985) and *The Wilmington 10—U.S.A. Ten Thousand* (1978). Similarly, Charles Burnett has been more renowned for *Killer of Sheep* than the documentary he directed, entitled *America Becoming* (1991). But apart from the masthead representatives from the Los Angeles School, it is the women within this cadre who have been true exemplars of the documentary forte. The most captivating achievement in this genre has been that of Carroll Parrott Blue. In contrast to Barbara McCullough, who interrogates the creative act as a ritual process, Blue examines it as a representation of history, memory, and tradition. Blue's *Conversations with Roy DeCarava* in many ways marks the pinnacle of documentary filmmaking within the Los Angeles School. In examining the work of Roy DeCarava, the film, on one plane, chronicles the history of African American photography from James Van der Zee to Carrie Mae Weems. On another level, the film focuses on life in Harlem and its myriad historical representations. Blue posits DeCarava as the link between James Van der Zee's moment of the Harlem Renaissance and the postmodern era of Black women artists and intellectuals headed by Weems. DeCarava is conscious of his place in this historic and artistic continuum when he says of his work:

> I just want my work to be as completely honest and as deeply emotional as I can make it. I don't have any particular goals in mind other than I want to take the kind of pictures that have never been taken before. When I say never taken before I mean in terms of the intensity and importance. I'm addressing myself to Black people first. There is a certain responsibility that each of us in his own discipline should survive and help other Black people to survive, and that includes photographers.[11]

DeCarava's use of photography to retrieve, retain, and represent the survival of Black people demands the kind of commitment to blues aesthetics that Albert Murray observes in the work of Romare Bearden. Murray finds in Bearden's art the dynamics and spontaneity that have come to characterize nearly all Black cultural production.

> As striking as the figurative and thematic dimensions of the paintings and collages of Romare Bearden so often are, their specific forms ... are by Bearden's own account always far less a matter of considered representation than the result of on-the-spot improvisation or impromptu invention. He approaches his subjects not as a portrait painter might, or a landscape artist of, say, the Hudson River School, but in the manner of a jazz musician.[12]

DeCarava, too, approaches photography in an improvisational manner similar to that of a jazz musician. This is most evident in the book *The Sweet Flypaper of Life* (1955), consisting of DeCarava's photographs and an accompanying text by Langston Hughes.[13] In her chronicle of DeCarava, Blue clearly captures the improvisational spirit of his photography. In a particular moment from the film, DeCarava acknowledges the influences of African American musical traditions upon his own work: "Jazz, I think, approaches the visual experience of photography at the precise moment when the shutter captures that slice of experience that you see, that you feel. At the moment when all the things come together.... There is a Black aesthetic. I will do whatever I can to make sure that it survives. If the Black aesthetic does not survive, then Blacks will not survive."

Following this philosophy of aesthetic practice and cultural politics, Blue traces DeCarava's development through the rigors of Van Gogh's emotional intensity, the humanism of Charles White, and his maturation through the jazz poetics of the bebop revolution and John Coltrane. The apex of DeCarava's professional career and personal mission coalesces in his deanship with the Kamoinge Workshop, a workshop that promoted and generated formative experiences for a generation of Black photographers. In these different phases of his life as a photographer, DeCarava came to be known as a documentarian, a jazz photographer, a street visionary, and a Black historian. All of these designations attempt to capture the rich complexity of DeCarava's work. The film is interspersed with many of his photographs, which construct a narrative of his creative life history. The photographs themselves reveal various social and cultural histories: the political history of Harlem and oppression, and the cultural history of jazz and the social history of the Black family. The searing social realism of his black and white stills is a tribute to a tradition of African American photography made memorable in Richard Wright's *Twelve Million Black Voices.*[14]

Highly esteemed in the tradition of American photography by both Ansel Adams and Edward Steichen, DeCarava's work clearly demonstrates his mastery of the craft. In addition to depicting DeCarava as a photographer *par excellence,* Blue also presents him as a cultural producer and facilitator. As a cultural worker documenting and intervening in American cultural history, DeCarava has sought to establish institutions that would insure the survival of an African American photographic tradition. In 1955 he opened a gallery in New York City that exhibited the work of pre-eminent American and British photographers including Harry Callahan, Berenice Abbott, Minor White, Victor Obsatz, and others. DeCarava comments in the film that many exhibits held in his gallery were widely reviewed in the *New York Times,* yet in the cultural history of American photography, racism has made many white cultural critics and historians overlook the invaluable contribution Blacks have made in this domain.

A fundamental theme of Blue's film work is the nature of the creative process and the various institutions that sustain the viability of artistic endeavors. This was apparent in an earlier film, *Varnette's World: A Study of a Young Artist,* and is sustained in her later film, *Nigerian Art: Kindred Spirits. Varnette's World* revolves around the question of African American spirituality as manifested through visual art and its kinetic expression in the tradition of the Black church. The film begins brilliantly with a Varnette Honeywood painting, as the camera pans from the foreground where a group of Black people are walking toward the church, which stands at the center and background of the canvas. In the following scene we find Honeywood among a singing and clapping congregation inside a church, a scene that will later close the film. In a voice-over, Honeywood describes herself and her work in the following terms: "What I paint are visual statements of Black lifestyles on canvas. I get my subjects from the people I see and the places I go to within the community. I could be walking down the street, on the playground, or even in church." After completing her Bachelor of Arts degree in Art at Spelman College in the early 1970s, Honeywood returned to her hometown of Los Angeles to work with a consortium that develops an art curriculum and programs for eight public schools.

28

Blue constructs the narrative of the film as a discourse between the autobiographical sketch of the artist, her use of art as a pedagogical instrument, and Honeywood's attempt to tap her African heritage. Blue's primary theme here circulates around notions of healing and spirituality. In her quest for spiritual rejuvenation through her African origins, Honeywood attended FESTAC 1977 (The Second World Black Festival of Arts and Cultures) in Lagos, Nigeria. Returning from Nigeria to Los Angeles, she speaks in the film of the personal transformation the trip facilitated:

For me it was a very moving experience. I felt mystical being able to go to Africa and set my feet on the soil of my ancestors. I had not been to Africa before. I met Black artists from all over the world. It was rewarding for me to find out how similar our experiences and goals as artists were. I was really happy because I thought that I had done the right thing, and that was to paint what I feel exactly. For one thing, it made me realize that our legacy as an African people remains a part of our culture today. An example of this is our use of color. . . . The spirits that directed the creation of the African arts, the visual arts, the clothing, the spoken words, the dance and the religion have been carried over and are influencing Black people today.[15]

Since Honeywood works in a figurative mode, the artistic legacy that she sustains extends from Jacob Lawrence to William H. Johnson. It is instructive to note how the art created by these two great artists, remarkably different from each other, inform the legacy that Honeywood sought in Africa. It was fitting that Blue would come to examine the nature of African art in order to make fully intelligible the creative practices of African American artists. Articulating their different forms of Morrisonian Africanism, Dash and Larkin render their portraits of Africa through imaginative conjuring in *Diary of an African Nun* and *A Different Image*, respectively. But Blue actually visited Africa in her efforts to authenticate the historical intelligibility and rationality of this Africanism. The end product of this journey is Blue's documentary, *Nigerian Art: Kindred Spirits.*

Nigerian Art: Kindred Spirits begins with the smoky voice of renowned Black actress, Ruby Dee, dramatically challenging us with the following questions: "What can we know of Nigerian art? Where does its vitality come from? Is tradition the answer or modernity?" She tells us that Leopold Sedar Senghor has defined African art in the following manner: "African art is concerned with reaching beyond and beneath nature and has, itself, become a part of the vital force. The artistic image is not intended to represent the thing itself, but rather the reality of the force the thing contains. Thus the moon is fecundity and the elephant is force." Even though Senghor defines African art in metaphysical terms and abstract language, Blue attempts to locate the nature of Nigerian art through the dual constructs of tradition and belief, colonialism and independence, repression and freedom. Consequently, Blue structures her film as a steady volley between the historical notions of tradition and the pull of modernity.

Emmanuel Arinze, Assistant Director of the National Commission for Museums and Monuments, validates this dichotomy as he explains that

Nigerian art draws its inspiration from the basic principles of indigenous African art. This extensive art history consists of Nok art from 500 B.C., Eboku art from the ninth century A.D., Ife art from the twelfth century, and Benin art (the destruction of classical Benin art by the British punitive expedition of 1897 was one of the tragic defining moments of modern Nigerian artistic consciousness). Drawing inspiration from these different and complex forms, the past and the present co-exist in modern Nigerian art. Many of the artists whose work is examined in the documentary film use various Nigerian artifacts and cultural traditions to construct their modern art, which seeks to illuminate the present. Blue includes in her film many leading modern Nigerian artists: Lamidi Fakeye (sculptor), Nike (textile artist), Emmanuel Taiwo Jegede (sculptor, painter, ceramist), Ben Enwonwu (sculptor, painter), Sokari Douglas Camp (sculptor), Dele Jegede (art historian, painter), Simon Okeke (painter), Aina Onabula (teacher, "father" of modern Nigerian art in the 1920s and 1930s), Obiora Udechukwu (printmaker, painter), Bruce Onobrakpeya (printmaker), Rowland Abiodun (art historian), and Uche Okeke (painter, sculptor, printmaker). All these artists, by various ways and means, seek to unite the diverse cultures of Nigeria into a tapestry of many threads. Emmanuel Taiwo Jegede, an artist featured in the film, says of his artistic project: "The Yoruba concept of creativity is seeing art through life, and life through art.... Art is the totality of the cycle of life.... Most of my work is about telling stories: stories about life, agony, pain, joy, dreams, about all the things that make life possible." Many other modern Nigerian artists offer stories about tradition and modernity through their art work. In *Nigerian Art*, Blue sheds light on the actuality of Africa as it is manifest in numerous facets of African American creative process.

experimental representation

While Dash in *Four Women* examines the preservation of African American stories through dance, McCullough in *Horace Tapscott: Musical Griot* considers the narrative properties of jazz. In *Shopping Bag Spirits and Freeway Fetishes: Reflections on Ritual Space*, McCullough radically draws the creative process itself as a form of ritual. This latter video documentary is one of the high points of experimentalism within the Los Angeles School. Dash's *Four Women* is inspired by the Nina Simone song of the same title. Dash renders *Four Women* with a remarkably fluid form, which offers a striking precursor to the ground-breaking work of *Daughters of the Dust* (1991). *Four Women* is largely made in an experimental mode, clearly distinguishing itself from the poetic realism of the latter film. The experimentalism of Dash in this film has affinities with that of McCullough, which was a permanent feature of the latter's work. While Dash uses the experimental mode in this film to interrogate the history of Black people in the Americas, McCullough's style meditates on the ritualistic nature of the creative process among Black artists in the Diaspora. Dash most often incorporates this experimental style in fictive works, while McCullough uses it as the impetus behind her documentary form.

In *Four Women*, Dash uses Linda Young's choreography and dancing to convey the four phases or personalities that forge a complete and whole African American woman. Following Nina Simone's lead, Dash suggests that African American women exist in a constant state of resistance and struggle against the oppressive forces of American history. The film is a hymn to freedom and celebrates the triumph over adversity for American Blacks. But in one segment, Simone's song charts the more tragic yet obstinate aspects of African American women's history:

> My skin is Black
> My arms are long
> My hair is woolly
> My back is strong
> Strong enough to take the pain
> Inflicted again and again
> What do they call me?
> . . . .
> My name is Bitterness.

Simone identifies a lineage of strength and perseverance within African American women's history descending from Egypt, a reference that prefaces Dash's film with a perspective of Morrisonian Africanism. The film begins with Young in a fetus position symbolizing the helplessness of captivity as well as the birth of freedom. While she rests in this position, the film's soundtrack is African music overlaid with sounds connoting the Middle Passage, slavery, and the flight to freedom. As Young gradually unwinds herself upright and starts dancing, Dash unleashes the haunting strength and defiance of Simone's song. The film celebrates the birthing of freedom and liberation in the wake of adversity and oppression.

The extraordinary importance of *Four Women* as Dash nurtures her artistic voice is readily apparent if understood in comparison with the aesthetics of the documentary form of the East Coast Documentary Movement of William Greaves and St. Clair Bourne. *Four Women* marks Dash's entrance into the aesthetics of the fiction form of the Los Angeles School of Charles Burnett, Ben Caldwell, Larry Clark, and others. She makes her debut within the Los Angeles School, staking her claim to a fluid and malleable form reminiscent of Ben Caldwell's experimentalist blues and jazz style. Dash's decision to embrace an experimental format rather than a conventional approach to documentary resonates with significant social forces and shifts within the Black independent film movement. Because of its alignment with the Black Arts Movement ideology of Black aesthetics, as defined and espoused by Amiri Baraka and Larry Neal within the East Coast Documentary Movement, it could not accommodate the novel images and representations that Dash wanted to initiate. In the foreword to a posthumous collection of Larry Neal's writing, *Visions of a Liberated Future: Black Arts Movement Writings* (1989), Baraka recalls the ideology of Black aesthetics:

> We wanted an art that would actually reflect Black life and its history and legacy of resistance and struggle! ... We wanted an art that was as Black as our music.... An art that would educate and unify Black people in our attack on an anti-Black racist America.... We wanted a mass art, an art that could "Monkey" out the libraries and "Boogaloo" down the street in tune with popular revolution.... What we wanted to create would be African American and Revolutionary. In fact it would be the real link to our history—part of the mainstream of Black art through the century.[16]

Dash did not necessarily disagree with these revolutionary tenets of Black aesthetics, in so much as she opposed the despotic grip of the East Coast Documentary Movement on all of Black independent filmmaking. At this time, there was no coherent ideology of aesthetics within the Los Angeles School, precisely because it was then a cauldron of ideological conflicts between the African Marxism of Frantz Fanon and Amilcar Cabral, the cultural nationalism of the US Organization, and the revolutionary nationalism of the Black Panther Party. Moving from the East Coast to the West Coast, Dash was not deliberately aligning herself with a particular aesthetic ideology within the Los Angeles School, but rather, she ideally situated herself within its experimental environment of film language. In effect, Dash's *Four Women* cast her at the head of an experimentalist tradition that would soon find in it ranks the work of Ben Caldwell and that of Barbara McCullough.

Praise House (1991), based on the choreographic work of Jawole Willa Jo Zollar, and made sixteen years after *Four Women*, continues some of the themes of the latter film: the body of the woman as the self-expression of her freedom, Black people's ongoing hunger for liberty, and the fundamental importance of Africa in the search for cultural identity of Blacks in the Diaspora. *Praise House* delves much more deeply than *Four Women* into the cultural elements of history, myth, and religion. Whereas dance as an art form profoundly occupies Dash's creative vision, photography and painting fascinate Blue, and musical forms (jazz and blues) have strongly influenced McCullough. Larkin and Melvonna Ballenger do not seem to have been pulled by a particular art exclusively, but undoubtedly their work reflects a *mélange* of African American creative expressions.

Although *Praise House* follows some of the thematic patterns established in *Four Women*, its narrative structure is much more densely textured than that of the latter film. Whereas *Four Women* examined the body as a formal device in choreography, in *Praise House* the body functions as a vessel of spirituality communicating with the other world. Hannah, the young daughter in *Praise House*, refuses to confront reality and instead dwells in her imagination, where she conjures a world full of angels, symbolized by the other dancers. The film anticipates *Daughters of the Dust*, by developing several narrative lines that intersect each other and, in the process, constitute a dense narrative structure. This rich form facilitates the examination of two varied themes: the power of the imagination to alter reality, and the perpetuation of tradition and its transformation through continuity and discontinuity. Dash consistently traverses the boundaries between reality, and the super-real or fantasy. Hannah escapes the world of daily chores that her mother constantly imposes on her and retreats into her imaginative world, which in many ways is similar to that of her grandmother who is also named Hannah. The film's magic comes from the ambiguity of narrative perspectives from both the granddaughter and the grandmother. Between them, the relationship is one of Nietzschean eternal recurrence. In *Praise House*, history and myth are closely intertwined, a proximation that is very much foreign to the aesthetics of the East Coast Documentary Movement. In effect, the film testifies to the spiritual nature and social power of the imagination.

While Dash's *Praise House* explores the creative process as a metaphor for the events of African American history, McCullough's work views creativity as ritual. This preoccupation is the central thesis of McCullough's video documentary, *Shopping Bag Spirits and Freeway Fetishes: Reflections on Ritual Space*, which consists of different episodes with various Los Angeles artists in the process of creating a work of art: Kinshasha Conwill (painter, sculptor), Kamau Daa'ood (poet), N'senga Negundi (sculptor, earth sculptor), Bettye Saar (painter, sculptor), and Raspoeter Ojenke (saxophonist). With all of these artists, improvisation is a major aspect of their work. One episode from *Shopping Bag Spirits* features David Hammons creating an earth work sculpture from the rubble of a fallen building in South Central Los Angeles. McCullough interviews Hammons as he creates the piece and asks him about ritual and his creative process. Hammons claims that ritual is an everyday act that empowers him to release energy from nature by creating order out of disorder without contrivance. It is this energy that enables him to find order, balance, the focal point, and the center of interest in harnessing the forces of nature. The earth work sculpture that he creates from the destroyed building in the film illustrates the improvisational process that he sees as an important quality of avant-garde music. Confirming Hammons's observations about the sacred and the ordinary in *Shopping Bag Spirits*, Kellie Jones writes the following words in the recent catalog of his exhibition: "Throughout most of his career, David Hammons has disarmed and constructed symbols and stereotypes through constant reuse. He has recycled images, ideas and materials, employing them first one way and then another. By seeing them over and over again, recontextualized in a plethora of postures, meaning is emptied but becomes more fluid."[17] Even before his reputation as an internationally renowned artist took root, Hammons received much praise and recognition from the women artists of the Los Angeles School. In *Daughters of the Dust*, Dash features a sculpture that Hammons specifically created for the film.

Fine art, its nature or its construction, is ever present in the imagination of the women members of the Los Angeles School.[18] Recently, Larkin tried her hand at animation with the parodic piece, *Dreadlocks and the Three Bears* (1991), which consists of a series of illustrative drawings and paintings penned by the filmmaker. The video reconstructs the traditional fable particularly for African American children to entertain and inform them about Black culture in the Diaspora. It begins by alluding to Africa as the origin of many things, the cradle of human civilization, then meditates on the links between the Black cultures in the Caribbean and in North America. In this video, one hears the echoes of Larkin's constant preoccupation with pan-Africanism.

Like Blue's *Conversations with Roy DeCarava*, Larkin and McCullough have also produced documentaries on artists outside of their particular fields, namely a poet and a jazz musician, respectively. Their documentaries, shot in video rather than film, examine Los Angeles as a cultural complex—an urban site engaged as a cultural space in which Black people have made fundamental contributions. In *Miss Fluci Moses* (1987), Larkin considers the incongruity of the history of the Old South and the new history of the North. This theme also surfaces in Dash's *Daughters of the Dust* and Charles Burnett's widely acclaimed *To Sleep with Anger* (1990). In the background of Larkin's portrait of a Black poet is the great migration from the South to the North in the 1920s, 1930s, and 1940s. In her old age, Fluci Moses (Louise Jane Moses) recalls her childhood in Alabama at the early part of our century and muses over how the expectations she formed then clashed with the realities of the Black experience in urban centers like Los Angeles after the Second World War. From the stress of this conflict, her poetry grew as an expression of hope, a desire for place and a search for a cultural and spiritual harbor.

In *Horace Tapscott: Musical Griot*, McCullough investigates another branch of Black artistic production in Los Angeles. Horace Tapscott belongs to the tradition of Central Avenue Jazz (distinct from West Coast Jazz) whose luminaries include Eric Dolphy, Arthur Blythe, Charles Mingus, Don Cherry, Billy Higgins, Dexter Gordon, Ornette Coleman, and many others.[19] In sketching the biographical portrait of Tapscott, McCullough locates his training as a musician along Central Avenue in Watts, a jazz and blues Mecca of the West Coast. There, the young Tapscott interacted with his mentors, Art Tatum, Earl Hines, and Erroll Gardner, in the many jazz clubs on Central Avenue of the 1940s. *Horace Tapscott: Musical Griot* consists of four interwoven structures: a series of interviews with Tapscott on his formation as a musician as well as on the jazz and blues traditions in which he belongs; long stretches of him performing, both solo and with a combo; archival material of African American contributions to the cultural history of Los Angeles; and a brilliant improvisational lecture on jazz and the blues by Tapscott before a group of Los Angeles teachers. The film looks at the links between the politics of the 1960s and the avant-garde movement in jazz of the same decade, and through Tapscott's tenure as a musician, McCullough seeks to theorize the position of jazz in American culture. One of the dominant themes of this video documentary is jazz as a pedagogical tool, which is similar to Larkin's project with narrative in *Dreadlocks and the Three Bears*. Pedagogy through film comprises one of the most fundamental tenets for women filmmakers of the Los Angeles School.

Through the liberation of the female body and an exploration of Black women's sexuality, women of the Los Angeles School have sought to reconsider the corporeal ties between history and individuals. Along these lines, there are fascinating affinities between Dash's *Daughters of the Dust* and McCullough's *Water Ritual # 1: An Urban Rite of Purification*. McCullough frees the female body from the male gaze, while in Dash's film, the liberation of historical vision results from women's collective action. McCullough's experimental short begins with a woman sitting in the crumbling frame of a building in a desolate urban landscape. She walks to the front of the structure, where she sits and pays homage to the barren land, nature, and the soil. Having mixed the soil with some ingredients inside a calabash, Yolanda Vidato, as Milanda, gently spreads the mixture around her. She cups some of the soil with both hands, and bringing it close to her face suddenly blows it away from her hands. Naked, Milanda walks through a door into the falling structure, crouches, and urinates.

The major achievement of the film lies in its celebration of the female body as a force of nature unencumbered by the constraints of civilization. *Water Ritual # 1: An Urban Rite of Purification* in some ways continues the theme and sensibilities of *Four Women* in that both films celebrate women's pleasure in their bodies and their capacity to do whatever they please, unconstrained by the expectations of the Other. The strong impact of McCullough's film on Dash is perhaps reflected in Dash's portrait of women in control of their historical visions, their social sensibility, and their place in nature. In *Daughters of the Dust*, Dash portrays a community of women in collective possession of history, rather than an individual enterprise in isolation, as is the case in McCullough's ground-breaking film.

daughters of the dust

In the conclusion of this essay, I would like to respond to the critiques of *Daughters of the Dust* that have recently appeared in the neoconservative African American magazine, *Reconstruction*. In the essay, "*Daughters of the Dust*: The Making of an American 'Classic',"[20] Klaus de Albuquerque levels a series of unfounded charges against Dash's brilliant film. De Albuquerque finds the film historically inauthentic in its representations of African American history. He begins by stating that *Daughters of the Dust* is a work of marginal merit that "attempts to create a positive past that is psychologically satisfying."[21] Not content with demeaning the historical significance of the film, he dismisses the fact that Dash put a decade of her life into the making of the film: the arduous process of researching the film; developing a screenplay with a dense and complex narrative structure of multiple perspectives; her constant battles with financing and money; the monumental process of actually shooting the film; and the hardships of securing a distributor. In this unqualified discrediting of Dash's work, de Albuquerque casts doubts that she is "a major Black director." He then sneers at the critical attention *Daughters of the Dust* has received from noted scholars including Toni Cade Bambara, Greg Tate, bell hooks, and Houston A. Baker. All have, in some way, hailed the appearance of *Daughters of the Dust* as a watershed moment in the history of African American culture. In contrast, de Albuquerque declares:

> Both Baker and hooks argue that Dash has the artistic license to romanticize the history and culture of Black Sea Islanders.... My principal quarrel is with claims and exaggerations (contained in the film, her book and her numerous print reviews) that contribute to the romantic revisionism so prevalent among Afrocentrists and kente cloth nationalists.... *Daughters* is not only disappointing but disturbing. It contributes to a growing cottage industry of historical distortion. Distressing, too, is the fact that much of the uncritical cheerleading that has accompanied *Daughters* is animated by a notion that genetic linkage to Africa affords intuitive knowledge of Africa and things African.[22]

He concludes his misguided and unfounded indictment with the devastating claim that "As art, *Daughters* is a flop."

When one examines the evidence marshaled by de Albuquerque in support of his indictment, one is astonished to find that it consists of a series of cultural misconceptions and historical fallacies. De Albuquerque fails to bridge the film's form with the remarkable historicity *Daughters of the Dust* seeks to convey. The first misperception is evident when de Albuquerque writes the following sentence: "Reportedly a ten-year labor of love, involving countless hours of research at the Schomburg Library, the National Archives, the Library of Congress, the Smithsonian, and elsewhere, *Daughters* is a film about the fear that accompanies the decision to leave one's ancestral home and the cross-generational conflict such decisions inevitably generate."[23] While Dash successfully conveys the ruptures in tradition and family that modernity can ultimately generate, *Daughters of the Dust* is not a film about fear but rather about history. In its historical theme, *Daughters of the Dust* highlights the transformation of Africans into African Americans. It interrogates the collective memory of the cultural and historical repercussions of the Middle Passage in the imagination of African Americans. In so doing, Dash further develops the fundamental theme of all her work: the meaning of Africa to the New World Africans in the Diaspora.

The decision of the Peazant family to leave the Sea Islands of South Carolina in 1902 for the mainland does not so much elicit fear as much as it generates uncertainties and the particular challenges of a new era. There cannot be any fear of African American history, whether in its receding Africanness or in its emerging Americanness, on the part of the Peazant family because they carry their sense of history with them either in their living or dead bones or in their living or dead souls. What precipitates their uncertainty is the understanding of how special their history actually is and that, in delving deeper into the American aspect of their history, they are bound to encounter the maelstrom of American racism that places no value on their history at all. Thus their doubt and uncertainty rises from a fierce pride rather than any sense of fear or trepidation of their own historic course. The Peazant family's schism over whether to stay or quit their ancestral home illustrates Du Bois's double consciousness as articulated in *The Souls of Black Folk* (1903). Nana Peazant, the matriarch of the clan, serves to demystify and negate the patriarchal interpretation of history so prevalent in the African history of kings and conquerors. In other words, the interpretation of African and African American history in *Daughters of the Dust* is one driven by Morrisonian Africanism and not Asante's Afrocentricity.

The second misperception on the part of de Albuquerque is to characterize *Daughters of the Dust* as a soporific and lethargic film. He attributes this shortcoming of the film to the fact that he viewed the film in Charleston, South Carolina, where people supposedly left the cinema in droves. He then falsely argues that this supposed lethargic quality of the film is due to the influence of Slavko Vorkapich, the Russian montagist, who was Dash's teacher at the American Film Institute. Although Vorkapich was an outstanding teacher, Dash was not as close to him as de Albuquerque supposes. What de Albuquerque fails to register is that by establishing an unusual rhythmic tempo and visual luminosity in *Daughters of the Dust*, Arthur Jafa and Dash were articulating a new aesthetics of cinematography consonant with the lived experience of time and consciousness by Africans in the Diaspora. Dash demonstrates that initially, this sense of time and place engendered by Africans in the New World did not differ so much from that of Africans on the continent. This new exploration of time and space in the film is not something necessarily synonymous with an African aesthetics, for it can be encountered in the films of Andrei Tarkovsky, Michelangelo Antonioni, and Miklos Jansco: films developing a particular thesis ought not be confused with films carrying a message. Dash's alternative temporal and spatial configurations clearly go against Hollywood convention and maintain the tradition of the Los Angeles School, which eschews Hollywood fast cuts that blunt the spectator's engagement with the imagined world the film suggests. *Daughters of the Dust* demands that the audience engage its critical faculties. This new aesthetic of cinematography that Jafa and Dash orchestrate reflects the rich historiography of James Van der Zee and the mixed-medium expressions of Romare Bearden.[24] It is Bearden who is at the center of the film's complex form, more so than the Russian montagist.

De Albuquerque falsely accuses Dash of romantic revision and historical distortion. He argues that the point of disembarkation of most slaves was not on the Sea Islands of South Carolina but rather Charleston; he takes issue with the degree of loss and tragedy characterized by the Middle Passage, alleging that the number of lives lost to the slave trade could have been 400,000 at most, even though historians have suggested it could have been somewhere in the millions. Similarly, de Albuquerque argues that the language spoken in *Daughters of the Dust* is not Gullah, but rather, a mixture of West Indian accents. According to de Albuquerque, practically no Ibos landed on the Sea Islands as slaves, and thus the film's account of their mass suicides, rather than submitting to slavery, is, at best, a myth. He also contests the importance of Yoruba religion and mythology in framing the spiritual world of African Americans. Indeed, this is a big bill of accusations, but the subtext of these false charges is that African Americans, since becoming Black Americans in the Diaspora, have not retained much of their Africanness over the centuries. De Albuquerque views any postulation of Africanness in the historical experience of African Americans as the romanticization of African history.

The one point on which I could possibly agree with de Albuquerque concerning *Daughters of the Dust* is its inordinately complex narrative structure and the questionable effectiveness of Dash's multiple narrators. The fragmented layers of narrative ineffectively convolute the narrative flow of the film. In defense of Dash, one can argue that this project marked her attempt to challenge spectators caught in the contemporary onslaught of mind-numbing Hollywood blockbusters characterized by trite formulations.

I will not presume here to speak on behalf of hooks or Baker in their assessment of the film, but their analysis of *Daughters of the Dust* underscores Dash's originality and insight into the historical representation of African American history as opposed to the alleged historical accuracy of ethnographic accounts. This film is, after all, a work of fiction and never makes any claims to documentary status, a distinction de Albuquerque deliberately collapses and ignores in order to make unsustainable accusations against Dash's work. Why is de Albuquerque assuming a superior attitude concerning the historical searches of the Afrocentrists and the nationalists? Why this disdainful attitude, when the Afrocentrists and the nationalists express the deep pain of African American history in the context of American racism? I am a Marxist and do not adhere to the cultural and historical project of the so-called kente cloth nationalists, but I would venture to argue that the Afrocentrists have a better grasp of the problematical nature of African American history than de Albuquerque can offer, at least based on the evidence of the essay in contention here. It is Dash's brilliance of historical vision that cast her as a major film artist. She is one of the major artists within the Los Angeles School and beyond and within the larger context of the African American independent filmmaking tradition.

notes

This paper was presented at the December 1993 Modern Language Association Convention special session in Toronto on African American Women and Film. I would like to thank Dr. Glynis Carr of Bucknell University for having invited me.

1. Concerning the first group of the Los Angeles School, which consisted mainly of men, I have attempted to theorize how its origins rose out of the similar historic circumstances which molded the late-1960s emergence of revolutionary politics and Third World aesthetics: "The Los Angeles School of Black Filmmakers," in Manthia Diawara, ed., *Black American Cinema* (New York: Routledge, 1993): 107–17.

2. Through the concept of "black renaissancism," Houston A. Baker demonstrates how both the Harlem Renaissance and the Black Arts Movement articulated a "national sounding of a New World experience" and the preser-

vation of an African identity in America: "Our Lady: Sonia Sanchez and the Writing of a Black Renaissance," in Henry Louis Gates Jr. *Reading Black, Reading Feminist* (New York: Meridian Books, 1990): 318–47. One of the merits of Baker's essay is the articulation of the strong female voicing within the Black Arts Movement, a perspective of inclusiveness and expansiveness that Amiri Baraka endorses: "Masters in Collaboration," *The Music: Reflections on Jazz and Blues* (New York: William Morrow, 1987): 212. The second group of the Los Angeles School, the subject of this essay, has been characterized by a very strong female contingency. The third group, which constituted the final phase of the School in the 1980s, also had a large group of women filmmakers.

3. Amiri Baraka, *The Autobiography of Leroi Jones* (New York: Freundlich Books, 1984): 278–80.

4. Angela Davis, *An Autobiography* (New York: Random House, 1974): 194–95. In a paper given at a symposium on "Discussions in Contemporary Culture" in December 1991 at The Studio Museum in Harlem, Angela Y. Davis reflects on the problematical relation between nationalism and internationalism in the African American political context of the 1960s:

> The nationalist appeal of the early Malcolm X, however, did not move me to activism.... That image [of the Black Panther Party wearing a black-leather jacket], which would eventually become so problematic for me, called me home. And it directed me into an organizing frenzy in the streets of South Central Los Angeles. Today, I realize that there is no simple or unitary way to look at expressions of Black nationalism or essentialism in contemporary cultural forms. As my own political consciousness evolved in the sixties, I found myself in a politically oppositional stance to what some of us then called "narrow nationalism." As a Marxist, I found issues of class and internationalism as necessary to my philosophical orientation as inclusion in a community of historically oppressed people of African descent. (See "Black Nationalism: The Sixties and the Nineties," in Gina Dent, ed., *Black Popular Culture* [Seattle, WA: Bay Press, 1992]: 319–20).

5. Toni Morrison, *Playing in the Dark: Whiteness and the Literary Imagination* (Cambridge: Harvard University Press, 1992), 6–8.

6. Molefi Kete Asante, "African American Studies: The Future of the Discipline," *Black Scholar* 22: 3 (Summer 1992): 20–29.

7. The imposition of European modernity on African traditional cultures as dictated by the logic of European history is the defining theme of Amilcar Cabral's major theoretical works.

8. Julie Dash mentioned these observations in prolonged discussions we had in the Summer of 1993. Alice Walker seems not to have been a serious influence on Julie Dash. Recalling the high moral seriousness of the encounter with the poetry of Sonia Sanchez, Julie Dash spontaneously recited with deep emotions Sonia Sanchez's poem on Malcolm X in *Homecoming*, a poem that had made an impact on her twenty years ago.

9. Kwasi Harris, "New Images: An Interview with Julie Dash and Alile Sharon Larkin," the *Independent* (December 1986): 18.

10. Although Dash's *Praise House* (1991) belongs to these series of films and videos, it inhabits a peculiar position distancing it somewhat from the rest of this constellation.

11. Ray Gibson, "Roy DeCarava: Master Photographer," *Black Creation* 4: 1 (Fall 1972): 35.

ntongela masilela

40

12. Albert Murray, "The Visual Equivalent of the Blues," in Jerald L. Melberg and Milton J. Bloch, eds., *Romare Bearden* (Charlotte, NC: Mint Museum, 1980): 17.

13. Roy DeCarava and Langston Hughes, *The Sweet Flypaper of Life* (New York: Hill and Wang, 1955). See also the photographs by DeCarava in Edward Steichen's *The Family of Man* (New York: Museum of Modern Art, 1955). It is fascinating to see how Langston Hughes constructs a narrative text to clarify and support the logic configured by DeCarava's photography. Likewise, it is remarkable to note how Edward Steichen assembles photographs from different parts of the world to form a wordly narrative photographic text.

14. The poetic realism of DeCarava's photographs is greatly suggestive of the tradition laid by Henri Cartier Bresson.

15. Carroll Parrott Blue, "Varnette's World: A Study of a Young Artist," 16mm, color, 26 min., 1979.

16. Amiri Baraka, "Foreword," in Larry Neal's *Visions of a Liberated Future* (New York: Thunder's Mouth Press, 1989): x–xi.

17. Kellie Jones, "The Structure of Myth and the Potency of Magic," in *David Hammons: Rousing the Rubble* (Cambridge: MIT Press, 1991): 34.

18. Melvonna Ballenger appears to be an exception to this rule, as evidenced by her current works in progress, *Rain* and *Nappy-Headed Lady*, which are both foreign to any atmosphere in which the arts factor is of critical importance. There seems to have emerged a third wave of the Los Angeles School—a constellation of women including Zeinabu irene Davis, Yemane Demissie, and others. With a steady influx of artists and scholars migrating to the West Coast, there seems to have evolved a Black literary renaissance in Los Angeles, with three writers representing the nucleus of the group: Wanda Coleman, Lynell George, and Itabari Njeri. Recently, Coco Fusco, a performance artist and cultural theorist, also transplanted herself from the East Coast to the California shore. Ayuko Babu, who studied with the first constellation of the Los Angeles School at UCLA in the late 1960s, has recently organized the annual Los Angeles Pan African Film Festival. The success of the second festival (October 1993) was largely due to the popularity of Gerima's latest film, Sankofa. Babu defines the philosophy behind the festival in "There's No Such Thing as Hollywood," *African Screen* 4 (Milan, Italy 1993): 12–17.

19. Robert Gordon, *Jazz West Coast* (London: Quartet Books, 1986); Ted Gioia, *West Coast Jazz: Modern Jazz in California 1945–1960* (New York: Oxford University Press, 1992).

20. Klaus de Albuquerque, "*Daughters of the Dust*: The Making of an American 'Classic'," *Reconstruction* 2: 2 (1993): 122–25. I would like to thank Dr. Boyd James in the Department of Psychiatry at Charles R. Drew University of Medicine and Science for bringing this essay to my attention.

21. De Albuquerque, 122.

22. Ibid., 123.

23. Ibid., 123.

24. I have entitled my chapter on Julie Dash in my forthcoming book, *The Los Angeles School*, "Julie Dash: The Collaging of Romare Bearden in Film."

the

ties that

three   **bind**

cinematic representations

by black women

filmmakers

gloria j. gibson-hudson

The world's earliest archives or libraries were the memories of women.

—Trinh T. Minh-ha

Cultural identity is a matter of "becoming" as well as of "being." It
belongs to the future as much as to the past.

—Stuart Hall

introduction

The Black woman, as presented within mainstream cinemas, is a one-
dimensional depiction. Black women are shown as sex objects, passive victims, and as "other" in relation to males (black and white) and white
females. Worldwide, Black women's images are prescribed by narrative
texts that reflect patriarchal visions, myths, stereotypes, and/or fantasies of
Black womanhood. Consequently, these representations limit the proba-
bility of an audience seeing Black women as figures of resistance or
empowerment.

gloria j. gibson-hudson

Because many mainstream cinematic images of Black women are informed by erroneous and stereotyped societal attitudes, to challenge such caricatures has become the struggle of many Black women filmmakers worldwide. Contemporary cultural critic Cornel West believes that the "modern Black diaspora problematic of invisibility and namelessness can be understood as the condition of relative lack of Black power to represent themselves to themselves and others as complex human beings, and thereby to contest the bombardment of negative, degrading stereotypes put forward by White supremacist ideologies."[1] West's assessment applies to Black women filmmakers who challenge misrepresentations or inadequate depictions of themselves. These filmmakers seek audience enlightenment by foregrounding Black female cinematic representations that celebrate blackness and womanhood.[2] Moreover, their cinematic images demonstrate that cultural identity is fluid, contextual, and multidimensional, and that continuity exists in one's metamorphosis from "old" to "new" womanself. Most important, the films testify to the intimate relationship between representation, cultural identity, and the politics of race, sex, and class.

Closely aligned with the issue of representation is the concern with developing an appropriate theoretical framework to interpret the works. This problem is not new, but vividly mirrors the dilemma present in Black women's literary criticism.[3] In her book, *Binding Cultures: Black Women Writers in Africa and the Diaspora*, Gay Wilentz acknowledges, "until recently, the writing [substitute film] of Black women of the African diaspora, having neither gender nor color in its favor, has suffered the greatest neglect; moreover, canonical hegemony and lack of critical attention have led to a distorted view of the work when acknowledged."[4] Although the "tradition" of Black women's film is in its infancy, nonetheless, the films warrant scholarly recognition and critical analyses.

The intent of this essay is to continue the development of critical analyses of Black women films. I will explore the primary elements used by Black women filmmakers to construct their cinematic representations of Black women. Segments from the following films by Black women independent filmmakers will be examined: *Daughters of the Dust* (Julie Dash, United States, 1991), *Sidet: Forced Exile* (Salem Mekuria, Ethiopia/U.S., 1991), *And Still I Rise* (Ngozi Onwurah, Britain, 1991), and *Sisters in the Struggle* (Dionne Brand and Ginny Strikeman, Canada, 1991). Each filmmaker wrote, produced, and directed her film. These films were selected because they authoritatively challenge existing, dominant, mainstream conventions of (mis)representation, replacing them with images that reflect the complexity of Black women's life experiences. Although the genres vary, each film invokes and realizes a vision of Black womanhood situated within a social, cultural, and political framework.

This paper posits the idea that cinematic representations of Black women by Black women filmmakers are constructed by utilizing aspects of Black women's cultural identity situated within a specific socio-historic context. When viewed as a dynamic manifestation of historical constructs, cultural identity embraces the personal and the political. The cultural bond that joins these geographically and ethnically diverse cinematic statements is the artistic and political desire to develop innovative, relevant, and authentic relationships between cinematic representation and cultural identity. The effect of filmic representations contextualized by historical trajectories is a powerful icon that resists marginality, promotes survival strategies, and, potentially, transforms audiences into proactive, socially conscious viewers.

analytical framework: black feminist cultural perspective

Black women's cinema is an emerging tradition; therefore, new and dynamic theoretical tools of analysis are equally embryonic. Many approaches have surfaced in the analysis of Black women's film and literature.[5] These perspectives include: womanist Black feminism, Afrocentric feminism, Third World feminism, womynism, and African feminism. The refinement of theoretical approaches applied to film and other research areas involving Black women "can lead to redefinitions and critical examinations of concepts, perspectives, and methodologies used in research and [can] inspire a vital change that will render research activities as a basic human right and a process of liberation for oppressed groups."[6]

As Black women's "art" functions as more than "art for art's sake," so, too, should the theorized analytical framework of its "political" expression function as more than "theory for theory's sake." Moreover, Black feminist cultural analysis, as applied to literature, film, or other creative expressions of Black women, must not be ghettoized or viewed as ancillary to a Eurocentric feminist analysis. The theorized framework unearths thematic concerns, stylistic forms, and ideological stances that are crucial for study in their own right. Similarly, as Black women's communities resist oppressive life forces, and Black women filmmakers resist repressive iconic forces, Black women scholars resist irrelevant hegemonic analytical forces and frameworks.

A Black feminist cultural analysis seeks to define and examine the relationship between Black women and political agendas, including the identification of various forms of oppression and appropriate resistance strategies. As such, the framework provides for not only the investigation of the relationship between form and content, but also most importantly, the relationship between form, content, *and* political contingencies. Trinh T. Minh-ha explains:

> While theory is bound to proceed from a philosophical and
> historical awareness of "the end of art," the quesuons of art
> continue to be called on to open up the boundaries of philos-
> ophy and politics. Theory is not necessarily art, and art not
> quite theory. But both can constitute "artistically" critical
> practices whose function is to upset rooted ideologies, invali-
> dating the established canon of artistic works and modifying
> the borderlines between theoretical and non-theoretical dis-
> course.[7]

A second crucial agenda for Black feminist cultural analyses is the
exploration of the tenets of the "matrilineal diaspora." Critic Chinosole
defines the matrilineal diaspora as the link "among Black women worldwide enabling [them] to experience distinct but related cultures while
retaining a special sense of home as the locus of self-definition and
power."[8] Chinosole's timely words are echoed in those of Wilentz, who
writes:

> There is an ongoing, consolidated, movement by those
> involved with scholarly research on Black women to formu-
> late a broadbased critical approach.... Black Feminist schol-
> arship has developed rapidly as a moving force in critical
> theory. Black women and other feminist scholars have
> explored the dimensions of generational and cultural conti-
> nuity for people of African descent, particularly regarding
> women.[9]

While a relevant Black feminist cultural perspective as applied to Black
women's cinema is in its formative stage, the following principles undergirding this perspective have immediate significance, as they:

1. acknowledge that Black women worldwide share a history of patriarchal
    oppresion;
2. validate Black women's experiences as real and significant;
3. investigate the cultural history of Black women, including the survival
    techniques Black women employ to resist oppression and (re)formulate
    concepts of womanself;
4. acknowledge and respect alternative knowledge systems and the means by
    which Black women "recall and recollect."

The Black feminist cultural perspective applied to film seeks to identify
cultural and "womanist" images and social and political affluences that
subsequently inform Black women's creative cultural expression. Thus, a
Black feminist cultural perspective becomes, in one, a theoretical as well
as a political declaration. The analysis seeks broad conceptual commonalities that signature Black women's films worldwide, but in no way suggests a monolithic cinematic icon. The specific artistic manifestations may

vary significantly, but fundamental concepts underpin their creative cultural expressions to communicate concepts of identity, history, consciousness raising, resistance, and liberation.

history, identity, and representation

The complexity of Black women's cultural identity is vividly exemplified in the opening statement of Julie Dash's *Daughters of the Dust*. The voice-over acknowledges:

> I am the first and the last
> I am the honored one and the scorned one
> I am the whore and the holy one
> I am the wife and the virgin
> I am the barren one and many are my daughters
> I am the silence that you cannot understand
> I am the utterance of my name.

Implicit in these lines is the extraordinary diversity of women of color. While on the surface the statements seem to be contradictory or binary oppositions, they can be construed not simply as "either/or" dichotomies, but as a series of intricate self-portraits. Depending on context, identities are formulated and reformulated. Black women's identities are not rigid, fixed entities, but fluid—contingent upon personal, cultural, political, and social variables. Identity (re)formation is a continuous process of (re)positionmg within meaningful socio-historic structures. Film scholars Jacqueline Bobo and Ellen Seiter argue that "no longer can a text constructed by a Black woman be considered in isolation from the context of its creation, from its connection with other works within the tradition of Black women's creativity, and from its impact not just on cultural critics but on cultural consumers."[10] Bobo and Seiter's insights on Black women's cultural expression acknowledge the powerful effects of social reality upon creativity and subsequent filmic representations.

As cultural identity emerges from social reality it also embraces unity, celebrates blackness, and acknowledges the struggle against hegemonic political structures—but it entails more. Cultural critic Stuart Hall recognizes two levels of cultural identity. The first describes cultural identity, "in terms of the idea of one, shared culture [where] our cultural identities reflect the common historical experiences and shared cultural codes which provide us as 'one people' with stable, unchanging and continuous frames of reference and meaning."[11] While the concept of cultural identity recognizes the struggle of black people against oppression, this definition is not, by Hall's own admission, wholly inclusive because it de-emphasizes cultural difference.

However, Hall's second explanation of cultural identity places the issue in a broader context. He writes, "there are many points of similarity, there are also critical points of deep and significant difference which constitute 'what we are': or rather—since history has intervened—'what we have become.' Cultural identity, in this second sense, is a matter of 'becoming' as well as of 'being.'"[12] The latter concept of cultural identity is more applicable for this analysis because it recognizes how black people were positioned in history, due to hegemonic doctrine, but it also acknowledges differences in exactly how identities were (re)constituted as a result of specific socio-historic circumstances.

Cultural distinction also exists on another level. Gender-specific experiences comprise a decisive realm within cultural history because "Black women have a history of their own, one which reflects their distinct concerns, values, and the role they have played as both Afro-Americans and women."[13] This idea is applicable not only to Afro-American women, but also to Black women worldwide. Moreover, a discourse of cultural identity must be cognizant of the historical impact of the convergent issues of sex, race, and class. The common thread in the cultural history of black people is oppression, but the manifestations of that oppression differ depending on specific socio-historic circumstances.

As related to the present study, the specfic challenge entails an examination of the relationship between Black women's history, cultural identities, and filmic representation. In her chapter entitled, "Questions of Images and Politics," Trinh Minh-ha states that a "responsible work [film] today seems to me above all to be one that shows, on the one hand, a political commitment and an ideological lucidity, and is, on the other hand interrogative by nature.... In other words, a work that involves the story in history...."[14] It is precisely from Black women filmmakers' interpretation or memory of "her story" in/as history that cinematic representation acquires relevance and meaning. Aspects of Black women's history fuel cultural identity, which in turn provides the undergirding foundation for filmic representation.

A second relevant and equally crucial question emerges, namely, "What exactly constitutes history?" The recorded history of most people of the African diaspora, as reflected by Eurocentric research publications, expropriates and distorts black diasporic experiences. Canonical texts record and historicize experiences as linear evolutions, suggesting authenticity in documentation. Black experiences are encoded as marginal, therefore inferior. They are thus rendered as an insignificant other(s). And in most cases, the experiences of women suffer an additional stratum of invisibility and unimportance.

Black women historians recognize Black women's alternative systems of knowledge.[15] Consequently, their research publications capture a more inclusive history—one that transcends superficial name recognition. This paper argues that Black women filmmakers incorporate alternative, non-conventional elements of cultural history that stimulate the formation of filmic representation. These elements are viable because as they help to recount the past, they also document the individual and collective maturation of Black womanhood.

One of the most salient elements employed in Black women's films that contributes to identity (re)formation and frames filmic representation is the use of cultural memory, which functions as a personal form of history. Most importantly, within the film narrative, cultural memory transcends superficial inclusion because it is deeply entrenched within the filmic representation, thereby providing texture, complexity, and authenticity to the character and the narrative. Whether narrative or documentary, cultural memory foregrounds the filmic representation.

Black women's literary criticism frequently acknowledges cultural memory as a determinant in Black women's writings. For example, acclaimed novelist Toni Morrison explains how she views memory:

> Memory (the deliberate act of remembering) is a form of willed creation. It is not an effort to find out the way it really was—that is research. The point is to dwell on the way it appeared and why it appeared in that particular way. Memory for me is always fresh, in spite of the fact that the object being remembered is done and past.[16]

Morrison's thoughts on memory—though realized in literature—are equally important to Black women's cinema because memory emerges as a powerful cinematic device to frame historical content. Further, as memory functions within the the filmmaker's creative process and also as a filmic device, it remains intimately connected to cultural history and identity formation.

The use of cultural memory is a bridge to unite the past, present, and future. The films of Dash, Onwurah, Brand, Strikeman, and Mekuria seek to unearth the essence of Black womanhood by using history and identity to empower filmic representation. As they explore the multiple dimension of Black women's cultural identities, their cinematic imperative becomes the promotion of socio-political identities that will ignite the consciousness and transform the status of Black women worldwide.

daughters of the dust (julie dash, 1991, usa)

Perhaps no film embodies Trinh Minh-ha's statement "The world's earliest archives or libraries were the memories of women" as vividly and beautifully as *Daughters of the Dust*. *Daughters of the Dust* recounts the story of a younger generation Gullah family preparing to leave the Georgia Sea Islands for the mainland at the turn of the twentieth century. On another level, the film unleashes the folklore and material culture, memories, and heritage of Black women as they grapple with their destinies. *Daughters of the Dust* represents a dynamic interweaving of fiction and cultural memory, grounded in African American and African history. Most effectively, the film explores cultural identity as it is rooted in the past, manifest in the present, and projected into the future. The resulting narrative serves as an engaging interplay between diverse temporal and physical dimensions and mythical and spiritual realms. Consequently, time, space, and place (finite and infinite) perform a vital role in the construction of meaning. Historical time is represented by the past, present, and future. Historical place and space are this world and the spiritual realm mediated by the forces of nature. What Dash achieves is not monochromatic dimensions of time, space, and place, but an intimate merging of those planes, establishing how each advances the quest for identity.

Within the multiple planes of time, space, and place, the filmic gaze foregrounds the generations of the women (unborn child/child, young woman, middle-aged woman, and "old" woman), their identities, and their relationships to each other. Identity formation serves as one of the major themes of the film. Through Nana, the central character, Dash plots the course for the Peazant family to remember and reclaim their ancient identity. Nana realizes that spiritual bonds with the past, which transcend written records, will generate mechanisms for survival and empowerment. This section will briefly consider the character Nana and how she functions as the axis around which the other women revolve and through which their identities are challenged, restructured, and empowered. The argument advanced is simply that Dash's representation of Black women is constructed by placing the characters within the context of cultural history. History structured as cultural memory is made manifest through folk beliefs, material culture, and personal narratives.

Nana is a Black cinematic heroine, functioning as the matriarch of the Peazant family, and apparently possessing traits and powers of conjurer, priestess, and/or practitioner of hoodoo. More than a superficial, superstitious figurehead, she serves as the source of familial cohesiveness, thereby ensuring "salvation" through the practice of "sacred" rituals. As Nana articulates the ideologies, norms, and values that provide grounds for cultural "legitimacy" and identity (re)formation, she affirms her role as a conduit between those who will go North and those who remain— between those of this world and those of the spiritual realm, at one point uttering, "It is up to the living to stay connected with the dead."

Keeping in touch with the ancestors, via (re)memory and prayer, reflects one means by which Nana's interactions with the spiritual world contribute to identity formation and empowerment. Nana's beliefs, ideas, and daily behavior are not passive, but constructed from aspects of the African American folklore tradition. According to historian Lawrence Levine, "folk beliefs provided hope, assurance, and a sense of group identification, but they had another dimension as well; they actually offered the slaves sources of power and knowledge alternative to those existing within the world of the master class."[17] Nana instills within the family numerous folk beliefs such as praying to the ancestors or placing bottles in trees for protection against evil.[18] The family must align its identity with historical circumstances as well as with its cosmological and ontological heritage because these facets represent sources of empowerment. Nana realizes, even if her family doesn't, that the North "ain't no land of milk and honey."

Folk beliefs, of course, did not spontaneously develop, but rather embodied the (re)memory of an African past. Specifically in regard to the Gullah, scholar Margaret Washington Creel acknowledges:

> An African world view, an African theory of being, and some African customs were significant in Gullah religious tendencies and communal existence. These features of Africanity sometimes superseded, sometimes coexisted with the Christian influence. Elements of syncretism were especially pronounced in Gullah attitudes toward life and death.[19]

Creel's thoughts shed light on Nana, for whom folk beliefs function to construct and structure social meaning. As an active bearer of tradition, she must pass folk elements to the next generation. Thus, throughout the film Nana invokes the power of the ancestors to deliver the Unborn Child—who is and *because* she is the future.[20] Nana's greatest fear, in fact, is that the Peazant family will forget its past, thereby negating its "true" cultural identity. Moreover, she realizes that the search for identity must occur on the island—a journey inward through introspection and acknowledgment. If the family directs the journey for self-definition off the island, outside her confines, Nana realizes that the essence of "who they are" will remain illusive and illusionary forever.

In addition to the folk beliefs, the items in Nana's box filled with "scraps of memory" function to define who the Peazant family is. These items, therefore, serve as the actualization of cultural memory. In his article entitled "Things Are Stories: A Manifesto for a Reflexive Semiotics," Eugen Bar argues that "things" appropriate and exude meaning. Consequently, things become stories. He states, "in its diachronic and synchronic expanse, in its history and in its stories the human condition as a complex sign itself and as a story of stories, is inscribed at the very heart of those things that are accessible for observation and cognition."[21] As beliefs are culturally or historically infused, so too are "things" and their accompanying narrative.

Although it can be argued that *Daughters* contains several climactic scenes, the ritual "washing of the feet," situated in the present but calling upon the past and projecting the future, dramatizes how the concrete/finite is rendered ethereal/infinite. Nana's objective is to convince her "daughters" that identity awareness imbues life with meaning. The scene is beautifully framed with the women, Yellow Mary, Eula, Viola, Haagar, among others, dressed in pure white lace dresses, surrounding Nana whose persona signifies not only her "blackness" but also her dignity and power. She is seated in a chair, embodying omnipotence and omniscience. Nana personifies a "Christ-like" figure in this scene, her essence symbolizing sacrifice, service, collectivity, and salvation.

Dash illustrates the salvation of the family through Nana by intersecting multiple dimensions of time (past, present, future), place (Africa, island, mainland), and history (memory, folklore, material culture). As the gaze of the spectator and that of the women in the scene situate Nana within these structures, she is empowered and glorified as heroine. Moreover, Nana's "similarness" and her "otherness" reiterate that she is "the first and the last," "the honored one and the scorned one," and "many are her daughters." As the women kneel and wash her feet Nana states:

> When I was a child, my mother cut this off her hair when she was sold away from me. Now, I'm adding my own hair. There must be a bond, a connection, between those that go North and those that remain ... between us that are here and us that are across the sea ... a connection, we are two people in one body, the last of the old (pointing to herself) and the first of the new (motioning to Eula). We came in chains.... We must survive, we must survive.

As cinematic heroine, Nana is the conduit through which knowledge and renewal take place. Nana's love teaches that history must be valued and even nurtured. Identity formation begins with a sense of one's historical roots, but Nana also realizes that she must let go. She has given her family love, and a strong concept of self that will sustain them. She must now be at peace.

The use of medium close-ups highlights the women against the open-airedness of the island. The music, which begins with an eerie quality, but progresses to full and epiclike proportions, functions in tandem with the camera to elevate the individuality of Nana. As she emerges from her chair and weeps, the soundtrack is laced with the sounds of a baby crying. This multidimensional, vibrant, sonic dimension, coupled with the beautiful visual imagery, create meaning within the cinematic narrative, suggesting that destiny will prevail—and it does as the Unborn Child is "delivered" later that same day and remains on the island with her extended family. (It is significant that the Unborn Child is a girl.)

Although many identities are developed in the film, they emanate from a shared history: Africa, slavery, survival, and resistance. Nana is empowered as an active cultural bearer, matrilineal medium, and African priestess. Dash invites the audience to become active participants in the story by questioning their own identity and cultural heritage. How effectively do we "remember, recall, and recollect?"

sidet: forced exile (salem mekuria, 1991, ethiopia)

The diverse and transformational identities of Ethiopian women are the subject of Salem Mekuria's film. The women interviewed remember and discuss their lives before and after exile. Painful memories shape their identifies, but also serve as mechanisms to "free" them from their past lives, thereby enacting empowered identities. Before proceeding with the film discussion, a brief background overview of African cinema is presented so that the film is understood within an African and diasporic context.

The number of African films, despite escalating production and distribution costs, increases each year. Included in that body are films by African women who possess the production skills and marketing savvy to succeed, in spite of the fact that their work is not always acknowledged and appreciated. As scholar Nancy Schmidt notes, "One of the myths [concerning Africa] is that Safi Faye and Sarah Maldoror are the only women filmmakers in Sub-Saharan Africa."[22] Nothing could be further from the truth. African women represent a significant and rapidly increasing percentage of the total filmmaking community.

While women filmmakers are found in numerous geographic regions and ethnic cultures throughout Africa, distinct commonalities exist in their works, as well as in films by African men. Scholar Francoise Pfaff notes that "although a product of many cultures, [African] cinema offers an undeniable thematic homogeneity, for it emerges from countries which have had an analogous colonial past and similar preoccupations as newly independent nations."[23] Consequently, African cinema emerges as more than art for art's sake. The primary objective reflects the dire need to expose social, political, and economic issues that confront many African nations. Pfaff continues:

> From its conception, Black African cinema has been largely envisioned as a functional art form. While redefining the portrayals of Africa on film, Black African filmmakers vehemently rejected alien stereotypes in favor of realistic images of Africa from an African perspective.[24]

53

Among the many themes Pfaff identifies that permeate the cinema of Black Africans is the "evolving condition of women." Film scholar Manthia Diawara's research reflects a similar conclusion. In what he terms social realist cinema, which "thematizes current sociocultural issues in Africa," Diawara explains, "the heroes are women, children, and other marginalized groups that are pushed into the shadows by the elites of tradition and modernity.... The social realist cinema also positions the spectator by addressing the issues of women's liberation in contemporary African society."[25]

Not surprisingly, the focus of many African women's creative effort is exposing the condition of women. Numerous films detail how women's identities are informed by oppressive forces such as povetry, political exile, sexism, and classism. Other films seek to ascertain how economic transformation of women can be achieved when access (financial, educational, political) is minimal or denied altogether. However, the films don't stop with victimization. After addressing the relationship between repressive social situations and identity formation, the filmmakers introduce audiences to women who resist marginalization by instituting personal and/or political imperatives.

Salem Mekuria, an Ethiopian filmmaker now living in the United States, traveled back to her homeland to produce *Sidet: Forced Exile*. As the documentary traces the lives of three Ethiopian women refugees living in the Sudan, it communicates how, "particularly in a region characterized by poverty and exploitation, some groups have been even more oppressed than others—landless peasants, the minority nationalities, Muslims and all women [my emphasis]."[26] Through Mekuria's lens, the audience is introduced to the women's struggles and their methods of self-empowerment.

The documentary format allows the informants to speak for themselves—to tell their own stories, which interpret and communicate the impact of historic issues, political processes, and remembered events. However, even within their status as "other"—as exile—diversity exists. Social critic Florence Ladd notes in her film review of *Sidet*:

> The women differ with respect to personalities, education, family responsibilities, coping strategies, and capacity to establish themselves and their families in a foreign country. Their differences suggest that women refugees are not a monolithic group; each, with her unique strengths and weaknesses, is at the mercy of national and international forces that tear lives asunder.[27]

Although the women embody difference, all three are refugees. Their cultural identities have been partially shaped by wars and exile. Memory, therefore, functions in a similar manner for each woman, namely as a tool to construct, deconstruct, and reconstruct identity. Their cultural memories serve as active agents to promote personal introspection, womanist bonding, and identity (re)formation.

The documentary genre also permits the audience to align itself with each woman's dilemma in a realist fashion. Mekuria states of the filmic format: "The piece is basically structured in portraits of individual women, and through them I intend to explore social and political issues. Their voices are guiding me through it."[28] Because the undergirding structure establishes the women's voices within a socio-historical context, the film embraces a realist style. As Bill Nichols notes:

> The realist style in documentary grounds the text in the historical world. It is a mark of authenticity, testifying to the camera, and hence the filmmaker, having "been there" and thus providing the warrant for our own "being there," viewing the historical world through the transparent amber of indexical images and realist style.[29]

Consequently, through the documentary genre and a female-centered realist style, the women's testimonies and remembrances are not subjugated to anyone else.

Mekuria allows the women to reflect on their circumstances and identities before and after the war. For example, an elderly woman performing at the beginning of the film sings about her life: "I'm thirsty, my sister, I'm hungry, my mother. Who can I tell this to? I'm in exile. Oh me, oh my, in silence all season, I have nothing at all except old age and my poverty." As she sings, the camera pans to juxtapose the text of the song with the barren social space of the women. The film becomes more than "talking heads" as shots are framed to include a backdrop of devastation. In other scenes Mekuria utilizes long shots, which also establish the women in a hostile environment.

Terhas, one of the women interviewed, remembers her life before exile when she considered herself prosperous. That identity was shattered when she was injured fleeing from Ethiopia and was latter abandoned by her husband, leaving her alone to provide for five children. As she recounts her story, her memories are laced with pain. Those memories serve as the bridge to monitor her transformation. Rather than succumb to the suffering, she uses these memories in a self-reflexive manner to change the future through her children. Terhas encourages them to succeed in school and she begins a catering service to generate income.

In her article, "Common Themes, Different Contexts," Cheryl Johnson-Odim observes, "In 'underdeveloped' societies it is not just a question of internal redistribution of resources, but of their generation and control;

not just equal opportunities between men and women but the creation of opporturnity itself; not just the position of women in society, but the position of the societies in which Third World women find themselves."[30] Mekuria's documentary examines not only the impact of structural poverty on women in exile but also the specific repercussions of these detrimental conditions, which are further exacerbated by a prolonged war.

Sidet: Forced Exile explores through intimate discussions with three women how: (1) the experience of war has affected identity formation; (2) introspection leads to a heightened awareness and identity (re)formation; (3) identity empowerment results when marginality and passivity are replaced with resilience and persistence. Mekuria uses film to capture multidimensional aspects of exile as women strive for individual and collective freedom. Cultural memory becomes a tool not only to question identity but also to mediate new relationships with others and, most importantly, with "womanself."

and still i rise (ngozi onwurah, 1991, britain)

Nana, in *Daughter of the Dust,* remembers her African ancestry and slavery. Terhas, *in Sidet: Forced Exile,* recalls her life before and during exile. The directors, Dash and Mekuria, demonstrate how memory serves as a bridge to promote generational and cultural connections, encourages consciousness-raising, and functions as a cinematic device to foreground filmic representation. Onwurah utilizes memory in a similar manner, but her film also poses other important questions. She asks, "What happens when memory is frozen or when hegemonic structures attempt to distort memory?"

And Still I Rise cautions the Black woman to understand how myths concerning her sexuality and sensuality have been utilized to infer an identity of promiscuity, licentiousness, and inferiority. Not only did her color and gender sentence her to subjugation, but sadly, in many cases, the (mis)representation and appropriation of her own body also contributed to an injurious self-concept. Hazel Carby provides historical background:

> The effect of Black female sexuality on the white male was represented in an entirely different form from that of the figurative power of white female sexuality. Confronted by the Black woman, the white man behaved in a manner that was considered to be entirely untempered by anv virtuous qualities; the white male, in fact, was represented as being merely prey to the rampant sexuality of his female slaves.[31]

Consequently, "a devaluation of Black womanhood occurred as a result of the sexual exploitation of Black women during slavery that has not altered in the course of hundreds of years."[32] To justify their violation of Black women, white men imposed a cultural identity upon African women slaves that dehumanized them. Moreover, in addition to raping their bodies and capitalizing on their physical labor, White men exploited their reproductive ability for "breeding." Denying the humanity of Black women sanctioned all manner of physical, mental, and sexual cruelty on the part of white men. Thus the stereotypes of the Black woman as sexual savage emerged and prospered. Even after slavery, white attitudes and behaviors toward Black women changed little. Perceiving them as sluts, mammies, or tragic mulattoes legitimized the harsh treatment of Black women leveled by white men and women. Not only was the Black woman devalued, but also because of societal perceptions, her subsequent film image held negligible cinematic value.

The films of black British filmmakers (individual and collectives) seek to redress (mis)representation by presenting cinematic representations that counter mainstream images. Black British scholar Kobena Mercer acknowledges:

> A cursory survey of the work of black filmmakers in Britain will reveal the preponderance of a "realist" aesthetic in films made within both documentary and narrative genres. This insistent emphasis on the real must be understood as the prevailing mode in which independent black film has performed a critical function in providing a counter-discourse against those versions of reality produced by dominant voices and discourses in British film and media.[33]

Onwurah's objective in *And Still I Rise* is the analysis of myths regarding Black female sexuality and their impact on identity formation.[34] The film is framed within the context of historic and contemporary British society, exploring the psychological damage of racism, sexism, and classism. Through memory exploration, the film surveys how stereotypes have been internalized and subsequently, exorcised.

And Still I Rise is informed by and incorporates the message of the celebrated poem of the same title by the acclaimed African American writer Maya Angelou. Onwurah's film is, as is Angelou's poem, saturated with and situated in history—Black women's history. The structure of the film combines documentary as well as dramatized segments. The documentary sections allow Black women of diverse backgrounds (performers, academicians, and professionals) to reflect on the relationship between Black women's sexuality and identity formation. The dramatic reconstructions, framed as memories of slave women on the seeing blocks and violent rape, implicate racist societal structures for the devastating indictments and pronouncements against Black womanhood.

Onwurah's initial cinematic image is that of a Black woman in African garb walking in a meadow. That image of a proud, beautiful, Black woman, who could be from the past or contemporary, is juxtaposed to a soundtrack that spews negative myths and stereotypes about Black women. The voice-over begins with one-word descriptors: sultry, savage, dirty, hard, exotic, erotic. These words and their accompanying conceptual myths potentially erode self-esteem and construct a world suffused with self-doubt.

Later in the film Onwurah, using film clips from Lisa Bonnet's *Angel Heart* and Grace Jones's *Vamp* demonstrates how the image of the sexual savage has been incorporated into contemporary cinema. In both films the women are exotic, erotic, and demonic. Bonnet is murdered when a gun is discharged into her vagina. This act becomes symbolic of the destructiveness of white oppression and its need to eradicate Black women's sexuality and Black women in general. These films and others perpetuate a destructive cycle of misrepresentation. Negative, one-dimensional societal attitudes structure demeaning cinematic imagery, and powerless, cinematic icons feed and reinforce fallacious societal perception. More than "just misconceptions," one-dimensional myths of Black womanhood contain an inherent danger, namely:

> Representations of powerlessness have an effect on those in control: they give them the authority to continue to suppress collective resistance through force. Most importantly, images of powerlessness have an effect on those who would resist rather than giving them incentive to further action, they may prompt an acceptance of the status quo.[35]

And Still I Rise dramatizes a rape sequence where a Black woman exercises courage as she refuses a gift of earrings and spits in her master's face. He then brutally rapes her, interpreting her screams of pain as sounds of enjoyment. After this savagery, he returns to his wife, sitting in tranquility. She has no doubt heard the assault. The voice-over explains that white slave owners viewed their female slaves as livestock that had to be "broken-in." As research indicates, rape is not an act of sexual pleasure, but an act of violence, a perverted psychological need for power. The scene, filmed as a memory flashback, demystifies rape by clearly dramatizing the slave woman not as a willing collaborator but as a powerless victim.

The film's structure also incorporates interviews from Black women who, through self-reflection, discuss identity formation. Novelist Buchi Emecheta explains that Black women's identity and sexuality are derived from an African heritage. She states:

> Your umbilical cord from Africa has not been cut and it can
> never be cut because your blackness is like a badge—you
> wear it wherever you are. You must not suppress your
> Africaness. You don't have to be in Africa—to live in Africa,
> to identify with Africa. Wherever you are you carry your
> Africa with you.

Emecheta and Onwurah recognize and remember that Africa is the motherland, and through identification with their heritage a more profound sense of self emerges. Remembering and reflecting on the source— the essence of one's being—leads to empowerment. To exorcise the pain and self-doubt, Black women must rise above oppressive, racist strategies.

Onwurah concludes the film with Black women reciting Angelou's poem. The first stanza reads:

> You may write me down in history
> With your bitter, twisted lies,
> You may trod me in the very dirt
> But still, like dust, I'll rise.

The line "I rise," is repeated three times at the end of the poem and the film underscores the importance of this line. Black women and a little black, who symbolically steps out of a cage, proclaim, "I rise." As the credits roll, the soundtrack decrees, "Don't give up the fight!" If Dash's *Daughters of the Dust* is characterized as a film structured like a folk narrative, Onwurah's *And Still I Rise* is reminiscent of a lyric text with its fragmented images and lines that poeticize and politicize the images of Black womanhood.

Onwurah's film deconstructs the hegemonic voice regarding Black women's history, identity, and sexuality. Mainstream images of Black women generally render them cinematically as one-dimensional and dehistoricized. Onwurah's dramatized representations of historic mistreatment and candid statements by interviewees reaffirm womanhood by situating Black women's identities as a manifestation of diasporic history. In addition, both foreground the uncomfortable memories of rape and misrepresentation. Through reflection, however, the women communicate to audiences the realization that patriarchal behaviors and images embody power only if women allow them to do so.

sisters in the struggle (dionne brand/ginny strikeman, 1991/ canada)[36]

In each film discussed thus far, the cultural memories of "home" are crucial to self-esteem and identity formation. In *Daughters,* home is Africa, the island, and the mainland. For the women in exile, home was Ethiopia, and now Sudan, but someday they hope to return to Ethiopia. For the women in Canada, home is also transitional and multidimensional. Some women trace their ancestry from Africa, to American slavery, and subsequently to Canadian "freedom." Many contemporary Black women migrated from Trinidad, Jamaica, or one of the other Caribbean islands to be domestics. Whatever their route into Canada, the women acknowledge that the memories of their struggles and those of their foremothers shape their contemporary identities.

African Canadians, throughout the decades, have endured prejudice and discrimination as have other members of the diaspora. The chronicles of Black women in Canada have been produced by Black Canadian women filmmakers in several documentaries. *Black Mother, Black Daughter* (Sylvia Hamilton and Claire Prieto, 1989) historicizes the "herstory" of several older, Black women in Nova Scotia.[37] *Older Stronger Wiser* (Claire Prieto and Dionne Brand, 1989), also structured as personal portraits, traces the impact of older generations of Black women and the wisdom they pass down to the next generation. Each of these films provides an intimate portrait of Black women examining the beliefs, values, and attitudes derived from their life experiences. Moreover, as the films showcase women as repositories of cultural traditions and history, they meet the challenge of Canadian scholar Dorothy Wills who believes, "Black women must continue to remember . . . and to relive the slave and peasant experience of their ancestors."[38] Documentary film, therefore, becomes a powerful vehicle by which women can record their experiences, sharing them with a wider audience while bridging intergenerational struggles that have shaped Black women's lives.

Sisters in the Struggle chronicles the "herstory" of Black women in Canada as they struggle against racism, sexism, classism, and homophobia to carve an identity, not as passive victims, but as political activists.[39] Through their resistance strategies, the women defy cultural, economic, and legislative practices which cast them as subordinate "other." Similar to the previously discussed films, the filmmakers focus on the memories of contemporary Black women, drawing corollaries between the past and present to frame and discuss how these memories function as interwoven voices to shape the future. Although the women live in Nova Scotia, Toronto, Ontario, Winnipeg, and other Canadian territories, their stories contain striking similarities.

Brand and Strikeman employ two elements to foreground the memories of the women: the use of music and highlighting the importance of Black women's collectives. The text of the title song "Sisters in the Struggle" recalls the various contexts of women's struggle—most situated while waiting in line. Reminiscent of the character Dorothy in Haile Gerima's *Bush Woman*, who spends time walking and waiting, the song narrates the inordinate amount of time Black women spend standing in lines. The text identifies the food line (shopping for white families), the abortion line, the job line, and the welfare line. The highly rhythmic, free-flowing, improvisational structure of the music is vividly juxtaposed to the text, which communicates the mundane and rigidly structured time of black domestics, many of whom work for white families. The final line of the text states, "Sisters in the struggle is what we are!" Similar to a memory motif in a filmic score, the music has critical significance as it communicates and evokes the culture history of Black women.[40]

Perhaps the most innovative tool used in the documentary is capturing the memories of women who are members of political collectives. As the women sit comfortably on chairs and couches, they recall the struggles and hardships of Black women, including extreme poverty, deportation threats, racism, and sexism. The collectives function to evoke cultural memory. One woman states, "When the whole white world is asleep—Black women are working." The women also acknowledge that struggle and survival encourage future generations. Another woman passionately remarks, "We have always had fighters in our communities, that is the basis of our survival. We have always had women doing the things I'm doing. They are not in anybody's textbook. They've not been celebrated, but I think that our survival, to a large extent, has depended on these women." These (re)memories do more than call attention to the circumstances of women. They serve as a forum where women provide emotional and political support for each other.

As the women remember that racism prescribed employment opportunities, they recall too that sexism within the black community was also injurious to them. Some discuss experiences during the civil rights era when women were called upon to cook, to make banners, and to administer to the men. It was not until they challenged these relegated roles that women were given or seized significant responsibility. Unlike *Daughter of the Dust, Sidet,* or *And Still I Rise, Sisters* examines sexism in the black community, suggesting that the condition of women must be an intimate part of the political agenda.

Sisters in the Struggle acknowledges the power and importance of memories of the foremothers. Their stories must be handed down from generation to generation to insure a healthy sense of womanself. Younger generations must be nurtured and molded and their identifies (re)formulated. The women in *Sisters* demonstrate how cultural memory can play a significant role in that process.

synthesis

Tamsin E. Lorraine states in *Gender, Identity, and the Production of Meaning*:

> In the act of writing theory the writer is attempting to assimilate experience in accordance with rules of conventional language as well as in accordance with identity themes that give coherence to that writer's experience.... Thus theory is simultaneously about the subject who is writing it and about the object under examination.[41]

This statement is applicable to the present study in several ways. First, an analytical theory of Black women's film must understand and appreciate the vision of the filmmakers, whose objective is often to ascertain how past life experiences impact upon the present life circumstances of Black women. The theory must acknowledge that aspects from both temporal spheres (past and present) are valid as they inform the future. Moreover, as theory acknowledges the validity of Black women's life experiences, it simultaneously recognizes their germination within a social, political, and cultural context—and that context becomes a key element in the analysis.

Utilizing aspects of a Black feminist cultural perspective, this analysis has recognized and integrated the experiences and socio-historic contexts as intricate components of the investigation. A Black feminist cultural analysis unearths not only the personal, social, and political aspects of life circumstances and their contexts, but also their resonant messages. This perspective, then, as applied to Black women's films, hopefully provides an illuminating conceptual framework to explore the dynamic process of meanings embedded in their creative cultural expression.

Most importantly, the analytical perspective unearths "the ties that bind," diasporic films of Black women. Their works are not monolithic, but like strands of hair, although singular, when braided together form an intricate design communicating power, liberation, and "unity in diversity." One of the primary signatures of Black women's film is the presentation of diverse images of Black womanhood—ones which emerge from a realist style. These films frame women in multiple identities, biological and nonbiological: mothers, daughters, sisters, friends, lovers. Moreover, the films suggest that, "for women, the need and desire to nurture each other is not pathological but redemptive; it is within that knowledge that real power is rediscovered."[42] Black women as heroines, Black women in exile, Black women sold into slavery, and Black women who fight for freedom, these cultural and political identities serve to counterpoint the one-dimensional, hegemonic, and patriarchal images that are typically seen in mainstream cinema.

Second, there is a recognition of Africa as the earth mother, thereby affirming a matrilineal diaspora. "Mother Africa" is the source of power, inspiration, triumph, and identity. In recognizing Africa, the power of the ancestors is evoked as identity (re)formation requires an anchor, an umbilical cord—a cultural nucleus. Eradication of internalized identity conflict is achieved through an acknowledgment of the generations of mothers from Africa and the diaspora.

Third, there is an appreciation of struggle and triumph. Struggle emerges from issues of sexism, racism, classism, poverty, marginalization. The struggle, however, is not the complete story because, "like dust, I rise." *Daughters of the Dust, And Still I Rise, Sisters in the Struggle*, and *Sidet: Forced Exile*—each film, through a female-centered structure, embodies both struggle and triumph, conflict and resolution.[43] These films function to help give birth to a new consciousness—a heightened sense of woman-self, through the presentation of women who may not have overcome all odds, but exude confidence and persevere.

Black women filmmakers use cultural memory, a form of history, in dramatized flashbacks or as personal reminiscences to construct and empower their cinematic images. Because they are contextualized by historical constructs, the cinematic representations, whether in documentary or narrative film, yield images that resist marginality and encourage realistic survival strategies. Expanding on Trinh's epigraph, the memories of Black women continuously serve as libraries and archives; however, women must be repositories *and* disseminators. And to repeat Hall's epigraph: cultural identity encompasses "being" and "becoming," the past and the future. As the films of Black women of the African diaspora explore multiple dimensions of time, place, and space, they not only keep alive the recollections of the foremothers, but also serve as an intergenerational cultural bridge to promote and affirm contemporary Black womanhood.

notes

I would like to thank Dr. Carolyn Mitchell for her helpful comments and suggestions on an earlier draft of this paper. Research for this article was supported by a postdoctoral fellowship from the Ford Foundation.

1. Cornel West, "The New Cultural Politics of Difference," in *Out There: Marginalization and Contemporary Cultures*, ed. Russell Ferguson, Martha Gever, and Trinh T. Minh-ha (New York: Museum of Contemporary Art, 1990), p. 27.

2. Not all films by Black women focus on issues pertaining to Black women. Further, many Black women do not feel their work is "feminist." It might also be argued that some Black male filmmakers' work is "feminist." My research thus far, however, indicates a paucity of male "feminist" filmmakers and a majority of Black independent women filmmakers whose objective is the presentation of "realist" images of Black women.

3. See Hazel Carby's chapter, "Woman's Era: Rethinking Black Feminist The-

ory," in her book *Reconstructing Womanhood: The Emergence of the Afro-American Woman Novelist* (New York: Oxford University Press, 1987), which gives an overview and assessment of Black feminist literary criticism.

4. Gay Wilentz, *Binding Cultures: Black Woman Writers in Africa and the Diaspora* (Bloomington: Indiana University Press, 1992), p. xiii.

5. See Mark Reid, "Dialogic Modes of Representing Africa(s): Womanist Film," *Black American Literature Forum* 25, no. 2 (summer 1991), pp. 375–88; Sheila Petty, "Black African Feminist Filmmaking?" *Society for Visual Anthropology Review* 6, no. 1 (1990), pp. 60–64; Alile Sharon Larkin, "Black Women Filmmakers Defining Ourselves: Feminism in Our Own Voice," in *Female Spectators: Looking at Film and Television*, ed. E. Deidre Pribram (New York: Verso, 1988), pp. 157–73; Jacqueline Bobo and Ellen Seiter, "Black Feminism and Media Criticism: The Women of Brewster Place," *Screen* 32, no. 3 (Autumn 1991), pp. 286–302; Gloria J. Gibson-Hudson, "Aspects of Black Feminist Cultural Ideology in Black Women's Film," in *Multiple Voices in Feminist Film Criticism* (Minneapolis: University of Minnesota Press, 1994). Also see the following for excellent discussions/definitions of Black feminism: Patricia Hill Collins, "The Social Construction of Black Feminist Thought," *Signs* 14, no. 4 (1989); select articles in Henry Louis Gates Jr., ed., *Reading Black, Reading Feminist: A Critical Anthology* (New York: Meridian, 1990); and Chandra Talpade Mohanty, Ann Russo, and Lourdes Torres, eds., *Third World Women and The Politics of Feminism* (Bloomington: Indiana University Press, 1991).

6. Filomina Chioma Steady, "African Feminism: A Worldwide Perspective," in *Women in Africa and the African Diaspora*, ed. Rosalyn Terborg-Penn, Sharon Harley, and Andrea Benton Rushing (Washington, DC: Howard University Press, 1987), p. 4.

7. Trinh T. Minh-ha, *When the Moon Waxes Red: Representation, Gender, and Cultural Politics* (New York: Routledge, 1991), p. 226.

8. Chinosole, "Audre Lorde and Matrilineal Diaspora: 'moving history beyond nightmare into structures for the future … ," in *Wild Women in the Whirlwind: Afra-American Culture and the Contemporary Literary Renaissance*, ed. Joanne M. Braxton and Andree Nicola McLaughlin (New Jersey: Rutgers University Press, 1990), p. 226.

9. Wilentz, pp. xiii, xiv.

10. Bobo and Seiter, "Black Feminism and Media Criticism," p. 286.

11. Stuart Hall, "Cultural Identity and Cinematic Representation," *Framework*, no. 36 (1989): 69.

12. Ibid., p. 70.

13. Paula Giddings, *When and Where I Enter: The Impact of Black Women on Race and Sex in America* (New York: W. Morrow, 1984), p. 6.

14. Minh-Ha, *Whzn the Moon Waxes Red*, p. 149.

15. See Paula Giddings, *When and Where I Enter: The Impact of Black Women on Race and Sex in America*; Terborg-Penn, Harley, and Rushing, *Women in Africa and the African Diaspora*; Filomina Chioma Steady, ed., *The Black Woman Cross-Culturally* (Cambridge: Schenkman, 1981); and selected volumes by Darlene Clark Hines.

16. Toni Morrison, "Memory, Creation, and Writing," *Thought* 59, no. 235 (December 1984): 385. Also see Toni Morrison's article in *Out There*, entitled "The Site of Memory." In addition to an explanation of the importance of memory, in her work she states, "The crucial distinction for me is not the difference between fact and fiction, but the distinction between fact and truth."

17. Lawrence Levine, *Black Culture and Black Consciousness: Afro-American Folk Thought from Slavery to Freedom* (New York: Oxford University Press, 1977), p. 63.

18. For more information on the folk traditions of the Gullah, see "Gullah Attitudes Toward Life and Death," and "Kongo Influences on African-American Artistic Culture," in *Africanisms in American Culture*, ed. Joseph Holloway (Bloomington: Indiana University Press, 1990). Select chapters in Zora Neale Hurston's *Mules and Men* (Bloomington: Indiana University Press, 1978) are also applicable.

19. Margaret Washington Creel, "Gullah Attitudes Toward Life and Death," in *Africanisms in American Culture*, ed. Holloway, p. 17.

20. In her discussion of the Africanisms in Gullah culture, Creel acknowledges that "the fate of the unborn child was in the care of spiritual beings and forces" (73). Throughout the film, Nana speaks to the ancestors to ask for the Unborn Child's safe delivery. Interestingly, Dash also continuously overlaps the voice-over of the Unborn Child with the visual image of Nana suggesting their maternal and spiritual bond.

21. Eugen Bar, "Things Are Stories: A Manifesto for a Reflexive Semiotics." *Semiotica* 25, nos. 3/4 (1979): 194.

22. Nancy Schmidt, "Films by Sub-Saharan African Women Filmmakers," *African Literature Association Bulletin* 18, no. 4 (1992), p. 12.

23. Francoise Pfaff, *Twenty-Five Black African Filmmakers: A Critical Study with Filmography and Bibliography* (New York: Greenwood Press, 1988), p. x.

24. Ibid., p. ix.

25. Manthia Diawara, *African Cinema: Politics and Culture* (Bloomington, IN: Indiana University Press, 1992), p. 144.

26. Jenny Hammond, *Sweeter than Honey: Testimonies of Tigrayan Women* (Oxford: Third World First, 1989), p. 11.

27. Florence C. Ladd, *"Sidet: Forced Exile,"* *Sage* no. 1 (Summer 1990): 64.

28. Margaret Tiberio, "An Interview with Salem Mekuria," *Visions* (Winter 1991): 16.

29. Bill Nichols, *Representing Reality: Issues and Concepts in Documentary* (Bloomington: Indiana University Press, 1991), p. 181.

30. Cheryl Johnson-Odim, "Common Themes, Different Contexts: Third World Women and Feminism," in *Third World Women and the Politics of Feminism*, ed. Talpade, Russo, and Torres, p. 320.

31. Hazel Carby, *Reconstructing Womanhood: The Emergence of the Afro-American Woman Novelist* (New York: Oxford University Press, 1987), p. 27.

32. bell hooks, *Ain't I a Woman:Black Women and Feminism* (Boston: South End Press, 1981), p. 53.

33. Kobena Mercer, "Diaspora Culture and the Dialogic Imagination: The Aesthetic of Black Independent Film in Britain," in *Blackframes: Critical Perspectives on Black Independent Cinema*, ed. Mbye B. Cham and Claire Andrade-Watkins (Cambridge: MIT Press, 1988), p. 52.

34. Ngozi Onwurah considers herself a Black British filmmaker. Her father is Nigerian and her mother is white British.

35. Jacqueline Bobo, "Black Women in Fiction and Nonfiction: Images of Power and Powerlessness," in *Wide Angle 13*, nos. 3 and 4 (July–October 1991), p. 73.

36. *Sisters in the Struggle* was directed by Brand and Strikeman, produced and distributed by the National Film Board of Canada. Brand is Black, Strikeman is not.

37. See Alice Walker's *In Search of Our Mother Gardens: Womanist Prose* (San Diego: Harcourt Brace Jovanovich, 1983), for discussion of the concept "herstory."

38. Dorothy Wills, "The Challenge for Black Women in the Eighties," Report of the Fifth Conference of the Congress for Black Women of Canada, 1982. As quoted in *Canadian Women: A History*, ed. Alison Prentice, Paula Bourne, Gail Brandt, Beth Light, Wendy Mitchinson, and Naomi Black (Ontario: Harcourt Brace Jovanovich, 1988), p. 405.

39. Lesbian identity is an important and recurring issue in many films of Black women. *Daughters of the Dust* broaches the issue in a "safe" manner. The filmmakers of *Sisters in the Struggle* allow several women to discuss their identities as lesbians. For other films that discuss Black lesbianism, see *Janine, She Don't Fade* (Chervl Dunye), *Among Good Christian People* (Jacqueline Woodson and Catherine Saalfield), and *The Audre Lorde Project* (Michelle Parkerson).

40. Black independent filmmakers tend to use music for purposes other than emotional impact. In many instances the music functions as a powerful communicative device, either in tandem with or antithetical to the cinematic narrative. See Gloria J. Gibson, "The Cultural Significance of Music to the Black Independent Filmmaker" Ph.D. dissertation, Indiana University, 1986.

41. Tamsin E. Lorraine, *Gender, Identity, and the Production of Meaning* (Boulder, CO: Westview Press, 1990), p. 41.

42. Audre Lorde, "The Master's Tools Will Never Dismantle the Master's House," in *This Bridge Called my Back: Writings by Radical Women of Color*, ed. Cherrie Moraga and Gloria Anzaldua (New York: Kitchen Table: Women of Color Press, 1983), p. 104.

43. Even without viewing the films, the individual words in each film title imply a diasporic cohesiveness. Daughters and sisters (*Daughters of the Dust/Sisters in the Struggle*) suggest female bonding; forced exile and struggle (*Sidet: Forced Exile/Sisters in the Struggle*) communicate conflict; and dust suggests mother earth and triumph (Daughters of the Dust/And Stile I Rise. "But still, like dust, I'll rise).

gloria j. gibson-hudson

the

functional

family

of

camille billops

monique guillory

In the early 1980s, several women of color would meet occasionally in Barbara Smith's modest kitchen to share their interests in literature and cultural issues. Such were the humble beginnings of Kitchen Table: Women of Color Press, which would form the bedrock of Black feminist criticism throughout the 1980s and 1990s. Similarly, the Hatch-Billops studio on Broadway in New York City heralds the rising stars of the con-temporary Black arts movement. Camille Billops and her husband, James Hatch, have fashioned their home into a creative center that nurtures a thriving community of artists, writers, and intellectuals. Complete with a library, archives, and an impressive collection of Black art, the studio dou-bles as a living and working space for cultural events, plays, exhibits and the publishing house for "Artists and Influence"—a series of over 1,000 interviews Billops has done with notable figures from the art world. As a site of support and creative exchange, the Hatch-Billops studio stands as a cornerstone of the New York art scene, with the husband and wife team offering themselves as creative surrogates for new talent.

This nurturing and familial spirit resonates in the four films that Billops and Hatch have codirected and produced. Each project has been a collaborative effort by members of the Hatch-Billops family, behind and in front of the camera. Dion, Hatch's son from a previous marriage, serves as the director of photography. Billops's first film, *Suzanne, Suzanne* (1982), examines the interpersonal dynamics between her sister, Billie, and Billie's daughter, Suzanne. *Finding Christa* (1991) features Christa Victoria, Billops's estranged daughter whom she put up for adoption in 1961. The premise for their third film, *Older Women and Love* (1987), grew out of an affair Billops's aunt had with a younger man. And in *The KKK Boutique Ain't Just Rednecks* (1994), Hatch and Billops anchor a provocative discussion of racism with their own love and happiness as an interracial couple. Adhering to the precedent of their earlier work, the next project from Hatch and Billops, *The String of Pearls*, features members of Billops's family discussing their opinions and experiences with abortion.[1]

An established artist prior to her venture into film, Billops's training in various media of creative expression gives her work a multidimensional richness that defies pat or singular interpretation. Since *Finding Christa* won the 1992 Grand Jury Award for Best Documentary at the Sundance Film Festival, Billops has been mostly associated with the genre of documentary. However, the fluid and experimental nature of her work resists such definitive classification. And even though Billops's life and family are the focal points of her films, the category of autobiography does not fully accommodate the overtly political stances her works advance. Encompassing aspects of both documentary and autobiography, with a heap of performance and a dash of surrealism, Billops's films are elusive and constantly changing, seldom delivering the perspective they appear to propose.

In her attention to the dynamics of family and social protocol, Billops constantly blurs the divides between private life and public domain. She courageously surrenders the sacred with the hopes of offering clarity and insight to some of the most complicated dimensions of feminism — motherhood, domestic violence, sexual intimacy, and interracial coupling. Not only does Billops herself brave these treacherous social tracts, but also she, in turn, wins the confidence of her family members as they entrust her with intimate facets of their private lives. In transgressing one of the most salient rules of propriety for the Black family, the business of "airing dirty laundry in public" yields powerful rewards in apparent emotional catharsis for the subjects and a valuable reconsideration of such prescribed cultural tenets for the audience.

Finding Christa, for example, often evokes volatile responses from audiences as Billops recounts in the film her decision to put her four-year-old daughter, Christa, up for adoption in 1961. This personal and difficult decision is retold in the wake of Billops's reunion with Christa twenty years after she left her in the care of the Children's Home Society as a four year old. Contrary to audience hopes and expectations, Billops makes no apology for having left her daughter behind and her subsequent career as an artist. Rather than delineating her own emotional anguish in giving up a child who had become such a pronounced part of her life, Billops uses this personal experience to explore the larger question of women's roles and the decisions they feel compelled to make within the context of particular social conventions. Billops does not attempt to justify this decision, unpopular by nearly all accounts, but rather, through the circumstances surrounding her own life and choices, Billops establishes herself as a conduit through which to examine, in close personal detail, the debilitating confines of gender in this country.

Through the constructs of testimony and family narratives, this piece examines the role of subjectivity in Billops's films. Billops strategically intertwines various layers of narrative voice to assert a decisive subjective position within a recognizable feminist ideology. While Billops draws her films from her own experiences, it is not her voice that surfaces in the end but rather a deliberately ambiguous articulation of personal politics as they resonate within a larger sphere of public discourse. As Valerie Smith notes of Billops's cinematic composition, "The directors' use of strategies associated with fiction films questions the very meaning of documentary filmmaking. They frustrate the viewers' desire to observe Billops's private emotions and challenge the voyeuristic relationship between viewer and documentary subject."[2] It becomes clear that we are not to take Billops's subjects simply for what they say, or don't say, but rather, each individual's comments come inscribed by a complex matrix of social values and tropes. Perhaps the most visibly problematized social construct in Billops's work is gender roles, as most of Billops's female subjects exemplify subtly subversive feminist ideologies. Along these lines, male subjects become curiously marked in Billops's films as she presumably attempts to rewrite the normative, social specificities of gender that she has consistently fought to resist in her life and her work.

mothers and daughters

In *Suzanne, Suzanne*, family skeletons rise slowly, but inexorably, to the surface. The piece begins *in medias res* as subjects talk freely about people and events the audience does not yet know. We come to understand that the family patriarch, Brownie, has died. His wife, Billie, and their daughter, Suzanne, seem ambivalent about his passing. Suzanne opens the film with a series of questions she would ask her father if she could: Does he love her and if he did, then why did he treat her the way he did? Why was she the one to receive the whippings and no one else? Throughout the film, whenever Suzanne speaks of her father, she appears dimly lit and in shadow before a curtain similar to that of a confessional. In contrast, her mother, Billie, speaks of Brownie from a brightly lit, nearly white setting, with one of Suzanne's children, Peter, standing silent and fidgety in the background. While the women are portrayed and interviewed in a variety of settings, whenever they discuss Brownie, it is consistently from these respective contexts, which symbolically demonstrate each woman's personal relationship with Brownie. Suzanne, in the darkness and shadows, appears haunted and uncertain about her relationship to her father. By contrast, Billie freely conveys the bittersweet relief she felt when Brownie died, although she admits that this feeling comes with some tinge of guilt. Although Billie acknowledges a turbulent and unpredictable relationship with her husband (she explains how she would run into the shower to "compose her thoughts" whenever he would come home late at night), she appears resolved and reconciled with this past. But as Billie expresses these thoughts about her dead husband, the camera focuses on Billie's pristine and neatly manicured hands as they gesture nervously with the story of Brownie's last breath.

The mother and daughter offer contrasting narratives to the text. Billie appears a picture of confidence and self-security, but she steadily alludes to instances of affirmation and validation. She glowingly talks of receiving "a nice little applause" when she appears with her daughter and mother in fashion shows. Billie speaks of having her "ego stroked" when she participated in the 1979 "Mrs. America" pageant. A sharp contrast to Billie, Suzanne talks indifferently about her drug addiction, her feelings of insecurity and poor self-esteem. One run-in with the police is told in harrowing detail from Suzanne's perspective as well as from that of her young son who was with her at the time. It is clear that Suzanne has perhaps more than once jeopardized the welfare of her children because of her addiction and its concomitant life style.

Through a motif of beauty and grooming, the film establishes a trope of appearances and deception. Suzanne's brother, Michael, speaks almost entirely from in front of a mirror where he is combing and waxing his moustache. Billie and Suzanne, by their physical appearances, seem to have led incongruent lives—Billie appears beautiful and confident. She wears fashionable outfits, complete with makeup and jewelry. She tends to her daughter's hair and touches up her mother's makeup. Suzanne, usually in a simple T-shirt or an unflattering jacket, however, looks disheveled and unkempt next to her mother's polished and pristine beauty. Usually seen alone on camera, Suzanne seems the negligent mother, as her children are never seen with her but are either playing alone or with their grandmother.

In the final dramatic moments of the piece, Billops levels the terrain and brings the women to a common ground. They are framed by total darkness—distinctly different from the shadows we have seen with Suzanne and the bright background associated with Billie in the text. In this all-consuming darkness, Billops taps the women's unconscious minds and the unspoken impetus behind the film and this fragile mother/daughter bond. While this segment was originally scripted, Suzanne abandons the prescribed dialogue and confronts her mother with a series of questions similar to those she would have asked her father. They begin predictably enough: "Mother, do you love me?" to which Billie offers the expected response, "Yes, Suzanne, I love you very much." The dialogue then spirals into a private conversation where family secrets are painfully revealed and discussed. Suzanne asks her mother about "death row," the name given to Suzanne's room whenever a whipping from her father was imminent. Suzanne asks her mother if she was beaten from the beginning—an indication that Suzanne is well aware that her mother was beaten, but she does not know when her father started beating her mother. As the mother tearfully empathizes with her daughter's suffering, its becomes apparent that each woman's life was shaped tremendously in response to Brownie's tyrannical hold over the house. While Suzanne turned to drugs to escape the pain of her father's abuse, her mother embraced the pretense of middle-class respectability. But through this exchange between mother and daughter, it becomes starkly clear that Billie became complicitous with her husband's abuse, as she permitted him to beat Suzanne in the hope that his focus on his daughter would curb his abusive tendencies towards her. Together, in the darkness and the absolving presence of Billops's camera, the women work together through the pain and confusion Brownie left in his wake.

Billops's position as a director filming her sister and niece in pain presents a crucial question in representing and analyzing such deeply personal traumas. Even as Billie collapses in tearful sobs over the pain of her husband's abuse, the camera keeps rolling and records Billie's despair. This aesthetic choice is certainly rife with problems of perspective and representation. How does Billops stand by and film her sister's pain? How do viewers resist the voyeuristic nature of seeing this seemingly proud and self-possessed women reduced to not only her own victimization with domestic violence but also her complicity in the abuse of her daughter as well? Are viewers able to get beyond the spectacle of pain to the more profound and productive insight the piece lends on domestic violence?

In their introduction to *The Violence of Representation*, Nancy Armstrong

71

and Leonard Tennenhouse caution scholars, writers, and theorists about rendering acts of violence into discursive forms. "The words we use to represent the subjects and objects of violence are part and parcel of events themselves . . . what we feel it is and how it makes us feel."[3] It is difficult to watch these women suffer. Suzanne's urgent need to confront her mother poses an awkward moment where the viewer no longer feels welcomed into this family's home. These are matters that ought to be handled behind closed doors, not before cameras. Suzanne tearfully recalls one grueling whipping from her father when he beat her with a fan belt and the hook became lodged in her flesh. Up to this point in the film, while it was apparent that this family had its share of tensions and conflict, these women, freely sharing their experiences and triumphs, did not appear to be harboring such a dark and painful past.

In showcasing Suzanne and Billie at such a vulnerable moment, Billops runs the risk of exploiting their pain to make her film (and her political point, even). But the fact that this is Billops behind the camera, that she does personally know these women and is likely already familiar with their relationships to Brownie, works to ameliorate some of the brutality of these accounts of abuse. Valerie Smith has pointed out that Billops's presence in the film is conspicuous and deliberate, as she is often visible in front of the camera with her relatives. As the director and a participant with the subjects of the film, Billops offers "a Black feminist intervention within the family romance."[4] The opportunity for Billops to make this film rises out of celebratory circumstances—the abuse these women speak of is over and they, through Billops's project, are attempting to heal themselves.

the rites of motherhood

The stark violence and abuse recalled in *Suzanne, Suzanne* does not recur in Billops's other films; however, her work does characteristically embody a violence of representation as it engages deeply painful and personal choices—such as leaving one's child to pursue a career as an artist, in *Finding Christa*. Some audiences have vehemently denounced and personally criticized Billops for this decision, losing sight of the courage it took for Billops to face her daughter as well as make a film about the experience. Barbara Letkasas notes that the outrage audiences express for *Finding Christa* as opposed to *Suzanne, Suzanne* demonstrates how "a mother who gives up her child is considered even lower on the scale of civilization than a brutal father."[5] Recognizing the potential problem of representation her film may possess, Billops now begins discussions about *Finding Christa* by eliciting responses and reactions from adoptees in the audience first, thereby giving them an opportunity to articulate their own experience contrasted with her representation of the adoption experience.[6]

The most compelling and, to some extent, disturbing feature of *Finding Christa* lies at the heart of the film—that some twenty years ago, a young mother brought her four-year-old daughter to the Children's Home Society and left her there. In this retrospective account of that decision and its consequences, one may expect to find an emotionally taxed woman, grieving over what others might deem a mistake, repentant and apologetic. But this is not the case with Billops in the film, for she is strong and successful, and apparently did well by nurturing her artistic talents rather than her maternal instincts. While such decisions can be grueling and unsettling, they are nonetheless a part of women's realities—particularly in the lives of women of color. These critical moments in Black women's histories have been explored extensively in literature and fiction, but they have not been significantly chronicled in film.

Joanne Braxton traces the figure of the outraged mother as the primary archetype for Black American women writers. This ancestral icon "speaks through the narrator of the text to 'bear witness' and to break down artificial barriers between the artist and the audience."[7] Braxton locates this figure in African cosmology, which extends as far back as the Grand Nanny figure common to Maroon communities in Jamaican folklore. While this literary convention has far-reaching implications throughout Black women's writing, Braxton identifies that the most trenchant features of the outraged mother in literature can be found in her desire to save herself and her children: "Implied in all her actions and fueling her heroic ones is outrage at the abuse of her people and her person. She feels very keenly every wrong done her children, even to the furthest generations. She exists in art because she exists in life."

Billops's roles as a mother and an artist in *Finding Christa* epitomize Braxton's construct of the outraged mother. In hinging this project on actual events and people from her personal world, Billops effectively dissolves the boundary between art and life. She deliberately structures historical chronology in the film to suggest that Billops's options to be a mother or an artist were mutually exclusive. Immediately following the segment where Billops leaves Christa at the Children's Home, she offers scenes from Egypt, where she had her first gallery show. But through the entity of the film itself, Billops rectifies this disparity between motherhood and art. Billops appears in the piece as both an artist and a mother—both attesting to a nurturing and creative spirit that is as evocative of art as it is of motherhood. As the "outraged mother," Billops recasts motherhood without assuming the mantle of sacrificial lamb that western understanding of maternity often implies.

Perhaps one of the most powerful expressions of self-assertion is Toni Morrison's *Beloved*. Inspired by the true story of Margaret Garner, Morrison's protagonist, Sethe, is a fugitive slave who chooses to kill her children rather than return them to the plantation at the hands of approaching slave catchers. She kills Beloved, a baby girl, but is stopped before she kills her two sons and her oldest daughter. Like Christa, who returns to Billops vulnerable and wounded by the trauma of their separation, Sethe is haunted by Beloved's needy spirit. Struggling with the selfish demands of the ghost-child and her own broken self in the aftermath of slavery, Sethe considers how she can reconcile this act with the reality of the child's ultimate destruction had she given her up to a life as a slave:

> Sethe was trying to make up for the handsaw; Beloved was making her pay for it. But there would never be an end to that.... Before Sethe could make her understand what it meant—what it took to drag the teeth of that saw under the little chin.... Sethe could make her realize that far worse than that—far worse—[was] that anybody white could take your whole self for anything that came to mind.[8]

Morrison's *Beloved* powerfully articulates the ruptures and damage slavery exacted upon the human psyche. Through the fragile members of Sethe's splintered family, Morrison illustrates slavery's toll on various factions of the Black community—men and women, the young and the old. Sethe, like Billops, also embodies the "outraged mother"—radically casting off the constraints that slavery and the apparently inalienable moral obligations motherhood impose upon her. Sethe's act of destruction ultimately transforms into a creative force, liberating Beloved's spirit and rekindling the life in Sethe's home. But Morrison recognizes that even in freedom, and long after the dismantling of slavery as a formal institution, its destructive legacy endures in America. In reflecting on the social realities that led to Garner's decision, Morrison's vision of Sethe's world sheds light on Billops's predicament as well:

> Those women, under those circumstances, had confronted the modern problem in the nineteenth century—something that I thought was a contemporary problem, the continuous problem that women have, with the number of choices having been increased in our lives, the continuous problem of what I call self-murder, self sabotage. That no matter whether one chose the complete, nurturing life, or whether one chose the complete, individual self-regarding life, there is always this element to betray ourselves by ourselves. This is not a new idea, but it was enhanced for me, lit by a dual problem of being female and being Black and what that suggested.[9]

Since slavery, the state of motherhood for Black women has been fraught with contradictions and compromises. Numerous historians have noted the socio-sexual obstacles of the Black matriarch, who is more often celebrated as the iconic strength of the Black family rather than fully understood in her historical and social complexity. Cultural, economic, and social factors continue to levy challenges against Black mothers, as stereotypes of them as welfare queens and national liabilities abound. Although she is an established and tenured professor of law at a prestigious university, Patricia Williams nonetheless found herself stigmatized when she adopted her son in the swarm of the "family values" police who characterized the 1992 Republican National Convention: "I am so many of the things that many people seemed to think were antifamily—unwed, black, single, everything but teenage. Add mother and it began to sound like a curse. Stand at the mirror and say it to yourself a few times: I am an (over-the-hill) black single mother."[10]

the nest and the west

In her prolific essay, "Mama's Baby, Papa's Maybe," Hortense Spillers traces the social paradox slavery proposed to Black women. As both slaves and mothers, Black women found themselves in double jeopardy—vessels for perpetuating their own oppression and yet denied the blood-rite of maternity. But Spillers suggests that slave women survived the personal atrocities of plantation life precisely through the willful and aggressive self-affirmation epitomized by Garner's heinous act: "Actually claiming the monstrosity (of a female with the potential to name), which her culture imposes in blindness, Sapphire might rewrite after all a radically different text for a female empowerment."[11]

In the hands of artistic expression, Black motherhood often becomes rewritten and revamped alongside conventional representations of Black women as self-sacrificing caretakers who not only tend to their own children but also protect and preserve the culture of the race at large. Like Billops, playwright Adrienne Kennedy reconstitutes motherhood and pregnancy through her own unfulfilled life as a young mother. In several of her plays, including *A Movie Star Has to Star in Black and White* (1976) and *Funny House of a Negro* (1964), Kennedy uses multiple titles for her characters to demonstrate madness and mental anguish over their fractured identities as Blacks and as women. For example, in *The Owl Answers* (1988), the female lead, Clara, is described in the list of characters as "CLARA PASS-MORE who is the VIRGIN MARY who is the BASTARD who is the OWL."

Like Billops, Kennedy also dissolves the veneer of public and private selves, between thought and action through her use of family and family drama. In *The Owl Answers*, individual members of a Black family share the stage with actors guised as white, Hollywood stars including Bette Davis, Marlon Brando, and Shelley Winters appearing in recognizable roles from their film careers. Occasionally, one of the film stars speaks as a member of the family or even takes up the subjective positions of the family members themselves. Billops's description of her stepfather as "a complicated Negro who booby-trapped his record player, counted his canned goods, and pulled the phone out of the wall when I came home from the hospital with my illegitimate child"[12] echoes with the warped family ties Kennedy explores in her psychological dramas. The shared space and multilayered identities of the characters in Kennedy's plays demonstrate that mutual reliance on film and theater that both Billops and Kennedy share. Linda Kintz observes:

> Family characters who are grieving over the injured son lying in a hospital bed in a coma or the pregnant woman worrying about the bloody effects of pregnancy are characters who would normally be located in domestic and interior spaces reified here by static photos of the Family. However, the family members find themselves part of several scenes from the most public space of all in American culture, film. Their individual identities are thus immediately fragmented as they are inserted into and compared to the symbolic places publicly provided for them by the films. This insertion sets up a shimmering, wavering movement between sites of subjectivity which simply don't match up, which won't fit.[13]

Both Billops and Kennedy hold up the most intimate facets of private life for public scrutiny. In addition to their common reliance on the spectacle of film and theater, they both draw heavily from their personal experiences to assert their own feminist stances. Similar to the matrices of motherhood that Billops's work suggests, Kennedy's plays sustain a metaphor of miscarriage through the motif of blood and failed pregnancies. These tropes undoubtedly resonate from Kennedy's personal experiences as a mother who felt stifled at home, pregnant, while her husband, an academic, traveled extensively and pursued his intellectual interests. In her autobiography, *People Who Led to My Plays*, Kennedy writes in detail about the trials of those lonely times:

> Often I reread a book on Marie Curie. Many times I felt so unfulfilled in my role as a young "housewife" that Emma's taking arsenic made sense to me. I felt I also understood Anna Karenina's unhappiness. Both these women were plagued by endless, mysterious feelings of unhappiness and confusion despite the fact that they found a certain joy in their children and marriages. They were in an inexplicable turmoil, as I was.[14]

Undoubtedly, it is these listless feelings of isolation and powerlessness Billops sought to avoid in leaving motherhood behind. In *Finding Christa*, Billops recounts with her sister Josie that she "would have died" had she continued on the path she was on with Christa. The child would have died as well. Josie heartily agrees. Like Kennedy identifying with the characters in the books that filled her life and imagination as a young mother, Billops, too, sees herself, and that which has been denied her as a woman, in terms of cinematic fiction:

> Women are not always nestkeepers. Some men want to be nestkeepers and some women, they want to be on the highways, or on the road finding the news. What was that movie with Marlon Brando, "One Eyed Jack?" And he took off over those hills. We were sitting in Rotterdam with a friend in the movies and I said, "See, that's the adventure they want to deny us. To hit the horses and ride the trails. You see that's the information, that's where the news is. I don't think the news is all in the parlor; I think it's out there on the road and those are the adventures and women are adventuresome and I like that idea."[15]

In these introductory remarks before the *Point of View* presentation of *Finding Christa* on PBS, Billops clearly demarcates the ideological parameters of the piece and her life's work as well. She lays out here a dichotomy of men and women: what men can do and what women can't do; what men are allowed to do and what women are expected to do. Throughout *Finding Christa*, the social gridlocks of gender are steadily exposed and Billops quixotically charges to dismantle them. Repeatedly, the film offers instances of women making vital life choices under the sway of a man's approval. A cousin reveals that Billops's mother, Alma, probably couldn't offer to take Christa because of Dotson, Billops's stepfather. Margaret Liebig, the woman who does eventually adopt Christa, conveys a touching story of how she was forced to give up another child she cared for upon the insistence of her husband at the time. Billops's own husband, James Hatch, weathered and gray with age, stands accused as he holds a large photograph of himself as a younger man. This photo shows the man Billops was involved with at the time Christa is put up for adoption. But in this crusade for feminist empowerment, Hatch is not unscathed. His defense is shabby and unconvincing as he nonchalantly says to the camera, "At the time, I told Camille, don't give Christa up for me."

With the formidable task of asserting feminist autonomy and empowerment simmering beneath the surface of her texts, Billops's representations of men seem deliberately critical and flat. *Suzanne, Suzanne* begins with the grisly sight of Brownie (we never know his first name) lying in his casket. As his wife and his daughter relay their own accounts of him, Brownie is unable to defend himself but rather is depicted as a good-time dandy through photographs of him shirtless, holding a beer, and carousing with friends. Similarly, Michael, Brownie's son, is framed consistently in the bathroom as he grooms and waxes an excessively long moustache. Michael's narcissistic attention to the excessive moustache elevates it to a symbolic phallus as he works to make it rigid and stiff. When he is done and Billops pulls him away "to find Suzanne," Michael resists and returns to the mirror for "one more look." Michael's actions and commentary in the film punctuate the oppressive cycle of patriarchy, as he glibly recalls teasing Suzanne before her beatings, because "she had something coming to her." This subtle critique of the masculine continues in *Finding Christa*, where Billops's accounts from men are few but significant. Her stepfather, Dotson, appears aloof and distant as he explains he knew very little about the time Billops was considering giving away Christa. As he recalls this time, we see two different shots of Dotson playing tenderly with puppies—a critical substitution for the child Billops would leave behind. In another segment are home movies of Billops as a young mother bathing Christa as an infant. She appears happy and adjusted but in voice-over explains how she wanted "the little Hollywood thing." When Christa's father, Stanford, never returned to take care of Billops and his child, "then I didn't want to do it. If you were a single parent, then you were just an unwed mother which was just next to being a whore." Following this comment is Vantile Whitfield, who introduced Billops to Stanford. His attire is conspicuously masculine: a three-piece suit with an open collar and a gold chain. A derby sits atop his head cocked to one side as he seems to chuckle in agreement with the comment Billops has just made:

> Yes, those were the good ol' days—or at least they were back in the traditional values days when it was rare to see a woman pregnant and not married. In fact, that was shotgun time—brothers, fathers, uncles, everybody was on their horse riding out.

Here, Whitfield echoes Billops's introductory reference to the West, with men riding out to adventures the women back home would never see. Whitfield's mention of "shotgun time" is ambiguous but likely refers to a time of quick "shotgun" weddings before men took their leave from their new brides and their unborn children. Billops's editing here is significant because she sets Whitfield up to seemingly affirm the comment she has just made, although the connection is not as crisp as the editing suggests it to be. In this context, it appears that Whitfield recalls that time

Billops spoke of, a time when unwed mothers were just next to being a whore, the "good ol' days."

Another telling scene, where Billops clearly delineates her feminist ideology through the narrative voice of a man, comes in a seemingly scripted exchange with the playwright George C. Wolfe. The scene opens with Billops in her studio conversing with Coreen Simpson, a friend who is presumably there to photograph Billops and her work. The segment begins as Billops relays the story of Christa's adoption and the imminent reunion to Simpson. Wolfe comes in and joins the conversation as the two women listen to a tape Christa has sent Billops. Wolfe comments that Christa sounds good, like her mother:

> *Wolfe:* So what are you going to do? Are you going to see her or is she coming to see you?
> *Billops:* I don't know.
> *Wolfe:* What do you mean you don't know?
> *Billops:* I don't know if I want to come from under the water.
> *Wolfe:* Well, why not?
> *Billops:* Because I'm scared. I don't know if I can do that.

Steadily, as the dialogue continues, Wolfe finds it difficult to articulate himself in response to Billops's rapid-fire assertions and her defiance to hold her ground as a woman against Wolfe as a man.

> *Wolfe:* Yes, but you've got no choice now. Clearly, she's come from under the water so you've got no choice, I mean, I don't know why, I don't understand why, I mean, aren't you curious?
> *Billops:* I'm curious but it's very difficult. You ain't never done this.
> *Wolfe:* Well, that's true but still.
> *Billops:* Well, how can you be the judge?
> *Wolfe:* Well, I'm not judging it, but I'm just saying she sings like you, she looks like you so I don't understand why you don't, like, you know, I mean, my curiosity, but I—I, you know, but I haven't done this.
> *Billops:* But that doesn't make any sense George—look like me, sing like me. That don't mean I necessarily want to get involved. Twenty years, I ain't known her in twenty years.

As Billops chides Wolfe, it becomes clear that this is a metaphoric sparring of the sexes. It is a rhetorical exchange because the reunion had already occurred eight years prior to the making of the film. Billops and Wolfe both know that she will, ultimately, see Christa. In the fervor and intensity of her responses, Billops is not directly addressing Wolfe but rather uses this opportunity to synecdochichally refute men who self-righteously attempt to dictate women's lives. In one interview, Billops recalls a similar exchange with another male friend who tried to make her feel that she owed Christa so much now that she had found her. She responded to him with "I don't take that from childless men."[16]

"One must assume the feminine role deliberately," Luce Irigaray writes, "which means already to convert a form of subordination into an affirmation, and thus beginning to thwart it."[17] In *Finding Christa,* Billops not only seizes the reins of her own sexual identity (the "monstrosity" that Spillers suggests) but in so doing, underscores the sexual politics of the many women her text engages. In contrast to the hegemonic prescription of the happy housewife and homemaker, the women in *Finding Christa,* including Christa herself, offer alternative constructs and nontraditional choices as grown, adult women. There are no representations of successful, happy marriages, and even Billops's own marriage seems tainted with Christa's abandonment. Billops's sister Josie admits that she could be of little help with Christa and described herself as a "stone Butterfly McQueen" who didn't know "nothin' 'bout birthin' no babies, and wasn't too keen on getting to know." Similarly, Liebig recounts how she wrestled with her second husband who insisted on spoiling Christa and giving her what she wanted "because she was adopted." Liebig also recalls how Christa's stepsister (who doesn't actually speak in the film) definitively stated that she would not get married, thus leaving Christa the big wedding. Billops uses footage from Christa's marriage, including an ironic rendition of "Because You're Mine" that Liebig sings during the ceremony. After the wedding footage, completely conventional, with Christa in the lacy gown and a nervous groom in a tuxedo, Billops underscores, once again, a reversal of gender roles as she shows Christa riding a motorcycle in full leather gear. Christa, on the bike, evokes that sense of adventure and carefree life style that Billops longs for at the beginning of the film. She stops to pick up a man who is presumably her husband. He plants a long kiss on her lips then hops on the back of the bike as Christa drives off with him. We then see them in a domestic setting but, again, in reversed roles—he is reading at a desk with a cat while Christa practices karate stances in her Ge. In voice-over, she explains how she appears strong and self-reliant but, deep down, she remains that scared, abandoned, four-year-old child. The marriage has apparently not helped to heal her, and the failure of her marriage is symbolically depicted by Christa mopping the kitchen floor in her wedding gown with her blue belt tied around her waist. She defiantly throws down the mop and walks off-camera. Through Christa's failed marriage, Billops illustrates the same struggle she had once experienced as the myth of domestic bliss tussled with her own sense of freedom and self. Christa in her gown and her karate belt seems bound both by her marriage and her developing identity as a self-possessed woman.

While it isn't quite accurate to say that Billops's films offer negative depictions of men, she obviously doesn't stop them from undoing themselves. Rather than spotlighting individual shortcomings or character flaws in the various men in her films, Billops frames and positions these male voices to levy a general critique against patriarchy and male privilege. As these men speak freely about themselves and their account of Billops's decision, it becomes readily apparent how obscure yet persistent sexual oppression can be. These men don't seem to pose the same sort of physical and psychological threat as Brownie in *Suzanne, Suzanne*; however, they don't appear to be consistently helpful or supportive factors in these women's lives. As Barbara Letkasas notes, "men in the films constitute the absent center. Even when present, they seem not to be there, as women talk around and about them. The dramas may be on behalf of men, but they seem to take place between the women."[18] Billops does not present a sense of antagonism between the sexes but rather illuminates the need for mutual understanding and constructive alliances between women and their male partners.

Even in Billops's second film, *Older Women and Love* (1987), which means to celebrate the sexual freedom of some of the older women in Billops's life, the chasm between men and women still seems irreconcilable. In its fractured and disjointed form, the film does not lend itself to any sense of cohesion or unity. The primary setting is a cocktail party where women mill about with glasses of wine and engage in gossipy conversations about the sexual conquests of older women. Ultimately, these women are alone and seem to take more substantial comfort in each other's company than in the fleeting security of a young lover's arms. The most poignant segments of the film come with the one-on-one interviews with Hatch, Billops, and other guests from the party. But the primary shortcoming of the film is precisely that there is no connectedness, no feeling of continuity. No one is named, and consequently the film seems to lack the gutsy, up-front honesty that is so appealing in Billops's other works. Even as women talk about their young lovers and how this latent sexual awakening has rejuvenated them, the lovers these women speak of are absent and cannot offer what the experience has meant for them. Ilka Pajan and her husband Gilberto Reyes are the only couple that appear together, but even their relationship cannot live up to the "love" promised by the title of the film. Pajan translates Reyes's responses and she stresses that their relationship is ending because he needs more freedom. Their exchange with Billops is abruptly ended when the woman emphatically resists being interviewed any longer and stresses to Billops, "Camille, you know it's over. That's what's going to happen, we are going to separate." Pajan dismisses both Billops and tells Reyes he can "go finish working." As both subjects leave the frame of the camera, what appeared to be a kitchen in a home is revealed to be a set in a studio. The lingering shot on the empty kitchen set resonates with the illusory nature of domestic tranquility and the instability of marital accord.

excess and surrealism

Billops's four films to date span a breadth of subjects, but they all share fairly recognizable similarities: they all feature or at least contain members of her family; they are iconoclastic and attempt to reconstitute gender roles and expectations. In so doing, Billops's pieces provoke and arouse intellectual sensibilities and prompt one to rethink universal conventions like family, motherhood, and responsibility. Never shying away from controversy and criticism, Billops's films may not strike a harmony with popular opinion, but perhaps more valuable is their ability to validate and affirm alternative approaches to life and sociability. One quality of Billops's films that may not be so easily identifiable can be best described by what Bill Nichols has called excess: "the random and inexplicable, that which remains ungovernable within a textual regime presided over by narrative."[19] In each of the films discussed above, and even moreso in Billops's latest film, *The KKK Boutique Ain't Just Rednecks* (1994), residual elements of emotion and ideology have become a signature for the provocative quality of Hatch-Billops productions. Within the narrative flow of Billops's films, there often occur those elements that tend to overwhelm or step beyond the film's structure. In *Suzanne, Suzanne*, the final emotional scene between Suzanne and her mother Billie would classify as excess, according to Nichols's term, because the film has not prepared the viewer for this painful, emotional trial. While it is apparent that there has been turmoil in this family, there is no way to know that the mother and daughter will experience this deeply moving, emotional display before our eyes. Because of its dense, emotional surplus, this scene powerfully punctuates the film—reverberating with all of the significance and sentiment that mother-daughter relationships conjure.

The excess in *Older Women and Love* operates in a similar manner in the exchange between Pajan and her husband Reyes. Again, Billops presents subjects who step beyond the structured parameters and protocol of what viewers expect to see within the framework of a documentary. They exhibit an abundance of emotional response that harkens to some information, some history that was not fully explored or established in the film. Within the dramatic contours of the works, these displays are residual, and while they do contribute to the overall foundation of the film's ideological premise, they reveal too much, not in what is said but in how it is presented. Nichols describes these moments as "the noise that remains when we agree upon limits for what will pass as information."

Finally, in *Finding Christa*, various moments throughout the film, concentrated with "authentic," genuine expressions of emotion, imbue the film with a disconcerting sense of restriction in reality. In one scene, Billops appears on camera with her sister Josie as Josie recalls the time, more than twenty years ago, when Billops found out she was pregnant. Josie remembers, "You missed a week of school," and her voice begins to break with tears. Billops breaks in and quips, "You know what I remember? You want me to tell you a funny story so you don't cry?" Josie is already crying, but Billops's casual and detached segue into a whimsical story about their mother, even though it helps to continue the flow of the film, discounts the obvious pain Josie feels about this issue. This same dynamic occurs with Bertha, Billops's cousin, who is considerably older than Billops and evokes a very no-nonsense presence on camera. Bertha is forthright and direct but is ever conscious of the camera on her. When Billops asks her, "Why do you think I gave Christa up?" Bertha quickly averts her eyes from the camera, then looks askance at Billops and says under her breath, "You want me to say this?" Billops encourages her to go on and Bertha responds, "Because at that time, you had met your husband." Hatch is apparently there, off-camera, because as Bertha says this, she glances outside of the frame. Billops inquires, "You think that was the reason?" to which Bertha emphatically responds, "I know it was." The scene dramatically cuts to black and opens with confirmation of Bertha's assertion in photographs of Hatch and Billops in the nascent days of their romance. Bertha's commentary, with its reticent fits and starts, comes inscribed within a denser language of cultural etiquette and respectability. Although she is not readily at ease discussing these family secrets, she nonetheless speaks her mind, boldly and unabashedly. She chides Billops for having been "smart at the mouth" when she told the family that she was going to give Christa away and there was nothing they could do about it. She reminds her that it was in the same room in which they are currently filming and that it was at six o'clock in the morning when the family had gathered to try to persuade Billops not to put Christa up for adoption. In her grave tone and direct stance, Bertha's responses seems to revisit the "scene of the crime" when a young Billops defiantly transgressed one of the most sacred precepts of Black womanhood—she gave up her child to traipse off with some man, and a white one at that.

While it is not unusual to find honest expressions of pain and emotion within a documentary, what is striking about these moments in Billops's films is that they erupt with nearly no historical or social context from within the film, but rather help to crystallize the aesthetic and political grounds of the work itself. Billops does not lead us confidently into these painful, uncomfortable places. As viewers, we find ourselves out there on the limb with the subjects, empathizing and emotionally involved with them in a way that Billops concertedly avoids. Even her husband acknowledges that in the films "she talks a lot, and gives you her opinion, but you really don't know that much about her."[20]

The preservation of these overtly personal and sentimental segments within her films is one way Billops's work exacts a sense of excess. Through tears and uncomfortable tensions before the camera, Billops's subjects exude a sense of excess through their solid grounding in a specific and fixed moment, dripping with "reality." Another cinematic convention in Billops's work that would classify as excess is her allusion to the surreal. As a visual artist and sculptor, Billops's paintings and figures embody elements of surrealism that also find their way into her films. Mel Hillstein, a colleague of Billops and Hatch since they met in a college production of *Fly Blackbird* decades earlier, made the following observation of Billops's artistic vision. It is applicable to her life and cinematic focus as well:

> It was obvious to me that this was somebody who really knew what she was doing with her own work and had a real vision of what she wanted to do and again it was one of those things that I always found really interesting about Camille as an artist is how she has moved to the kind of work that she does today which is not at all realistic but which is much more powerful, I suppose.

This sense of excess as manifested through surreal representations accounts for one particular segment in *Finding Christa* and features more prominently in the recent, experimental piece *The KKK Boutique*. In *Finding Christa*, Christa Victoria's first adult appearance in the film (she is seen throughout the beginning of the film as a child in old photographs and home movies) occurs during a fantasy segment where George Wolfe plays the emcee for "Auditions for the Mother Daughter Recital." He is dressed in a slipshod, vaudevillian suit with oversized sunglasses and a top hat. He introduces Billops as the first contestant by her childhood nickname, Bootsie. Billops appears on a stage dressed in a white, crinoline, Shirley Temple dress with blue ribbons. Behind her, in the foreground, someone is at the piano but is not discernible in a large hat. A musical track of yodeling begins, but Billops's lip-synching is off and she expresses some frustration until she gets it right. She then yodels with the track until the music stops and as Billops curtseys her finish, the figure at the piano tips her hat to Billops. Billops mugs a look of shock and surprise as the camera focuses on a woman's face whose eyes are made up in the same Egyptian style that has become Billops's trademark. The young woman also bears the phenotypic indication that she must be the long-lost Christa and Billops's child—the faintly pilose upper lip.

While critics have been quick to dismiss this portion of *Finding Christa* as enigmatic and incongruous, its symbolic intervention in the film not only underscores the significance of Christa's first appearance in the text but also prefigures the dominant aesthetic strategy of Billops's most ambitious piece, *The KKK Boutique*. There are numerous possible readings of this section, yet some interpretations assert themselves more easily than others. Undoubtedly, the film itself and the process of putting the film together have been an "audition" for both Christa and Billops as a mother/daughter team. The mother here appears as the child, up front and in the spotlight, while the child, Christa, recedes to the background—a symbolic parallel to Billops's desire to develop herself as an artist and her consequent decision to leave Christa behind. This "recital" undoubtedly symbolizes all of the recitals Christa would have hypothetically given as a child and is also a significant common ground for the mother-daughter duo, as both of them are professed singers. Christa's appearance in the film is of critical importance and Billops justly stages it as such. Certainly, their actual reunion eight years prior to the shooting of the film had some sense of the surreal—a mother and daughter reunited after twenty years of separation—and Billops aptly illustrates the stunning and hyper-real nature of this moment through this fantasy sequence.

Billops returns to a rhetorical strategy of fantasy in *The KKK Boutique*, again, to delineate another phenomenal reality of life that cannot adequately be represented in language, images, or text: racism. The rhetorical structure of *The KKK Boutique* operates on three narrative levels: first there is the metanarrative of Hatch and Billops's relationship, which frames the film. As the filmmakers, they introduce and conclude the film with their reflections as an interracial couple. Second, throughout *The KKK Boutique*, there are numerous historical genealogies of race and racism, such as how stereotypes of Native Americans were once used to sell tobacco and a Chinese American's recollection of New York's Chinatown. Finally, and perhaps the most vital aspect of the *The KKK Boutique*, is its element of fantasy and the surreal. The boutique is the Hatch-Billops studio in New York transformed into a multi-level museumesque space of race memorabilia and art installations. Hatch introduces the boutique as "a place where we could change our race" but warns that "each stop has its own madness, its own punishment." A group of people sit in a conference-style room before a podium and a panel of attendants who observe and analyze the boutiquers throughout their visit. Hatch informs us that the boutiquers in the film are not actors but "those are our friends." Before they enter the boutique, the boutiquers are given an official orientation to this "workshop on racism" by Dr. Ruth Helfinch and the attendants. Throughout the film, Helfinch dialogues with the attendants in clinical terms like "detoxing" and "BMS—Black Male Syndrome."

The boutique itself contains racist memorabilia as well as clothes and objects overlaid with racial epithets and iconography. A shirt is covered in racial slurs. A bra has two pickaninny heads in place of cups. A little boy and his mother read a malignant rendition of "Ten Little Indians." Here again, Billops returns to her convention of surrendering the sacred as racial slurs and icons are flagrantly displayed. As a Jewish scholar talks about the history of the Swastika, Hatch's disparaging voice can be overheard commenting, "Here he goes with a 2,000-year-old swastika. Who cares?" George Wolfe conspicuously delivers a dignified and formal reading of the poem "Coon, Coon, Coon" as though it is a masterpiece. Billops begins this workshop by acclimating the viewers and the boutiquers to the spurned trappings of racism—the words we are afraid to say, the thoughts we are afraid to admit. Billops has likened racism to the archaic attitudes people once had about tuberculosis: "We don't have permission to talk about our racism because it's such a shameful thing. You're not supposed to have it."[21]

In the boutique, Hatch and Billops draw the viewer's attention to the complicity of capitalism and racism. The racist icons and images are conflated with commodities in a boutique—a symbolic space for capitalist exchange. This idea is extended in a segment about immigrants who think to themselves that they can't pay their rent and they can't clothe their kids even as they shuffle along to the American dream. Their thoughts and combined steps merge into the chant, "It's all about money." Throughout the film, economics resonate as a subtext with racism so that the fact that this is a "boutique" and not a "funny house" or a "museum" underscores a major principle of the film that economic factors play a prominent role in perpetuating racism.

Hatch and Billops loosely structure this "docu-fantasy" according to the levels of hell from Dante's *Inferno*. Billops guides a seeming tour group through several thematic spaces epitomizing some facet of racist expression. "Asian Fantasy" features an older Black woman dressed as Puccini's Madama Butterfly warbling through a bluesey rendition of "Poor Butterfly is a Flygirl Now." She plays the coquette, demurely glancing over an open fan as she shimmies through the song. "May I Touch Her Here?" mimics a game show where male contestants answer a series of sexually and racially loaded questions and are then rewarded with permission to touch figures of ethnic women in places that have been particularly overwrought in the social imaginary. The women's portion of this segment follows as a panel of women analyze the men's responses and their attention to specific physical attributes of ethnic women. In addition to these fun house, carnivalesque segments, subjects offer personal stories of their feelings and encounters with racism.

Apart from Dante's *Inferno*, a more contemporary model for examining the barrage of images and information in *The KKK Boutique* is the "sensitivity workshop," which characterized the "Politically Correct" movement of the late 1980s and 1990s. In the blitzkrieg of PC mania, several Fortune 500 companies invested $200 to $300 annually in the early 1990s for diversity training targeted primarily for those in management positions to raise their consciousness about women and people of color within the workplace.[22] These programs strongly resemble group therapy sessions where managers and employers converge on neutral turf to hash out their personal demons with racism and sexism. People are invited to be honest and candid as they attempt to purge their prejudices, thereby yielding a kinder and gentler workspace.

The KKK Boutique is packaged and publicized as the Hatch-Billops version of diversity training. The film comes with a facilitator's guide offering questions and commentary to promote group discussion, and particularly targets those "in leadership positions" to take advantage of what the film offers. The overview of the film asserts that before we can work to solve racism in the world, we must all confront our own racism, a "difficult and fearful process." In the face of racism's formidable challenge however, the film promises "we can find ways of softening our fears and guilt by talking about them with others, which can create a social and racial bonding against our common illness."

The most impressive contender against the epidemic of racism in the film appears in the model of Billops and Hatch as a couple. As a preface to the film, Hatch and Billops appear in a field of sunflowers combing each other's hair. They talk about the intimacy of combing hair and how Billops has been cutting Hatch's hair for more than thirty years. The film intermittently returns to them in this setting as they speak impromptu about race and the myriad ways it has impacted their relationship. In this casual exchange, neither Hatch nor Billops seems self-consciously sensitive on this touchy issue, but on the contrary, they allow the intimacy of mutual understanding, fostered over thirty years, to supersede the "correctness" of the conversation. For example, when Hatch tries to explain what it is like to touch Black people's hair, his remark that "it is the softest most sensual kind of thing!" cannot help but sound patronizing and objectifying. As is the case with all of Billops's films. The "true" nature of her marriage to Hatch cannot be discerned from its representation in the film. However, Hatch and Billops are unequivocally partners with four poignant films attesting to the personal and professional success of their union. Therefore, in *The KKK Boutique*, even as Hatch and Billops fail to articulate how they consistently ward off racism, from without and

87

within, to maintain a healthy, productive relationship, their very presence in the film together, in such a tranquil and fecund place, resonates as the most powerful argument for dismantling racial divides and surrendering one's own racial prejudices.

The films of Camille Billops may not be a good place to look for answers. Nor should one expect to have any one ideology or school of thought confirmed there. However, the confrontational brashness of Billops's work precisely yields the dynamics of interrogation and discourse that may lead us to a path of productive valuation. It is clear that in her films, Billops does not view herself as an exemplar of feminism nor does she endorse her own life as a universal model for all to follow. But ultimately, Billops is unequivocally a feminist and her life tacitly embodies those social factors and forces that encroach upon the life and freedom of all women. As a woman and a filmmaker, Billops commands the fearlessness and courage to produce meaningful work. Her films are like family reunions, with all the joy, pressure, and tension that such events entail. With each new production in the "Mom and Pop" business that Hatch and Billops run, we will look eagerly for Suzanne and Billie; we will note how big Suzanne's boys are getting and always hope the best for the ever-vulnerable Christa. Regardless of what we may feel about the choices she has made in her life, how she treats her child, or how she puts together a film, Billops offers us through her work a full and extensive appraisal of family that in the end amounts to a bittersweet treasure and a bounty of mixed blessings.

notes

1. Samella Lewis, "Camille Billops An Interview," *The International Review of African American Art* 10: 4 (1995): 36.

2. Valerie Smith, "The Documentary Impulse in Contemporary African American Film," in Gina Dent, ed., *Black Popular Culture: A Project by Michele Wallace* (Seattle, WA: Bay Press, 1992), 61.

3. Nancy Armstrong and Leonard Tennenhouse, eds., *The Violence of Representation: Literature and the History of Violence* (London and New York: Routledge, 1989), 24.

4. Valerie Smith, "Telling Family Secrets: Narrative and Ideology in *Suzanne, Suzanne* by Camille Billops and James V. Hatch," in Diane Carson et al., eds., *Multiple Voices in Feminist Film Criticism* (Minneapolis: University of Minnesota Press 1994), 386.

5. Barbara Letkasas, "Encounters: The Film Odyssey of Camille Billops," *Black American Literature Forum* 25: 2 (Summer 1991): 398.

6. Julia Lesage, "Contested Territory: Camille Billops' *Finding Christa*," forthcoming manuscript.

7. Joanne M. Braxton, "Ancestral Presence: The Outraged Mother Figure in Contemporary Afra-American Writing," in Joanne M. Braxton, ed., *Wild Women in the Whirlwind* (New Brunswick: Rutgers University Press, 1990): 300.

8. Toni Morrison, *Beloved* (New York: Plume, 1987), 251.

9. Toni Morrison upon receiving the 1988 Robert F. Kennedy Book Award.

10. Patricia Williams, *The Rooster's Egg* (Cambridge: Harvard University Press, 1995), 171.

11. Hortense Spillers, "Mama's Baby, Papa's Maybe: An American Grammar Book," *Diacritic* 17: 2 (Summer 1987): 80.

12. Lynda Jones, "Dream On, Dreamer," *Village Voice*, September 6, 1994, 60.

13. Linda Kintz, "The Sanitized Spectacle: What's Birth Got to Do With It? Adrienne Kennedy's *A Movie Star Has to Star in Black and White*," *Theatre Journal* 44 (1992): 75.

14. Adrienne Kennedy, *People Who Led to My Plays* (New York: Alfred A. Knoppf, 1987), 84.

15. Preface to the PBS *Point of View* presentation of *Finding Christa.*

16. Amanda Meer, "Profiles and Positions: Camille Billops," *Bomb* (Summer 1992): 23.

17. Luce Irigaray, *The Sex Which Is Not One* (Ithaca, NY: Cornell University Press, 1977), 76.

18. Letkasas, *op. cit.,* 396.

19. Bill Nichols, *Representing Reality: Issues and Concepts in Documentary* (Bloomington: Indiana University Press, 1991), 141.

20. Meer, *op. cit.,* 24.

21. Ibid., 23.

22. Gwendolyn Thompkins, "We're All Sensitive People with So Much to Give," unpublished manuscript, 1995.

part two

critical

practice

carol

munday

lawrence

producer,

director,

writer

c a r o l   m u n d a y   l a w r e n c e

"You have to have a *reason* for being an artist. This is not a game we are playing." Hughie Lee-Smith, the great surrealist painter, said this to a class at New York's Art Students League in a film about African American fine artists that I produced and directed. In those short phrases, he articulated and validated the philosophy that has been the linchpin of my career.

Having a reason for being an artist does not mean that our work must always have racial content; this is a matter of individual choice. People of color, like everyone else, have a full complement of human emotions and ideas to express. Nor is it to say that everyone has to make reality-based films: Mr. Lee-Smith is a surrealist, after all, but the composition of his paintings—what he refers to as the "juxtaposition of disparate objects"—always carries a subtle message. Whatever the reason for your decision to become an independent filmmaker, it must be strong enough to spur you to excellence and nourish you through many painful hours of disillusionment, not to mention high levels of frustration and budgets so tight they cut off your circulation.

My reason for making films is twofold: as an artist, I have something inside that demands to be expressed and shared with others; as an African American, I feel a personal responsibility to use my tools, motion pictures and words, to create works that empower and celebrate my people. To this end, I have worked on many film and television productions over the years as a producer, director, and writer.

When I was growing up in Tuskegee, Alabama, it never occurred to me that I could be a filmmaker. Movies were an escape mechanism for whites; there was no room for Black people unless we were securely strapped into our designated roles as servants and comic relief. When it came to television, any time one of us—invariably a performer or sports figure—appeared on the air, everybody in my family would run to see, a drama that was repeated in every African American household in the country. With our appearances on screen being so stereotypical and so rare, we did not need to be told that there were no Black people working behind the camera.

It wasn't until the 1970s that we began to appear on film in any numbers. We knew that there was something counterfeit about those images, but we cheered our cardboard heroes on regardless, as they defeated organized crime, outwitted the feds, and kicked bad-guy butt in the neighborhood. The producers called it "Black exploitation" without apology: exploitation of our frustrations, our dreams, and our pocketbooks. Although the genre reaped unprecedented profits, we knew full well that our people were neither rolling the camera nor counting the cash.

Black people are still being exploited today, in a much more subtle guise with deadlier, more immediate repercussions. I want to do something about it through the films and television shows I make and through my efforts to effect change behind the scenes. I want my work to uplift, and to give the lie to the lies; I want us to be able to speak our own words in our own voices; I want those of us who know the language of film and television to have access to the best tools of the trade; I want us to be able to distribute our work to the general public unfettered by racist censorship that protects the status quo, and I want those who aspire to learn the craft to have the same opportunities that are available to any other would-be film, television, or video professional.

My first job in media was Director of Operations for Blackside, Inc., Henry Hampton's Boston-based production company, in its first year of operation in 1968. Henry was well ahead of his time because there were very few independent production companies for him to use as a model, none of them Black-owned and none of them located in Boston.

Our minuscule staff consisted of Henry, Howard Dammond, and me.

Our lofty titles belied both our experience (none) and our salaries (ditto), but Henry had big dreams, progressive ideas, and a lot of heart. His motley crew somehow managed to produce one or two short films and a series of radio spots called "The Black Side" that were not half bad. Howard and I wrote scripts for the radio series and were sent out on assignment with a Nagra tape recorder, the only piece of equipment Blackside owned, to interview people in the Roxbury community. I sometimes wonder what happened to those tapes, especially my interviews with Vietnam veterans like "Shazam," a handsome young man not long out of high school whose horrific memories and gaping emotional wounds were still fresh, and who was still trusting enough to expose them.

I hung in with Blackside for a year or so before the burden of poverty became too oppressive, but Henry persevered, eventually landing foundation grants and government production contracts that enabled him to get Blackside on its feet. The rest, of course, is history: when the critically acclaimed series *Eyes on the Prize* went on the air in 1987, Henry Hampton made it onto the map in a big way and my lean year at Blackside suddenly became a feather in my cap.

In 1970, Ray Richardson, producer of a Black-oriented television series called *Say Brother*, invited me to join his staff at WGBH-TV as the show's Associate Producer. We didn't know each other very well, but Ray was desperate to fill the position. I was honest about my ignorance of television production, but that didn't matter to him any more than it had mattered to Henry Hampton that I had no idea what a director of operations was. All Ray wanted to know was, "You can read and write and do basic math, can't you?" I had been looking for something new and the job sounded interesting, so I took the chance.

WGBH in Boston and WNET in New York were (and still are) the cream of public television stations, generating the bulk of the network's national programming: shows like *Julia Child, Evening At the Pops, Masterpiece Theatre*, and the Children's Television Workshop series *Sesame Street* and *The Electric Company*. I will never forget the taste of Julia Child's chocolate cake or the spectacle of Alistair Cook, silver-haired British host of *Masterpiece Theatre*, trying for fifteen minutes to say "loo-tenant" (lieutenant) instead of "leftenant." Cook's curses (enunciated in impeccable BBC English) and his good-natured howls of laughter were hilarious. The three major black-oriented series of that era, *Say Brother, Black Journal*, and *Soul!* provided a much-needed forum for the exchange of information and ideas among African Americans.

Say Brother was a weekly, one-hour magazine format series born in the wake of the murder of Dr. Martin Luther King Jr., when Boston's Black community pressured local television stations to unlock their doors. Producer Ray Richardson had carte blanche when it came to the content and layout of the shows, and a full-time technical staff that included a film crew and two film editors. *Say Brother* also had its own minivan, which made it possible for us to go out into the field. The shows were videotaped in studio by a full complement of WGBH's top-notch technicians. These resources, coupled with the freedom to experiment and the station's nonunion status, allowed us to learn the medium inside and out.

My job, like everyone else's, was jack-of-all-trades. I learned to structure a show; write voice-over copy, news copy and political commentary; conduct on-the-street interviews; and work with film and videotape editors. I became a wizard in the control room, timing out shows with two stopwatches, cuing the floor manager ("ready the ten minute cue . . . give the ten minute cue!") and the engineers ("five seconds to deadroll . . . deadroll!"). I did the work of assistant directors, script supervisors, camera coordinators, producers, writers, and camera assistants. I also supervised production in the field, often directing the filming. No one could ask for a better, more thorough learning experience. *Say Brother*'s flexible magazine format included news, commentary, interviews, film clips, music — you name it. Well-known performers from out of town appeared on the show because it was excellent publicity for their local club dates. People like Stevie Wonder and Sly and the Family Stone came by; so did the Funkadelic, who got incensed when we didn't let them take off their clothes the way they did in the clubs. *Say Brother*'s regular hosts, Jim Spruill and Sara-Ann Shaw, interviewed guests, introduced taped segments, and provided voice-over narration.

Stan Lathan was *Say Brother*'s director. Stan took full advantage of his artistic freedom, experimenting with visual concepts that were highly innovative at the time: he greased the lenses, reversed the polarity, and in one brilliant production that required two television sets to watch, collaborated with the equally talented Gus Solomons, who leaped from set to set in a beautifully-staged, virtuoso modern dance. It was inevitable that Stan would outgrow *Say Brother*. He eventually left for New York to direct *Black Journal* and *Sesame Street* (among many others) and is now the most successful Black television director in Hollywood.

Russell Tillman followed Stan as director; Morris Alston was a cinematographer; Henry Johnson, now Vice President of Production at Warner Brothers Television, was an editor. Tony Lark, also an editor, is a post-production supervisor in Los Angeles. The entire staff, including production assistants Mignonne Gumbs, Jewelle Gomez, and several more whose names I don't recall, numbered between eight and ten.

There were a number of other Black women working at the station at that time: Marita Rivero, a producer-trainee assigned to a highly innovative community access show; Maureen Bunyan, an on-air news reporter; Charlayne Haynes, who worked in the videotape department, handling tape stock and the station's extensive tape library; and Madeline Anderson, who was on the production staff. Our presence made the station management vaguely uneasy, especially on days when we brought in take-out chitterlings from Bob the Chef's ("what is that smell?!"), but we were allowed to do our work in relative peace.

WGBH taught me how powerful a medium television is, how powerful an educational tool it can be if utilized with skill and sensitivity, and how much I loved working with picture and sound. Of course, the job was not all fun and games. We did some awful shows from time to time, experiments that missed their mark by a mile. I still have nightmares about the one I was conned into hosting. That day marked the beginning, middle, and end of my career in front of the camera.

It started when they accidentally shuffled the pages of the script, so that my introductory statement made no sense; when it came time to roll in the two film segments, the voice-over for one was heard during the other. You saw shots of a dilapidated housing project that violated every building code in the book, while a narrator cheerfully announced the opening of a brand new playground. By the time we got to the studio interview, my guests were so terrified that they refused to tackle any question that couldn't be answered "yes" or "no." No root canal was ever so painful. I was forced to end the interview ten minutes ahead of schedule and had to ad lib until the floor manager cued me to stop. For those who don't know, ten minutes is an eternity, especially when you have nothing to say and are saying it badly. Did I mention that this horror was on the air live? The instant the credits started to roll, I slunk out of there with my coat over my head and hid for a week.

The work schedule on a weekly, hour-long television series is grueling, with long days and little or no privacy. It was my first experience in an environment where employees could be paged in the restroom. For mental health's sake, one learned to seek refuge in secret, quiet places. Mine was the announce booth, a soundproof cubicle from which the station ID ("This is WGBH, Channel 2 Boston") and other announcements are made. The booth announcer was in hiding too, but he had it easy: all he had to do was close the padded door and turn off the mike, and he was perfectly insulated against the madness outside. I don't know why he offered me sanctuary; maybe it was because I laughed out loud when he displayed his considerable skill in the art of character assassination, our

way of coping with the insecurity we felt knowing that our careers often hung by a boss's grudge.

About a year into my stay at WGBH, I learned about the Nguzo Saba ("Seven Principles" in the Kiswahili language) adapted by Dr. Ron Karenga from the teachings of President Julius Nyerere of Tanzania. Each of the seven principles constitutes one of the ingredients of a unified community, something vital to the cultural and economic survival of African Americans. When I heard neighborhood children reciting these concepts by rote, without really understanding them, it occurred to me that each one could be illustrated by a folktale from somewhere in the African diaspora.

I had read a short story entitled "Tiger and the Big Wind" in a book of folklore by William J. Faulkner called *The Days When the Animals Talked*. "Tiger and the Big Wind" perfectly illustrated the first of the seven principles: Umoja, or unity. I adapted it for the screen, asked Dr. Faulkner to do the narration, and hired a budding animator named Salvatore Raciti to help make it into a children's film. I knew nothing about the animation process and tried to pin Sal down about the cost, but he was one of those artists with an aversion to money; he was even embarrassed about discussing his fee. Dr. Faulkner helped me raise the ridiculously inadequate $7,000 budget through a philanthropist friend of his, and we stumbled blindly into production.

Roxbury schoolchildren provided the artwork. They were old enough (fourth and fifth grade) to draw the pictures with a relatively sure hand, but still young enough for their work to have a childlike quality. We gave them brand new magic markers in a hundred colors and instructed them to draw various figures in preordained sizes, from several different angles. These were then cut out and animated against backgrounds drawn by Sal, who shot the film on a Roxbury animation stand at one of the universities. It was big fun and a wonderful learning experience for everybody, children and adults alike.

I found the perfect theme music on a record album by folksinger Odetta. When the record company demanded a small fortune for the rights, I invited Odetta to come and record the tracks in person, bribing her with the promise of homemade apple pie and collard greens, and a bed with a handmade Mississippi quilt. It was my first experience working solo with a professional of her stature (I was terrified), and the first of three film scores we have done together so far.

Despite our inexperience and inadequate resources, the film, entitled *Umoja: Tiger and the Big Wind*, turned out well. It was my first independent production. I saw Sal's credit on television recently and was pleased to discover that he is still working his magic. Something tells me he's gotten over his shyness about asking for compensation.

When the politics began, *Say Brother* as we knew it came to an end. In the early 1970s, students were demonstrating all over the country, and Boston, with its many universities, was no exception. The *Say Brother* staff were among the few members of the press allowed behind the scenes whenever there was a conflict. I remember when we climbed through a second floor window of the administration building at Boston University to interview Black students holed up inside. Experiences like this inspired Ray to produce a series of news shows, something he had never tried before.

It wasn't long before we realized just how difficult it is to crank out an hour of hard news every week without your own sources. We tried to compensate by building a window into each show for late-breaking news, then throwing in whatever came over the wire services that day, but this was haphazard at best. Those of us who wrote copy learned to write fast, with someone standing over us snatching the pages out of the typewriter as soon as they were finished.

This exhausting experiment was short-lived, but it did not go unnoticed by management: *Say Brother* was acceptable when it was limited to singing, dancing, and complaining about conditions in the African American community, but it was something else altogether for the series to express a sophisticated point of view on national and international news, with acid critiques of American foreign policy. To make matters worse, a lot of people took the programs seriously.

Management was well aware of the fact that the show could not be canceled without fearful repercussions, so they solved the problem by cutting it to half an hour and clipping Ray's wings. This turn of events led to a bitter confrontation between Ray and the program manager, who fired him, triggering a mass protest by loyal viewers who were under the impression that the future of *Say Brother* was in jeopardy. Station executives had no choice but to reinstate the show or commit public relations hara-kiri. When Ray went on vacation shortly afterward and drowned in a swimming accident off the coast of Mexico, the unrelated tragedy of his death was linked to the crisis at WGBH, precipitating a brouhaha that made it all the way into *Time* magazine.

I was assigned to work on two concurrent shows, one of them hosted by tennis commentator Bud Collins, until a producer could be found for *Say Brother*. After several months, the new man swept in with a new staff and a new attitude: where Ray's style had been informal and egalitarian, this individual was remote and distrustful of those of us who were carryovers from the past. I was very skilled at my job by this time, but completely naive about the perils of working with a boss whose plans for the future do not include you. Exhausted by the ensuing guerrilla war, I finally surrendered, accepting an offer from WCVB-TV, a brand-new ABC station.

WCVB was born of a license renewal challenge, the first successful one in the country. The competence and integrity of a television station's management is subject to challenge whenever the station's license comes up for renewal, provided the challengers have legitimate grounds and can demonstrate their ability to take the station over if successful. The new managers scoured major television markets, especially New York, for new producers, directors, and department heads, but they did not anticipate the inevitable jockeying for position as all those Type-A+ personalities fought to become top dog. The resulting bloodbath was gorier by far than *National Geographic*'s recent documentary on piranha in the waters of Brazil.

I left Boston for San Francisco at the end of 1972, with a firm grounding in hands-on television production—150 shows by conservative estimate— and the firm conviction that the do-unto-others-before-they-do-unto-you world of the television station staffer was not for me. My nemesis at *Say Brother* was followed by Topper Carew, who was in turn followed by Marita Rivero. Topper is now an executive producer in Los Angeles and Marita, who left Boston to run WPFW-FM in Washington, is back as General Manager of WGBH Radio. She is a close friend and godmother to my daughter, born a month after my then-husband and I left Boston. Friends are worth their weight in gold in the world of film and television production. You need them to rub your back during the inevitable down times, and to assure you that you are not crazy, no matter what anybody says.

The animated film *Umoja* languished on a shelf in San Francisco until Preston Wilcox, president of Afram Associates in New York, came for a visit and screened it. Always hypercritical of my work, I thought the film was too rough around the edges to distribute, but Preston not only liked it, as an educator he also knew that there was nothing comparable on the market for African American children. Rough-edged or not, it would fill an important niche. By the time he left, he had made me promise to distribute *Umoja* (which went on to win a CINE Golden Eagle) and to complete the other six films in the series.

The remaining Nguzo Saba ("Seven Principles") films illustrate the principles Imani (faith), Ujima (sharing work and responsibility), Ujamaa (economic cooperation), Kujichagulia (self-determination), Nia (purpose), and Kuumba (creativity). They were produced piecemeal, whenever there was enough money to put together a staff, with funds from the National Endowment for the Arts, the Cummins Engine Foundation, and the James Irvine Foundation, among others.

I wrote the scripts, with the exception of *Kuumba: Simon's New Sound*, which was written by Joel Dreyfuss. Poet Opal Palmer was the voice of Simon, and my daughter Maia and her friends played the other children's roles. Alice Walker gave us the use of her short story "Finding the Green Stone" to illustrate the principle Nia (Purpose), and writer Daphne Muse put together a teacher's guide. Artist Will Noble created beautiful images for two of the films, while Sal Raciti, Margaret Craig, Bob Bloomberg, and Jane Aaron did the animation. There is music by Odetta, Babatunde Olatunji, Taj Mahal, the Louis Arnold Steel Band, and Don Lewis. The last of the seven was completed in the 1980s. They are still in distribution.

Since there was going to be a considerable amount of production, it stood to reason that there should be a production company to serve as an umbrella. Of course, if I had known then what I know now, I would never have given the idea a second thought; it was blind ignorance that gave me the courage to forge ahead, blithely overlooking the fact that I had no experience in either business or large-scale independent production, nor did I have financial resources or a support staff. These minor details notwithstanding, Nguzo Saba Films, Inc., named after the animated series, was incorporated in 1973. Its description in the company's first brochure calls it

> an association of individuals with media skills, [emphasizing] the use of techniques which support the cultural values of minority groups as they define them. Nguzo Saba Films makes possible community involvement on all levels by giv- ing talented musicians, writers and artists . . . the opportunity to work on professional productions and exposure for their work. In the spirit of the community-as-classroom concept, the production process is often a learning experience in itself.

Of course, there was no "company" at that time: I had had some classy-looking stationery made up, learned to say "we" instead of "I," and lined up a plush office to borrow whenever there was a potential benefactor to impress.

To their credit, my family cheerfully tolerated my long hours, out-of-town travel, emotional stress ("Why do employees act like that? Will we get the money? Now that I'm in the middle of the lake with no paddle, maybe this wasn't such a good idea") and all the rest of the headaches and mood swings that go with the territory.

The grant that enabled me to get Nguzo Saba out of our house and into an office came from the National Endowment for the Arts' Expansion Arts Program, under the direction of Vantile Whitfield, who flew to San Francisco and conducted a site visit after reading the proposal. Unperturbed by the fact that there was no site to visit (the meeting took place in my home), he threw his full support behind the concept of an educational production company that would produce materials for people of color, awarding the company $10,000 for administrative expenses.

This seminal grant enabled me to hire Peggy Dammond (now Preacely), my first employee. Enthusiastic and loyal, Peggy saw possibilities in me that I could not see in myself and proved to be an indispensable ally. She worked on two of the Seven Principles animations and served as Associate Producer of the pilot episode of Nguzo Saba Films' first major production, *Were You There*. She also introduced me to valuable contact people and talented colleagues like Kathy Collins and VeVe Clark. I owe her a great deal.

There were so few African American filmmakers at that time—that is, people who were trying to make a living at it—that we all knew or had at least heard of each other. I met most of them through their work; for example, Julie Dash's *Four Women* (1975) was screened by an American Film Institute panel on which I served. Whenever a viable proposal by a Black person came up for review, I went to war to get it funded. I think we all did that, because we knew how hard it had been for the filmmaker to get that far, and how much our people needed to see themselves portrayed on screen in solid, positive productions. I would hope that we are still fighting for each other, because the safeguards that once assured diversity among grantees are now under bitter attack.

Throughout the 1970s, filmmakers raised production money from the National Endowment for the Humanities, the National Endowment for the Arts, the American Film Institute, the Corporation for Public Broadcasting, and whatever funding sources we could develop on our own. I remember pleading with the Executive Director of the James Irvine Foundation to take a chance on one of the animations. He did, and the Foundation has since supported many other filmmakers and television programs. Not only were there ample places to shop a proposal, but you could raise your entire budget from only one or two sources. Today, unless the film is financed by a cable or network television company (an option that has certain drawbacks), producers must piece their budgets together from many sources in a lengthy, expensive, hit-or-miss process.

The production that put Nguzo Saba Films on the map was the series *Were You There* Marita Rivero sent me a copy of a request for proposals issued jointly by the Corporation for Public Broadcasting (CPB) and the

Public Broadcasting Service (PBS) for a minority-oriented television series. The grant amount was an unprecedented $1 million. We had nothing to lose by applying, but Nguzo Saba Films was unknown to PBS and obviously lacked experience at this level of production; therefore I rounded up seasoned producers, performers, and technical staff and convinced them to lend their credibility to the project.

The concept was simple: we would produce seven half-hour programs, each exploring some aspect of recent African American cultural history. Each show would feature a person or persons who had experienced the era in question—someone who had "been there," hence the series title, also the title of a spiritual song. The shows would be fast-paced and visual, enhanced with dramatic re-enactments, vintage film clips, and music. There would be no hosts or narrators.

Individual programs included the Black West, featuring Colorado native Mrs. Eunice Norris, and Frank Greenway, a rodeo cowboy who rode with the legendary Bill Pickett; Harlem Renaissance—era fine art, featuring painters Jacob Lawrence and Hughie Lee-Smith; the Cotton Club, with Cab Calloway, Avon Long, the Nicholas Brothers, and former showgirl Estrellita Morse; the world of the blues, featuring prolific songwriter-singer-producer Willie Dixon; African American folklore, featuring storyteller-scholar Dr. William Faulkner; the life and work of pioneer film director Oscar Micheaux, with actors Bee Freeman ("the Sepia Mae West") and Lorenzo Tucker ("the Black Valentino"); and a profile of sports greats Alice Coachman, the first Black woman to win an Olympic gold medal, and Negro League baseball player Artie Wilson, star shortstop of the Birmingham Black Barons.

Several months after the proposal was submitted, a letter arrived from the Corporation for Public Broadcasting informing me that the grant had been awarded to Nguzo Saba Films. It goes without saying that a whole lot of shouting and dancing went on in the office that day. The celebration was in full swing when the second call came. There had been a slight change of plans: the review panel had been reconvened and was going to finance not one but three pilot programs, one to be produced by each of the top three contenders. If Nguzo Saba Films could produce the winning pilot, the grant was ours. We had been thrown back in competition, only this time it was a battle of productions, not proposals. We had no choice but to recork the champagne and take up arms. The saga of my efforts over the ensuing years to deal efficiently with two intransigent bureaucracies is at once humorous, tragic, and infuriating. Adjectives like "Byzantine" and "Machiavellian" come to mind. I kept a detailed chronology of the whole outrageous odyssey, which I may well publish one of these days.

Madison Davis Lacy, a PBS executive associated with the project from its inception, and Donald Marbury, who joined CPB's program department after preproduction had begun, were our angels inside the system. The two of them worked miracles on our behalf behind the scenes, sometimes taking significant professional risks to do so. Dave Lacy eventually left PBS to become a producer in his own right, while Don Marbury has for some years been Director of CPB's Television Program Fund.

We spent almost a year doing research for *Were You There* and at least a month of preproduction before going out on the road to shoot. All of the featured guests were interviewed during the location scouting process, enabling us to get to know them, gather material for the dramatic re-enactments, and develop a clear-cut structure for each show before going out on the road. Careful preparation makes it possible to work within your budget, and makes it easier to deal with unanticipated problems. It also frees you up to be creative, and to take advantage of any unexpected good fortune that comes your way.

Were You There was charmed from the start. That which did not work out according to plan eventually worked out better than we could ever have planned it. I think that this was a matter of Life paving a way for each of those elders, many of whom have since passed on, to leave a legacy on film. Several of them wept during the interviews, overwhelmed that someone was not only interested in their stories but also willing to give them a national forum. Even the high-profile celebrities like Cab Calloway were pleased. The personal lives of all the staff and crew members who worked on the series have been enriched by our association with these wise warriors. So much of our precious history has been lost because we do not take an interest in our grandmothers and grandfathers. Many people helped bring *Were You There* to the screen, among them Linda Marquez, Brenda Grayson, Barbie Fujimoto Petino, Carmen Langford West, and Kathy Irving, the Rocks of Gibraltar who ran the Nguzo Saba Films office (Trudy Ramirez, Ann Hayward, and Sandi Cupit were with us for a brief moment); directors Bob Zagone, Stan Lathan, Kit Lukas, and Gilbert Moses; directors of photography Emiko Omori and Rick Butler; camera assistants Michael Chin and Orlando Bagwell; production sound mixers Curtis Choy and Bill Lewis; editors Irving Saraf, Jennifer Chinlund, Paul Evans, and Chic Ciccolini; assistant editors Stacey Foiles and Bob Shoup; production manager Ed Dessisso; production designer Kent Kay; and costume designer Marianna DeFina. I am very proud of the fact that all those listed as "assistants" have gone on to become top professionals in their respective crafts. We mourn the loss of Linda Marquez and Gil Moses.

Were You There was shot on location in California, Arizona, New York,

New Jersey, Alabama, Illinois, Colorado, and Washington State, on 16mm color negative film with one and sometimes two cameras (a slo-mo camera was used for parts of the cattle drive sequence in the Black West episode).

Scripts for the dramatic re-enactments were based on preproduction research and preliminary interviews with the featured guests. An unknown New York–based stage actor named Danny Glover got his first national television role in *Were You There*, portraying film director Oscar Micheaux. He took the time to interview actors who had worked with Micheaux and played the role beautifully, remaining in character on the set all day, every day. I take full credit for launching his career and I remind him of it at every opportunity.

Animator Neil Krepela, artist Will Noble, composer Don Lewis, and I worked together to create the opening cel animation sequence for the series. Most of the episodes were mixed at Saul Zaentz's Fantasy Films by Mark Berger. The finished programs were transferred to 1-inch broadcast-quality videotape for delivery to PBS, which has extremely strict delivery requirements.

After years of battling with CPB—the funding source—to complete the films, I naively assumed that my work was done: just hand the programs over to PBS—the network—and they would automatically appear on the air in a high-profile, prime-time slot. Little did I know that the Scylla of funding always works in concert with the Charybdis of distribution: you may survive the process of getting your film or TV show made, but it will never be seen by an audience unless you can survive the equally perilous ordeal of getting it distributed.

I remember waiting in PBS's Washington headquarters under the unblinking scrutiny of a huge, stuffed Cookie Monster that dominated one corner of the room. When I was finally called into their office, the execs informed me that *Were You There* had been adjudged to be a Black series. Not only that, but many of the individuals featured in it were old. This double indictment rendered the series ineligible for a coveted prime-time slot, I was told, because no one but old, Black people could possibly want to tune in. Surely I could understand that. They spoke to me in the same patronizing tone department store salesladies use when trying to reason with a size 12 woman who insists on squeezing into a size 8 dress: "An 8 p.m. prime-time slot is out. Perhaps we can interest you in something a little more appropriate . . . how about 12 noon on Sundays? or 12 Saturday . . . ?"

I argued that we had taken great pains to develop a series that would appeal to a broad, general audience. I argued that their age and their

African descent and the freshness of the material were precisely what made our interviewees so interesting. I argued that the original request for proposals specified that the shows would air in prime time. I argued that the production values were top-notch—why relegate a $1 million investment to the graveyard shift? I argued that their policy made it impossible for Black people ever to appear in prime time—on public television yet. I argued, but to no avail: the series was scheduled for 10 p.m., too late for schoolchildren, one of our target audiences. When I left, that big Cookie Monster didn't even have the decency to say he was sorry.

Were You There went on the air in 1981, broadcast by over 200 stations around the country. Positive reviews and poignant letters from viewers told us that we had struck a nerve: people of all ages and races found the shows to be informative and entertaining. Theater audiences laughed and got quiet at all the right places, even applauding Willie Dixon's musical numbers. Needless to say, the elders were pleased by this well-deserved and long-overdue attention; some were even reunited with long-lost friends and colleagues who recognized them on the show. Their race and their age were immaterial, as we knew they would be.

The series earned many honors and awards, both for those who worked on it and for those who appeared in it. Willie Dixon was hired to score TV commercials and a feature film; Oscar Micheaux's career was chronicled in a wealth of new books; Cab Calloway and the Nicholas Brothers were immortalized in documentaries about their lives; the Cotton Club episode helped inspire the feature film of the same name; Alice Coachman was at long last acknowledged for her accomplishments as an Olympian; there was a revival of interest in the Negro Baseball League; and former Cotton Club showgirl Estrellita Morse attracted an ardent New York suitor who pestered the office for her phone number (he didn't get it). The accomplishment I am most pleased about is that by fighting to produce *Were You There* independently of a PBS station, Nguzo Saba Films set a precedent that made it possible for others, both Black and white, to produce their shows through their own production companies, without an outside administrator.

Other people who were making films at around this time included sisters Julie Dash, Ayoka Chenzira, Carroll Blue, Michelle Parkerson, and Monica Freeman, and brothers Haile Gerima, Charles Burnett, Larry Clark, Billy Woodberry, and Warrington Hudlin. In the mid-1980s, I attended the screening of a student film called *Joe's Bed-Stuy Barber Shop* (1983), which had won that year's student Academy Award. The filmmaker, Spike Lee, came up and introduced himself. Frustrated because the prestigious award had not helped his career as it had done for his prede-

carol munday lawrence

cessors, he expressed his determination not to give up. The next time I saw Spike, he was back in San Francisco, this time at the première of *She's Gotta Have It* (1986).

I have worked as a producer or freelancer on all sorts of productions since the halcyon days of *Were You There*—animations; features (*The Cotton Club* [1984], directed by Francis Coppola, and *To Sleep With Anger* [1990] written and directed by Charles Burnett); dramas, shot on both film and videotape; documentaries of various genres; three-camera studio shows; industrials; awards specials; down-and-dirty-do-the-best-you-can projects with little or no money but lots of heart; and a number of productions that defy categorization.

I have worked on movie lots, in television studios, in people's homes, in theaters, on a moving train, on horseback, in the city, in the desert, in luxury, on the cheap, in blistering heat, in mountain snow, in the north, south, east, west and sometimes (it seemed) down below. I have written, produced, directed, edited, production managed, post-production supervised, narrated, followed focus, pulled cable, operated the boom, hauled, lugged, assisted, encouraged, defied, cajoled, scheduled, budgeted, begged, borrowed, laughed, cussed, and wept for joy. It's that last one that keeps you going back for more. Ecstatically pregnant with a new idea, you conveniently forget that many hours of childbirth lie ahead.

When government funding for the arts, once the lifeblood of independent production, began to be rescinded, I was forced to come to terms with the fact that there was no longer enough work in my beloved San Francisco Bay area to support me. In 1989, I moved to Los Angeles, where I now work as a producer under the banner of my company, Clay-Alexander Productions, and as a freelance writer, director, production manager, and post-production supervisor. Nguzo Saba Films is still alive and well. I firmly believe that Black filmmakers and videographers have a responsibility to participate in the ongoing struggle for equal access to the professional playing field. In an effort to practice what I preach about service to the field, I teach aspiring filmmakers in universities and workshops; I serve on two Writers' Guild committees, including the Committee of Black Writers (which I chair); I serve on the boards of directors of the Independent Feature Project and the Independent Documentary Association, and I frequently accept speaking engagements.

Projects currently in development include a television miniseries on the shared history of African and Native Americans, a feature film and a Black comedy (no pun intended) called "The Departure." That is today's list: as every producer knows, some things will be tabled and new ones will be added, because priorities are constantly shifting. In addition to screenwriting, I am a journalist, a poet, and am at work on an autobiographical book tentatively entitled *Adventures Of A Well-Travelled Colored Girl*. I also plan to chronicle my most colorful production experiences—the "war stories"—in a book about independent filmmaking on the road.

I believe in striving for excellence. I believe that we filmmakers and videographers owe it to ourselves and our audiences to do our best. We owe it to our crews to showcase their work in a way that does them proud, and we owe it to those who invest in our dreams to be worthy of their trust. We owe it to those who follow in our footsteps to make a path. This has nothing to do with perfection, or competition with others: it is a matter of doing the best you can with what you have. I want my work to make a difference. You have to have a reason for being an artist.

how

deep,

how

wide?

perspectives on the

making of *the massachusetts*

54th colored infantry

j a c q u e l i n e   s h e a r e r

editor's note on *the massachusetts 54th colored infantry*

In 1863 the first Black Union regiment was formed to fight in the Civil War. This was four years after John Brown, the abolitionist, led a raid on Harper's Ferry in Virginia, and two years after Confederate soldiers fired on a federal garrison in Charleston harbor, South Carolina, thus signaling the beginning of the Civil War.

The story of this first Black regiment, the Massachusetts 54th Colored Infantry, is given a fictionalized treatment in the film Glory *(1989). The film starred Matthew Broderick as Robert Gould Shaw, the twenty-six-year-old commander of the regiment. Denzel Washington was featured as the character Trip, and Morgan Freeman played the part of a grave-digger who eventually becomes a Sergeant Major. Washington later won an Academy Award in the category of Best Supporting Actor for his role in the film.*

The Massachusetts 54th Colored Infantry *(1991) is a television documentary on the same subject. The program was a segment of the PBS series,* The American Experience, *hosted by historian David McCullough. The program was written, produced, and directed by Jacqueline Shearer, a Black woman who has been making films since the early 1970s. Her film,* A Minor Altercation *(1977), is considered a classic example of the work of Black women filmmakers.*

According to Joseph Glatthaar in The Journal of American History, The Massachusetts 54th *tells a more accurate story than did the film* Glory, *and contains fewer errors about the Civil War than did Ken Burns's documentary series on the war.*[1] *Glatthaar states: "Jacqueline Shearer and her team deserve kudos for their excellent research. The filmmakers scoured archives from Washington, D.C., to Massachusetts and located numerous fresh and exciting collections of letters from Black soldiers."*[2]

The documentary is structured using Morgan Freeman as the voice-over narrator who maintains the continuity of the story. On-camera interviewees are descendants of the Black men who fought in the Massachusetts 54th regiment. Black historians Byron Rushing and Barbara Fields are also seen talking on camera. Fields was a historian used by Ken Burns for his series on the Civil War, and as Shearer relates in her article, Burns barely scratched the surface of Fields's extensive knowledge of the subject.

Rather than visual re-enactments of the actual people, the documentary featured photographs of the soldiers and the abolitionists of that period that were discovered during the research. Shearer also uses excerpts from their letters, diaries, and speeches. The excerpts are read as voice-over dramatizations by Hollywood actors including Larry Fishburne, who played the father in Boyz 'N the Hood *(1991); Carl Lumbly, one of the police officers on the television program* Cagney and Lacey; *and Blair Underwood of the television series* L.A. Law.

The Black Union soldiers were denied positions as commissioned officers, even though they were promised as much by the government. They were also paid a fraction of the amount paid to the white soldiers. One of the misconceptions about the Massachusetts 54th that Shearer corrects in the documentary concerns the length of time between the initial refusal of the Black soldiers to accept a lower pay and their success in getting a fair wage. In the film Glory, *the soldiers are portrayed protesting for a short period of time and their requests are granted. In actuality, the Black soldiers fought for eighteen months before the government was pressured into paying them the same amount given to white soldiers.*

Shearer's documentary rectifies a second misconception that Glory *asserts. During the time of the Civil War, it was widely believed that the Black soldiers who fought with the Union Troops were attempting to prove their valor and demonstrate that Black people were worthy of being freed. As Fields states in the documentary: "I don't think we have much reason to assume that they were unaware that they were men. What they were aware of was that there were some people who required extraordinary demonstrations of them in order to establish what, for themselves, they considered to be self-evident."*

The Massachusetts 54th Colored Infantry *tells the story of the 178,975 Black men who fought in the Civil War. It also tells the story of a very active Black abolitionist movement in Boston during the nineteenth century.*

digging ditches

I have worked with a Black woman film editor who has a particular gift for metaphor. Sometimes when the going gets tough in the editing room, Lillian[3] will deflate a metaphysical musing of mine with a question in response that puts things in their proper perspective. Hunching her shoulders down to the task at hand, she'll ask me, "How deep, how wide?"

Filmmaking is a lot like digging ditches. It entails hard physical labor. Once past the planning stage, progress happens on the real side. Either you have the piece of film you need or you don't. Either you have the three extra seconds you need or you don't. Sometimes you hit a rock that breaks your shovel and you have to find another one. Everyone is working against the pressures of budget and time and the more time you take, the greater the strain on the budget. When you're done, the results are observable and measurable.

I feel caught up in the doing of filmmaking most of the time, so I appreciate the different perspectives offered by critical discourse on the field. I value the insights that I might not otherwise have, or hear. It's always enlightening to hear from an audience, and often audiences in the Academy will make connections and comparisons that are particularly illuminating and useful. I also believe that that discourse is strengthened if it includes more thought and opinion from producers. It is in that spirit that I offer this report from the trenches.

introduction

The Massachusetts 54th Colored Infantry is a one-hour documentary that I wrote and produced for the PBS television series, *The American Experience*. It is the story of the first official Union regiment of Black soldiers in the Civil War. I researched, wrote, directed, and produced the show from April 1990 to March 1991. We shot location photography and interviews in 16mm color negative, and the photographs and engravings in 35mm, edited in film, and transferred everything to videotape in the final stages of post-production. Professional actors performed all the voice-over recording, among them Morgan Freeman as the narrator; Larry Fishburne as the voice of the activist writer, Martin Delany; Carl Lumbly as the abolitionist, Frederick Douglass; and Blair Underwood as Douglass's son, Lewis.

The 54th was broadcast nationwide for the first time in October 1991 and is repeated at the will of local public television stations. It is also shown in high school and college classrooms and in various community-based settings. It takes its place in the body of African American social history on film. Many of the documentaries produced each year cover some part of this ground. Every February, the airwaves are awash with this genre: biographies of race heroes, oral histories, portraits of cultural giants. These offer a scrapbook, sometimes piecemeal history of forgotten places and events.

Even though or maybe because the content of *The 54th* is not about women, I think that a look at its genesis and production yields some insight into the kind of work that many African American women in the field do, and some of the power and decision-making dynamics that we face, both with the material and with all the people along the production chain that leads from conception to completion.

true glory

One day I was interrupted by a phone call while at work on post-production for the second series of *Eyes on the Prize*.[4] The call was from Llew Smith, an African American producer who had worked on the first series of *Eyes on the Prize* and was now story editor for *The American Experience*, a PBS television series on the country's history that is based at WGBH-TV in Boston. He asked if I had an hour that afternoon and I heard urgency in his voice. I like Llew, I could spare the time, so I went without asking any questions.

His boss, Judy Crichton, the Executive Producer of *The American Experience*, had a proposition for me. It was a few months after the successful release of *Glory* (1989), the Hollywood film with Matthew Broderick as Captain Robert Gould Shaw, and Denzel Washington and Morgan Freeman as two of the soldiers in his regiment. Denzel Washington would win an Academy Award as Best Supporting Actor for his role in the film.

Judy wanted to do a "True Glory," a documentary about the men of the 54th infantry that would not take Hollywood's license with the facts. She also imagined that the piece would convey what the Black community of Boston in the mid-nineteenth century was like. I explained that my true passion in nineteenth-century African American history lay in the Reconstruction period, not the Civil War. But Judy was clear about what she wanted. It would be the 54th or not.

This idea was a recent brainstorm of hers; the schedule would have to be tight if this show were to catch up with the others in the season, which had all had a head start. Judy said she would commit most of the $480,000 the show would take, and promised to support my fundraising efforts for the rest. Not quite enough money, not quite enough time—but still a serious offer worth consideration. In a perverse kind of way, the fact that the schedule and budget were both short was a professional challenge to me: Would I be able to pull this off? More time and more money would have been better, but this way I wouldn't be able to linger too long, I would have to be crisp and decisive. I'd have to get in and get out. I was tired from the long haul of *Eyes on the Prize* and this meant that I wouldn't get the rest I badly needed. But I couldn't justify turning down an opportunity that other women of color, or even white men, would have died for.

Television documentary production is a world inhabited by many women, a disproportionately large number when compared to our scarcity in the field at large. Judy came from the old days at CBS, had worked with big shots, won many awards and now had her own highly respected and respectably funded series. Her second-in-command was also a woman. Many of the staff in *The American Experience* offices are women, as are many of the staff members at WGBH and other public television stations across the country.

I discovered right away that it was much more difficult for me to have an older woman boss because a "dutiful daughter" routine kicked in. Often, on a real unconscious, kneejerk level, I cared more about pleasing Judy than was professionally appropriate. It was much more difficult for me to be assertive. I found myself susceptible to being intimidated by my own need to be polite. In light of these interpersonal dynamics, Judy had a subtle sway over me that a white man never would have. I hadn't had a female authoritarian over me since I'd left my mother's home. Surprisingly, none of this ultimately got in the way; it all functioned as neurotic grease to my wheels. It's a good thing Judy wasn't Black, otherwise I would have been in a world of trouble.

collective shame

I loved the "True Glory" concept of telling this story from an African American perspective. Like many of us, I have no patience for the wrongheadedness that insists on relaying African American history through a white protagonist in order to sell it to a general (read white majority) audience. But while I basically agreed with the principle of the project, my initial reaction to the story itself was negative and not overly enthusiastic. A big yawn.

Why would I want to do a war story? I had always hated war movies, hated war stories, and had never been able to get beyond the basic absurdity of warfare. I could never get into the spirit of "Into the valley of death rode the six hundred . . ." And I hated the Civil War more than most other wars. I'd been an American History major at Brandeis and my aversion to this historic moment—a milestone for my country and my people— seemed personally neurotic at best, intellectually shortsighted, at worst. Why did I hate the Civil War?

I flashed back on my secondary education, my formal introduction to American history at an all-girls, mostly all-white high school. I remembered classmates stealing significant looks at me and the few other Black students when our American history course came to slavery and the Civil

113

War. I knew the reason for the looks. The implication was clear. Black folks had brought a lot of grief and suffering to the nation with our need to be free. There's a statue in Park Square in Boston of a tall, proud Abraham Lincoln bestowing freedom, or at least a congenial pat on the head, to two kneeling African figures. In the early hours of the morning, Black women would organize an informal street market in that park for day workers. In the late hours of the night, others gathered there looking for prostitution jobs. Boston was a hard place to nurture Black pride, and the image of those passive, helpless slaves as my forebears marked that square as especially infertile ground.

I once read an interview with the playwright August Wilson that gave me some much-needed insight into my visceral disdain for the Civil War. Apparently this contempt for the Civil War and its legacy of slavery surfaced in rehearsals for *Joe Turner's Come and Gone*:

> Black folks have this thing about slavery. We don't want to hear that word. There's this shame. In "Joe Turner's Come And Gone," I had a line that says, "Ever since slavery got over with there ain't been nothing but foolish-acting niggers." And the actor refused to say it. He said "Ever since the Civil War got over with..." Night after night. So I asked the director what's going on? He said, "He don't want to say it." I talked to [the actor], and he said he'd try to say it. [That night] he said, "Ever since the Civil War got over with ain't been nothing but foolish acting niggers." He don't mind saying nigger. But the word slavery he couldn't bring himself to voice it.[5]

Even before reading Wilson's insights, in thinking about *The American Experience* offer and my reactions to it, I had come to some kind of intuitive understanding that a big part of my resistance to the story was rooted in shame. Once I acknowledged that, I had no recourse but to confront it head on.

on the record

The other big part of my resistance had to do with my fear of becoming part of a deadly strain of hagiography in Black historical media making. I'm not comfortable with the ideological premise that anything Blacks have done is worth celebrating because Blacks did it. I spent a good part of my young adulthood protesting the war in Vietnam, spent a year in everyday terror that my brother would get killed over there, so why would I want to make a film that glorifies militarism and holds up for honor men ignorant enough to volunteer to fight for a country that enslaved them?

I knew that Blacks had always fought in every national war and had always acquitted themselves honorably, to borrow a phrase from the VFW. But was that something to be proud of? Would I be able to critique the role of the military in this society, or challenge the prevalence of warfare in this world? Would my politics have to experience a hiatus while I produced a puff piece on the honor of being cannon fodder?

I never silenced those lurid fantasies, but I was able to quell them by reassuring myself that no matter what I found out in the research, there would have to be a way to frame the truth so it would be respectful to the ghosts whose stories I was exhuming, and at the same time present the information as it would be useful and instructive to today's youth. Young people have always been my primary audience. I never really focused on the general programming for national television broadcast so much as on the years of Black History Month screenings at community groups, churches, secondary schools, colleges, and universities. Too often, young people are assaulted with a lot of mindless sentimentality parading as history. I knew from my experience with *Eyes on the Prize* that this piece would become part of the historical record.

a question of style

It's crucial to understand that a reflective look back over the production process misrepresents the true nature of things. Imagine a bumper-car ride at 90 mph at night with headlights that aren't always working or racing against a clock that vaporizes your prize money with every tick. Against such odds, aesthetics become a casualty of the war between what is desired and what is possible.

I'm always stumped when asked questions about an African American cinematic style or an African American women's cinematic style. I mainly think this is a question for the audience to answer, not me. I just dig the ditch, I don't know about its deeper dimensions. But lately, I've come to think of my work as quilt-making—a little bit of this and a little bit of that, eclecticism to the hilt. And like making quilts, the tone is not of high art, but folk art. This is art with a high use value, a way of using up all those pieces of cloth that might otherwise go to waste, to keep bodies warm that might otherwise be cold and provide something easy on the eye to contemplate at the same time. A quilt can be beautiful to look at, but I think the height of aesthetic appreciation of its beauty comes when you're wrapped up in it, warm and secure.

People now pay top dollar for these pieces of handiwork and museums treasure them as artifacts of folk life, but these are impositions on the quilts, not an inherent part of their design or intention. It's easy to demean this kind of work, and to romanticize it. But in any event it is always possible to judge them, the stitching, the colors and patterns of cloth used, the design holding everything together. Those women who made these quilts were putting themselves on the line with every stitch.

That's how I feel about my own work. As a child, I was groomed to be an intellectual and spent a lot of my youth in ardent philosophical debate. But the subjectivity of these pursuits were frustrating to me in their slipperiness. I welcomed the tangibility of filmmaking and today I use it to take stands, to say something definitive. I validate myself by producing a record of what I felt and thought about a subject at one time in history. If it were just an aperçu tossed out in conversation, I could always change it with my next breath. But a film is a developed line of thought and dramatic intention that has a life beyond me and my control. I appreciate its permanence and have always enjoyed being kept on my toes that way.

the doing of it

As an eldest daughter, I have no problem telling other people what to do. As a self-taught filmmaker, however, I keep myself open to suggestions and carefully gauge criticisms from others. This is how I've learned to develop my skills and my craft. Judy once paid my mother a compliment for having raised me with enough self-assurance to take criticism nondefensively. On some level, I tend to be confident that I'll be able to take what I need, toss out what I don't, and still maintain control of the film's overall direction.

I don't know if it's particularly gender-based, but it is a variation on the traditional macho to be able to absorb 360 degrees of opinion without entertaining any urge to lash out. My role as producer includes the task of absorbing everyone's problems and coming up with solutions. People look to me to create a work environment where they feel respected and are therefore able to give their best to the production. Like most other modern forms of production, I approach filmmaking as a twentieth-century art form where I set a vision on the creative assembly line and everyone along the way adds something. Sometimes, they strengthen the project with elements I would not have chosen or could not have foreseen, sometimes there are elements that I must discard. But always, the result winds up being much more than my original vision—a whole that is greater than the sum of its parts. This model of leadership is not about big displays of ego or rage, intimidation or manipulation. Sometimes I think it's a maternal tendency, that I worry too much about people who are supposed to be helping me. But if there has to be an imbalance, I prefer it on the side of the maternal rather than the tyrannical.

beginning points

Film, even documentary, works on an emotional level. It is a waste of the medium, therefore, not to consider the emotional subtext of a piece even while trying to figure out the practical details of plot and narrative flow. My own emotional subtext for *The 54th* began with the need to exorcise my own shame. My first intuitive groping toward a handle on this difficult emotion was to turn it on its head. This would not be a story about slavery, but a story about an irrepressible drive for freedom.

Once during the early planning stages for *The 54th*, I was having breakfast with one of the student interns who was working on *Eyes on the Prize*. He happened to have done some research on nineteenth-century Black history in Boston and I was picking his brain. I had asked him how he thought Black people in Boston before the Civil War felt about being Black in Boston. His one-word answer struck a chord in me: "vulnerable." Later, further research would confirm the veracity of this statement, but its emotional truth was powerfully clear on a totally intuitive level for me.

I am from Boston and although my roots there don't go back as far as the nineteenth century, even in the 1950s and 1960s Blacks were a small community with a proud but curiously timid voice. I remembered the terrible days of court-ordered school desegregation in the 1970s—the pervasive atmosphere of fear, the amazement in other parts of the country that liberal Boston was having these hateful problems.[6] I had just done a story on busing for *Eyes on the Prize II*[7] and found it curious to step back from this century to explore the similarities and differences in race relations in the nineteenth and twentieth centuries.

I could easily place myself in the setting of this story; I had walked the same streets, been in the same buildings that the mid-nineteenth century African community in Boston had once inhabited. I believe that regions have certain tones, and I could understand the tone of the Boston Black community then—they were a small minority in a city that was at the same time more liberal in its racial attitudes and policies than many other places in the North. Nonetheless, this was still a place that could be dangerous for Blacks, a place where it was sometimes easier to make alliances with the Brahmins than with Irish immigrants. Ironically, I found some striking similarities between this Old World Boston and the city where I grew up.

A Black woman filmmaker who had worked on Ken Burns's series on the Civil War (which had not yet been broadcast) strongly recommended Barbara Fields as an historian. Burns had totally underused her in his series but her interviews were brilliant. As I was reading through some of Fields's work, the sentence, "Freedom is more than the absence of slavery" jumped out and hit me in the head. I had a purely visceral reaction and knew that this statement marked the beginning of my journey.

Why would Blacks who enjoyed freedom in what was arguably the most liberal space in the free North risk life and limb to fight for the freedom of other Blacks? Of course many of them had formerly been slaves and quite likely still had family in slavery. But even those who had been born free understood that the freedom of Blacks in Boston wasn't the same as the freedom whites enjoyed. Particularly after passage of the Fugitive Slave Act,[8] all that separated free Blacks from slavery in Boston was the word of a slave-catcher. No, they weren't slaves, but they weren't truly free either.

I remembered James Baldwin's claim that as long as one Negro in this country was not free, then he was not free. Fields's statement, "Freedom is more than the absence of slavery," lies at the core of the African American experience since our presence in this country. We have long understood our existence within a context of community and connection. Slavery, its individual and communal assault on African Americans, forged this bond between us all. We recognize it in one another and awkwardly avoid eye contact whenever we are forced to confront this legacy of shame. This shame cripples us and we find ourselves unable to say words like "slavery" or "nigger," we become restless and defensive in conversations about race and equality, or we develop curious contempt for particular wars and historic eras.

a man's story

It wasn't until a few weeks into the project that it suddenly hit me that this was a story about men. I had been thinking about the big picture—freedom, slavery, abolitionism, retrenchment, Blacks in Boston—and it took some time to understand that the primary agents of this particular story were men. Their community esteemed women as vitally important (even then, Black families needed two incomes to make it), but it was the men who were at the center of the action. Now this was an important revelation for me. By this time, whenever I venture into a new project, my sensibilities kick into auto-pilot and foreground how this particular issue pertains to women, beginning, of course, with me. As had often been the case, my first insight with this topic emerged from my own insecurities about it. My inclination to underscore a woman's perspective in all aspects of history could serve me in this project as well but from a different angle. I recognized that having a strong position on the need for African American women's empowerment does not automatically do away with the horror we all feel at the statistics of homicide, shorter life span, incarceration, and joblessness that outline the crisis of Black men in America.

I thought about the severity of their predicament—the endangered species of the African American male. In my mind, those students who were my primary audience became young men. And what did I have to say to them? I could present Black men as credible heroes, not larger-than-life people, rich or famous or accommodating, but ordinary men who had hard lives but still put themselves on the line for the sake of principle and integrity—men whose heroism rested in their unrelenting resistance and militancy.

I felt honored that I had the resources to make a piece of media that in its own way would be designed to give Black men a mirror of their past selves—a reflection of their own potential from which they could draw pride and inspiration. I also seized this project as an opportunity to make a statement about the personal relationships between Black men and Black women as a counterpoint to the posturing and quibbling that too often wins the headlines. I looked forward to positioning warfare in relation to the home-front—a look into the lives of Black soldiers and their importance to the women and children they'd left behind in the name of freedom.

Men are always making films about women, but women don't often have the opportunity to return the gaze. Women have a lot to say about men to men. Usually in the pieces I produce or direct, more of the perspective would be from women's viewpoints rather than from men's, but this would not be the case in *The 54th*. Fields is the only woman historian, and most of the descendants of Civil War veterans we interviewed are men, not women. Two women who are shown on camera, Ruth Jones and Helen Givens, make a strong impact and I have been told countless times how these older women have reminded viewers of their great-aunts and grandmothers. The abolitionist, Charlotte Forten, is the only woman's voice we hear from the past. This imbalance of perspective is significantly different from my usual practice, but they were all conscious decisions. In various programs, male voices and perspectives dominate, usually because no one has made the effort to find female participants. But in this instance, the prevalence of the male voices in *The 54th* is a deliberate and affirmative statement.

construction workers

Who gets hired to do what is always an important political consideration in the construction of a film. Some argue that it is harder for a Black woman to get hired on a project headed by another Black woman. Also of concern to many is the gender distribution along the hierarchy of positions. I personally don't believe in hiring women exclusively, but I do pay attention to make sure that there's at least parity in leadership positions.

As part of my effort to seek out Black male perspectives, I created two in key positions; director of photography and cowriter.[9] Most of the scholars we consulted on the project were men, and I sought male opinions throughout the production.[10] But as is often the case, the new girls' grapevine was, as always, very helpful. It led me to Barbara Fields, who I might not have found on my own, and also put me in contact with the amazing array of actors who performed the voice-overs, including Morgan Freeman, Larry Fishburne, Blair Underwood, and Carl Lumbly.

storytelling

I learned a lot about storytelling from my work on *Eyes on the Prize*. Henry Hampton, the Executive Producer, drummed it into our heads that what we were about was telling stories. If we could not pitch an idea to him in the story form—with a premise, a hook, characters, and dramatic rise and fall of action, in a pithy paragraph, then we didn't stand a chance of convincing him that it was something that belonged in the series. Hampton's rigor was good discipline. From my years of peer-review screening panels, I have come to understand that most documentaries produced in this country are mediocre because at the conceptual stage, right at the beginning of things, too many producers think that the issue is so compelling that it will tell itself. It never does.

This is the reason for the arduous work of ditch-digging, churning through mountains of material for the gold, searching for the clarity of the story. Where is the point of view located? Who are the protagonists? What is the conflict? What are the forces of good and evil? When I started shaping the story of *The 54th* from the research that had been culled, I found that I had much too much material. Unfortunately, all of it was good. The brunt of the story was the changing face of war. But the production subtext, as always, would be the tension between the ideal and the possible in terms of time and money. With me at the helm, I steadily floundered between wanting to put out all this great information I had discovered and knowing that I should emotionally distance myself to allow the story to breathe.

Apart from the various dimensions of history and production that the project entailed, the piece itself was about the evolution of the Civil War. But even more specifically, this was a battle waged by white men to preserve a slave-holding nation. Ironically, the slaves had to wage their own war to earn the right to fight. Once Blacks were allowed to enter the war, their fight no longer consisted only of Union and Confederate troops. Rather, they faced the formidable challenges of discrimination in their own ranks, most dramatically seen in the eighteen-month war the entire Black nation waged for pay equity between Black and white soldiers. This was one of the most flagrant inaccuracies in *Glory*, whereby the pay dispute for Black soldiers was seemingly resolved without incident. And finally, in the brutal reality of the battles themselves, these men, and the numerous communities they represented, risked everything to strike a blow for freedom.

Once the structure for the project was set, it was clear that this program would be narrated. I assumed the task of wordsmith and gradually pieced together the narrative strands of text. I have always felt deeply resolved that authorship is a profoundly feminist issue and having something to say can be empowering on numerous levels. But the power in writing comes not so much from style as from clarity, and I have always preferred a low-key, "nothing but the facts" tone, short on adjectives and superfluous emotion. When text is as concise and clear as it should be, each word matters very much.

There were a lot of words to manage in *The 54th*. I always feel a strong need to contextualize information, which ultimately causes a lot of narrative problems. The dramatic impulse is to cut to the chase, to start the story as much in the action as possible. This impulse clashes with the desire to set up the context of the narrative for some grounding and perspective. Somewhere amidst all the bits of history, personal details, and drama, I knew I also had to leave space for the emotional arias that Lillian, as an editor, builds so well. Through music and poignant images, Lillian could string together the myriad strands of information while also giving viewers time to settle comfortably into the developing story.

Writing to picture generates a particular kind of rhythm as you weave words in between images, music, and other sounds. Given the imperative to keep things moving, and my always didactic desire to say as much as I can, if not more, there is no time to make any point more than once. This is a different quality than writing for readers, where you can build and layer with much more substance. My working assumption when writing for programming is that I am raising questions and sowing seeds of interest that will give teachers material to work with and students an incentive to read more about the subject.

history: hagiography or redemption

For most filmmakers, the process of working on a project can be a spiritual journey of sorts. In my case, I never know where I'm going at the beginning or how I'm going to get there. I bob back and forth through waves of sheer terror and existentialist faith. I steady myself through pure faith—a persistent belief that I will be able to make it all work out if I keep a proper respect for the material and the process.

I guess it makes sense that the clarity I get from divining the story and then from executing its production is redemptive, as I feel lifted out of my ignorance and move away from the despair of not knowing. But this particular journey with *The 54th* came with two particular challenges in addition to the usual perils of the cinematic form. First, here were no visuals, an obstacle that only strengthened my resolve to picture it. Second, given the volatile nature of the subject under consideration, I lived daily with the fear that when all was said and done, I could end up creating something that turned out to be politically wrong.

We found the visuals. When we started gathering the photographs of the men of the 54th and other Union regiments, we were all amazed by how familiar these men seemed to us—so similar to men we knew and saw on the streets. It charged us all with a certain emotional urgency to tell the story: the characters became more real for us, people we could care about.

To complement these images, we found wonderful period music.[11] The music research that we did and the original recording of popular nineteenth-century African American songs had proved to be a powerful tool in setting the tone for the piece. In preparing the soundtrack, we were all reminded of how critical music and song have been throughout the course of African American history.

Much to my own relief, I found that there was nothing for me to be ashamed of in the story of Blacks and their participation in the Civil War. Black soldiers hadn't been the unwitting dupes I had once imagined them to be. It was these men who were the bedrock of abolitionism, not well-intentioned, benevolent whites as history has claimed. Blacks had pushed the issue of their freedom onto the national agenda and they were willing to fight for it no matter whose side they had to stand on. This substantial injection of Black soldiers helped Union troops win the war. Ultimately, through their courage and faith, we had won our own freedom.

notes

1. Joseph T. Glatthaar, "Movie Review: *The Massachusetts 54th Colored Infantry*," *The Journal of American History* 78: 3 (December 1991): 1167.

2. Ibid.

3. Lillian Benson, A.C.E., is the editor for *The 54th*. She is the first Black woman selected for membership in American Cinema Editors, the international organization of film editors. Lillian was also nominated for an Emmy award as the editor of "The Promised Land" segment of *Eyes on the Prize II*.

4. I was the producer/director for two segments of *Eyes on the Prize* II: "The Promised Land" and "The Keys to the Kingdom."

5. "Beating Our Heads Against Concrete," *Newsday*, April 23, 1992, 109.

6. My film, *A Minor Altercation* (1977), is a dramatization of the effects of busing on the families, Black and white, in Boston.

7. "The Keys to the Kingdom."

8. The Fugitive Slave Act became law in 1850. The act allowed slave-owners, or their agents, to capture and return runaway slaves, even if they had escaped to the North.

9. The director of photography is Arthur Jafa, who was also the director of cinematography for Julie Dash's *Daughters of the Dust* (1991). *Daughters of the Dust* was awarded the prize for Best Cinematography at the 1991 Sundance Film Festival. The cowriter of *The 54th* was Leslie Lee.

10. The academic advisors, in addition to Barbara Fields, included James Horton, George Levesque, and Leon Litwack.

11. The music for *The Massachusetts 54th* was actual music played and sung in the nineteenth century. Josephine Wright, from the College of Wooster, Ohio, served as musical consultant for the program. Also advising us was Horace Boyer, a musicologist at the University of Massachusetts, Amherst. We then recreated the music for an authentic sound. For the documentary, the music was performed by a conglomerate of accomplished musicians and performers including the Howard University Choir (directed by J. Weldon Norris), The Year of the Jubilee Choir (directed by Horace Boyer), the McIntosh County Shouters, and John Ross.

fired-up!

o.fu n m i l a y o   m a k a r a h

On 29 April 1992, when "Not Guilty" verdicts were handed down for the four policemen accused of beating Mr. Rodney King, I was numb. From my Los Angeles apartment in a working-class, immigrant neighborhood, I shared this reaction with many of my artist friends. We were surprised that although we were outraged about the verdict, we were unable to pick up our cameras and record the action as people took to the streets. In the end, this decision was perhaps the best one, as law enforcement agencies, lawyers, and even the FBI have vigorously sought out and subpoenaed network and individual footage to prosecute looters and vandals.

In the days that immediately followed the ruling, I spent many hours at home talking back to my television in rage and disgust over the media's substantial role in inciting fear and perpetuating stereotypes of African Americans and Latina/os, thus widening the already severe divisions between Blacks and whites, the rich and the poor. I was furious as newscasters referred to dark-skinned people as "thugs," "looters," and "roving gangs." Why did these same newscasters never call the thieves from the savings-and-loan scandal "looters"? Where were these same newscasters when merchants burned their own businesses to collect insurance money and federal judges ruled that police dogs could continue to maim and terrorize human beings? Where were these newscasters when a young Black girl, Latasha Harlins, was needlessly killed by a shot in the back, and where were they when her murderer was set free?[1] Network news showed us the same scenes again and again of people going in and out of stores— monopolizing precious screen time that could have been better used to provide in-depth analysis of distorted pricing policies in the inner city and investigative reports on the exploitation of our urban areas by big businesses that abandon inner-city areas after aggressively pillaging them. Could the media have instigated discussion of the effect of gentrification on the inner city; the unequal amounts of money spent in different public school areas; the metal (and mental) gates that surround the University of Southern California in Los Angeles and other private institutions throughout the United States that effectively keep the surrounding African American and Latina/o communities locked out of higher education; the lack of adequate child care and affordable housing? Is there a legitimate reason the media didn't bring to our attention the effects of tuition increases at public universities such as UCLA that limit the enrollment of under-represented students at UCLA, while failing to promote supportive learning environments conducive to successful matriculation for currently enrolled African American, Filipino, Latina/o, and Native students?

As I watched my city burn, I thought about how all these things amount to federal apartheid policies that promote inequitable judicial, educational, political, medical, social, and economic systems. Is it any wonder that Black men in America are jailed at the rate of four times that of Blacks in apartheid South Africa?

The brutal image of Mr. Rodney King's assault was reminiscent of slaves who were beaten to death because they tried to escape to freedom. I thought of Ida B. Wells's work to communicate the horrors of lynching, the need for justice, and the right of women to vote. In the months that followed Mr. Rodney King's beating by the police, I was keenly aware of the "trial" as the evening news rebroadcast the "tape" of Mr. King being beaten and provided "highlights" from the "Rodney King Trial." As the saga continued, I remained outraged that once again we were being scapegoated for all of society's problems. The media trained us to call the trial of the police who beat Mr. Rodney King the "Rodney King Trial" instead of the "Suspended Police Trial" or the "Trial of the Videotaped Policemen" or the "Documented Racists' Trial." Why were we being trained to view this case as if Mr. Rodney King were on trial?

On 29 April 1992 I listened to the "Not Guilty" verdict and stared at my television in amazement. I watched my television and I wanted to know why we weren't shown the people in South Central and why we didn't hear about their experiences as their water, electricity, telephone, and mail services were abruptly cut off during and after the rebellion? I wondered if the people in South Central that night recalled (as I did) the night in December of 1969 when the electricity and phones went out right before the Chicago police murdered Black Panther Party members Fred Hampton and Mark Clark as they slept in their beds.

For me the 1992 LA Rebellion was no real surprise: it was yet another indicator of the differences that continue to stress tensions in this country around race and culture. I was acutely aware of the different ways that different people looked at Mr. Rodney King's beating by white policemen and the different reactions to the trial of the policemen accused of beating Mr. Rodney King. The jurors' decision that Mr. Rodney King caused his (near death) beating, the reactions to the rage that exploded after the verdict was announced, the indifference to the postverdict jailing—without trial or conviction—of the many young African American and Latino men and homeless persons—all these differences saddened me. Even my progressive white friends asked me what Mr. Rodney King had done to provoke the police beating. To date, not one African American has asked me this question.

According to the media misrepresentation of the LA rebellion, Black residents in Los Angeles came in two categories: either they were kids in the streets wreaking havoc or they were elders locked away in a church praying. From the disparity of these constructions, I longed to hear straightforward, unbiased coverage of California Congresswoman Maxine Waters's statements about our burning city. I was acutely aware of the blatant omission of the voices of the people I wanted to hear: I wanted to hear filmmaker Julie Dash, politician and educator Barbara Jordan, law professor Anita Hill, former LA Public Works Commissioner (and widow of Medgar Evers) Myrlie Evers, and children's advocate Marian Wright Edelman speak about the 1992 LA Rebellion and the racial climate in America.

As a filmmaker/videomaker, I was saddened, outraged, and disgusted as commentators set aside all pretense of objectivity and continued to pick and choose what we would be shown and how what we were shown would be contextualized. Why did the media choose not to tell us about the white people looting and burning in the Los Angeles area? Why did the police isolate South LA from the rest of the world, not respond to pleas for assistance from South Central LA residents, yet continue to eagerly respond to calls in Beverly Hills and other "white" areas of the city? Yes, I am one of the artists who did not record the 1992 LA Rebellion.

It was not until June of 1992 that I was able to turn my "rage" into art by working on a Video Installation called *Fired-Up*. The inspiration for this work was an invitation to participate in two Los Angeles shows, "Breaking Barriers: Revisualizing the Urban Landscape" at Santa Monica Museum of Art (September 1992–November 1992) and "No Justice, No Peace? Resolutions ..." at the California Afro-American Museum (October 1992–July 1993). The latter invitation provided the impetus I needed: a simple plan began to form in my mind about how I could create a unique piece for this exhibition that would share my feelings about the 1992 LA Rebellion.

where were you?—interviews about the 1992 los angeles rebellion

I began by taking a Hi-8 video camera and a microphone with me whenever I traveled (conferences, parties, vacations, festivals, parades). I interviewed friends, family, acquaintances, and strangers. Between June and September of 1992, I interviewed more than sixty people from around the country and around the world about their different reactions to the LA Rebellion and how the rebellion affected them personally.

My interviewing method was very simple: I asked everyone the same five questions, allowing each person to respond as broadly or as narrowly as they chose. As a television viewer, I am always bothered by the quick "sound bites" that reveal only a fraction of what a person may be trying to express. As the off-camera interviewer for my video, I attempted to present my questions without interjecting my own personal (and deeply felt) feelings about what had happened. For instance, in my own casual conversations I always refer to the victim of the 3 March 1991 police beating as "Mr. Rodney King." Similarly, I refer to the events in Los Angeles on 29 April 1992 and after as "The LA Rebellion" or "The Revolt." Because of the inherent "messages" connoted by our casual phrasing, I chose not to use these words when interviewing the subjects for the video. Instead, I tried to present each of my questions neutrally, and to allow each respondent to speak as they pleased.

The five questions I asked each person were:

1. What did you think the first time you saw the tape of Rodney King being beaten?
2. Where were you and what did you do when the verdict was announced?
3. What did you think of the events that occurred in Los Angeles and in other places after the verdict was announced?
4. What grade would you give the media for their coverage of the events that occurred after the verdict was announced?
5. What question do you wish I had asked you?

Some of the people I interviewed spoke for as little as three minutes. The average response was about fifteen minutes, and one person spoke for one and a half hours. I tried very hard just to let each person speak, asking additional questions to follow up or clarify the person's reply. For instance, when someone went blank when answering question number 3 (about what they thought of the events in LA after the verdict was announced), I would expand on this question by asking them how they found out what was happening (i.e., was it from the television or from friends), and I would ask what specific things they thought happened. I found that people were eager to respond to my questions even though I was conducting my interviews several months after the 1992 LA Rebellion.

In Los Angeles, the people I interviewed were very eager and somewhat sad about what had happened to their city. Young people, in particular, talked with me about how hurt they felt when people assumed they were "looting" because they live in South Central. A strong sense of community also came across as African American and Latina/o youth spoke of the need for these two groups to work together.

Outside of Los Angeles, many people spoke about television reports that promoted a sense of panic. They also recalled the rebellions of the 1960s. One New York City resident revealed his fear of young African American men. Several African Americans spoke of not wanting to talk to whites about what had happened, and several people told me they cried when they heard the "not guilty verdict."

In Upstate New York, I interviewed a white man who spoke about the "murder and the beating of Rodney King " and said that he and a lot of people wanted to know if the police brutality and "the death of Rodney King was justified or not." As this man spoke with me about the looting by "the Blacks against the Hispanics and the Hispanics against the Blacks," two white people in the background were moving furniture and equipment out of a building and into a truck behind him.

In Chicago a teenager spoke with great sadness and told me, "As a Black male I feel like I have a target on my ass." A young white woman from Kentucky admitted she does not personally know any Black people, but she also said she thought the "eruption" (as she called it) was long overdue because of how Blacks are treated in this country. In San Francisco a Latina told me that the verdict showed her that whites have no respect for the humanity of people of color. A Korean American college student from Philadelphia told me how saddened and embarrassed she was when the Korean government offered to help only the Korean merchants, even though everyone was suffering.

I have collected over sixty interviews, and I want to continue to collect even more. The police accused of beating Mr. Rodney King were scheduled to go on trial again in Los Angeles the following February[2] and I (like many other people) think we have not yet reached a conclusion to this story. Fortunately, the size and convenience of modern video equipment has made it possible for me to record events as they happen with little or no crew. But as an independent producer/director, I face the same financial and technical limitations that many of my colleagues confront. For instance, because I have no film or video equipment of my own I have to be creative and resourceful. I barter for equipment and editing time and juggle my funds to either pay rent or pay production costs. It was a real miracle that I was able to complete even one of the interviews, and another miracle that I was able to complete even a rough edit of my initial interviews. These videotaped interviews became the center of *Fired-Up*, my Video Installation at California Afro-American Museum (CAAM).

fired-up: a video installation

Video Installations are still a relatively new and unknown form of art that can be constructed in many different ways. The central elements of Video Installations are environment and experience. For instance, just as artists such as painters begin with a blank canvas, media artists creating Video Installations begin with an empty space that they transform. When I first entered the "canvas" or space that would be mine at CAAM, I realized I had to redesign my original concept, which was based on a floor game. As I stood in the actual installation space, it became clear that I could neither paint on nor carve into the museum's concrete floor. The final design, I think, was improved by this accommodation.

The complete Video Installation is divided into four parts and arranged to invite the viewer to experience and contemplate the events that led up to the 1992 LA Rebellion. The exhibition area is set up as a rectangular dining room. In the center of the room is a long covered banquet table holding two video monitors. The long wall behind the table is covered with LA 1992 memorabilia and consumer items. In front of this wall are two monitors that continuously play the prerecorded "live" network coverage of the Rebellion. The opposite long wall invites visitors to comment on the Rebellion. The two "short" walls have quotes about the Rebellion.

At the entrance of the installation space is a wall of local and national newspaper clippings. The papers are carefully selected articles on the assault against Mr. Rodney King; the subsequent investigation of the Los Angeles Police Department; and the trial of the police officers accused of beating Mr. Rodney King. The written material also includes magazine articles (about racism, starvation in Somalia, inequality in bank lending policies, homophobia, increases in hate crimes, the savings and loan debate, etc.); posters (such as "Free the LA 4!"); and bumper stickers ("Jail to the Chief", "Silence Equals Death"). Intermingled and on top of the written materials are items relevant to the Rebellion: T-shirts ("Justice or Just-Us?"; "Free Rodney King"; "White Men Can't Judge, Either"); flyers ("Support the LA 4"; "American Accent Training: Learn Correct Standard Pronunciation Without an Accent in 24 days"); buttons ("No Justice, No Peace"); and consumer items such as Kool-Aid, toilet paper, Pampers, milk, laundry detergent, canned soda, Tampax, cold medicine, condoms, peanuts, perfume, butter. Many of these products bear price tags: six-pack of soda: $2.05; potato chips: $1.99. In front of this long wall are two monitors that play the "live" news footage from the LA Rebellion in Spanish and English. Slightly above the two monitors on a small black platform is the VCR that controls the two news monitors. Next to this VCR, on a very small black silk-covered box is a bottle of orange juice. The orange juice also has a label: "Orange Juice, Empire Liquor Market, 9127 S. Figuroa, Los Angeles; $: One Young Girl's Life." Boxes of larger and more expensive consumer goods are placed on the floor a short distance from the news monitors: a microwave, a video camera, a suede shoe box, a toaster. On top of each monitor is a pack of disposable diapers. The larger pack of diapers has a price tag: "Diapers (large), Store Brand: $7.89; Name Brands: $17.89, $19.03, $21.03").

The anchor to *Fired-Up* is a twelve-foot long banquet table that stands in the middle of this rectangular room. The table is covered with a white table-cloth. Each corner of the tablecloth is tied with a different type of fabric (Oriental silk, African batik, a striped Mexican shawl, and calico) to symbolize both the four corners of the world and the different cultures and ethnicities in Los Angeles. The table is bare except for monitors placed at each end. These monitors face away from each other and simultaneously play interviews of people speaking about their reaction to events before, during, and after the LA Rebellion. I chose the banquet table to express my feeling that before the people in Los Angeles can begin to rebuild, they need to sit down at the same table, share nourishment for the body and for the soul, and really listen to each other. This is also why I chose to use a table that is not set—what nourishment is received will depend on what each person brings to the table. Similarly, the monitors are turned away from each other while simultaneously playing the same interviews to symbolize the way in which people often have the same concerns but sometimes cannot really listen to one another.

The two short walls on either end of the installation space are also covered with written materials, consumer items, and memorabilia. However, on these two walls the written materials form an open "frame" of white space. In one of these white "frames" written in red and blue are quotes by men that I collected from magazines and newspapers:

As you know, I planned a trip out there for some time, so it fits in very nicely.

> —George Bush after visiting LA after the LA riots

If their only remembrance of the crime was the pain of being bitten by a dog, that may be a negative reinforcement and they may never steal again.... I was thinking of their own welfare ... and that a painful experience might be a deterrent.

> —Judge Kenneth L. Ryskamp, President Bush's nominee
> to the Federal Appeals Court

The following five quotes are printed from unedited LAPD computer transmissions.

> My shooting policy is based on nationality and looks.
>
> And that's camel jockey for Iranian.
>
> OK ask him what's the difference between Mexicans and coyotes—there are just some things coyotes won't do.
>
> The best wife beating I've ever seen ... look like a whipped slave.
>
> Wonder if he lives in WLA like all the other Jews.
>
> It [the video] clearly showed what was going on there, the fact that Rodney King was not being abused.
>
> —A juror on *The Today Show*

In the white "frame" on the other short wall are quotes by women that are written in red, black and green:

> The LA Rebellion says "Dred Scott" is alive and well and living in the U.S.A.
>
> —Ruth Cooper

> Now we must use our time and energy to re-fight old battles instead of moving on to the problems that so desperately need to be addressed.
>
> —Barbara Jordan

> When [LA Police Chief] Gates calls someone a "drunken el Salvadoran" that sends a message to the police force.
>
> —Melanie Lomax

> Big Businesses have abandoned the inner city. They have borne no responsibility for their actions and now they are being invited to come back in to further exploit the same people they abandoned a long time ago.
>
> —Cheng-Sim Lim

132

The second (long) wall is painted in white. Written in an arch across this wall is a quotation from James Baldwin:

> Some of us know how great a price has already been paid to bring into existence a new consciousness, a new people, an unprecedented nation. If we know, and do nothing we are worse than the murderers.

Under this quotation is a sign inviting visitors to contribute their thoughts or a memento about my Video Installation and the 1992 LA Rebellion. Placed underneath this statement is a black pedestal holding an open "guest book" for visitors to add their comments. People have drawn pictures, responded to other writer's comments, and written in Spanish, in English, and in Wolof (an African language). The comments have varied widely from political and religious, to bland, angry, and insightful:

> I think that this video installation is a very important one and its a shame that this type of information isn't really available or presented to the mainstream public.

> Your presentation burns deeply

> I am the way, the truth, and the light. No man comes to the father except by me. Jesus is the only answer.

> The video installation brings echoes of the past and realities of the future. And I continually ask myself have we made any progress? I think not.

> I lynched James Baldwin. KKK

> Power in a United white government white power.

> It's no good. Something should be done over racism.

> All your African relatives, brothers and sisters, share and experience your pain. [A comment written in the Wolof language and translated into English.]

> The orange juice, that cost a girl's life, made me want to cry. I wonder where the hatred stems from or can it ever be eradicated. An African-American Woman.

> This brings back my initial feelings from the days following April 29. I feel chills remembering the pain and anger that was expressed. I remember the hope that maybe we would finally learn. This was the Fire Next Time, but the establishment still doesn't understand. There is so much remaining to be done. We must all strive for change. No Justice No Peace! . . . (white male and OK with that).

Fuck L.A.P.D.

This shows how much the media is our Enemy. Not our color.

Thought provoking, intuitive & a great jogger of our memories, lest we forget easily.

Observing the visitors to *Fired-Up* and reading their written comments, I reflect not only about my Video Installation and the various aesthetic decisions I made in constructing it, but also about the people and the experiences that propelled me to become a media artist.

how a black girl changed my life

Growing up in Chicago, I watched the 1950s CBS television series "Amos and Andy" and the film *The Green Pastures* (1936) with disgust and amazement. These shows frustrated me because the people I knew were not slow and stupid like the images on screen, yet it baffled me that there were such limited portrayals of Blacks available on television. One weekend this all changed when I was introduced to a whole new world of visual possibilities. I read in the newspaper about an African film playing in a downtown museum. I remember taking a bus from the south side and sitting in the audience absolutely transfixed as I watched a film entitled *Black Girl* (1966). As I watched this very moving and very vivid story about the effects of exploitation, colonialism, racism, and disrespect, I could only think, "Who is this person who shows the hope, despair, and displacement of a young girl so elegantly? Who could this person be who showed me Africa with beautiful Black people and without Tarzan?" This was my wonderful introduction to the Senegalese filmmaker, Ousmane Sembene, and the possibility of what cinema could and should be.

This film had such a profound effect on me that I continued to carry it deep inside of me. But I never planned to follow in Sembene's footsteps: most of my life I fought against becoming an artist and chose instead to focus my attention on academic pursuits. Indeed, when I left Chicago to attend Smith College in Northampton, Massachusetts, I had every intention of pursuing a pre-med course, entering a good medical school, and returning home to Chicago as a physician dedicated to working in the inner city.

My pursuit of a medical education was, perhaps, my way of compromising with my family. They had always honored education, teaching each of us to study hard and use our talents wisely. The women in my family, like the women in many African American households, were encouraged to be nurses and teachers. I never wanted to be a teacher or a nurse, and so I entered Smith en route to becoming a doctor. The irony is that even today, my ninety-six-year-old grandmother tells me that it's so nice that I "have a good education." Whenever we talk, she reminds me of so-and-so's daughters and sons who have "a good job teaching." More often than not, these are people I don't know, but the point is that I, too, can always teach.

At Smith I studied the usual subjects, but it was the college's Art Department that began to demand more and more of my attention. Before long, I left the medical books and took to painting, printmaking, serigraphy, design, and sculpture. Imagine my joy when I discovered not only still photography but also film and video at Smith. Unfortunately, although the film and television equipment was there, none of the professors really knew how to use it. The professors, however, gave me much freedom with the equipment and I soon began to experiment, making short, modest pieces at Smith. On my own, I figured out as much as I could about the clunky video cameras and the technically intimidating film equipment. I never quite knew what I was doing, but I liked being able to blend with and expand on the work I started with: art, design, photography, and theater. Proudly, I accepted my degree from Smith in Multi-Media: I left college secure in my new-found realization that the Black community needs artists as much as it needs doctors and lawyers.

The next step in my artistic development began in Los Angeles, where I enrolled in the graduate film and television program at UCLA. It was a wonderful time to be in Los Angeles and at UCLA. I worked on films with Haile Gerima, Tommy Pollard, and Charles Burnett. I met Larry Clarke, Barbara McCullough, Sharon Alile Larkin, Julie Dash, Carroll Parrott Blue, Jamaa Fanaka, and many other filmmakers who helped to make my UCLA experience worthwhile. This is not to say that we lived in a dream world. We were not all the same and we were far from the idyllic "one voice of Blackness." But in spite of our theoretical and ideological differences, we maintained a basic respect for the individual and collective goals we each wanted to achieve. I remember lively discussions about politics and films. We critiqued one another's works as well as what was out in the mainstream. I also remember the many wonderful events that these heated discussions precipitated. Undoubtedly, these discussions could often make or break one's commitment to a potential project.

We worked on each other's films, shared meals, swapped ideas, and offered each other moral support when the teachers just weren't there for us. Affectionately (and with respect) we called Charles Burnett "the Professor." Charles shot many of my early films and was always there to lend a hand and give encouragement. Even today, he continues to offer me (and many other filmmakers) encouragement and still takes time to look at my work.

Alile and I worked on our first UCLA films together. We spent long days and sleepless nights at the film school—living and breathing film. We took short cat-naps on the edit-room floors—too tired to drive across town to our own beds. Alile reminds me that we would buy oatmeal cookies from the vending machines at the school, put them into the microwave oven, and try to convince ourselves we were eating nutritious oatmeal.

My most memorable (and useful) classes at UCLA were with Shirley Clarke, who became my mentor and encouraged me to push myself beyond my own self-imposed boundaries. She made quite an impact on many of us as she taught us about experimental and independent media. In those pre-palm-sized-camcorder days, you needed a football team to carry the portable video equipment. Special effects such as instant slow motion didn't exist. Shirley taught us how to create slow motion by hooking up four or five video porta-packs (which were clunky reel-to-reel video machines) and worked with us to set up programs at Theta Cable, LA's new cable station.

In Shirley's class I worked closely with two other Black students, Denise Bean, the first person to direct a video about the women in the Nation of Islam, and Ben Caldwell, director of KAOS Network, a youth-oriented media center and cafe in Los Angeles. I also met Eddie Wong, one of the founders of Visual Communications (VC), the oldest Asian American media center in the United States in Shirley's class. From Wong and others at VC, I learned techniques for working in the community. For instance, when taping in South Central LA, I would use the VC model: I would videotape, then set up a monitor on the back of my equipment truck to screen the day's work for the neighborhood. As we wrapped and packed up equipment, the neighborhood residents would wander over to help us and stay to watch themselves and their neighbors on screen.

In the nurturing environment created by Burnett, Clarke, and other Black and Third World students, I was able to really grow as a film and videomaker. I interviewed the people around me, documented the places I visited, and got my friends to talk about their work on video. My work included *Apple Pie*, an irreverent look at the Bicentennial; *Survival—The Black South African Theater '77 Project*; *Naches*, a talk with a herbalist and natural healer; *Rummage Sale*, about women in South Central Los Angeles who owned and visited thrift stores; *Dialogue*, a round-table informal dialogue among Black filmmakers Charles Burnett, Billy Woodberry, and Larry Clarke; *Together*, a documentary on Black women networking around women's issues; and *Feet*, a playful experimental video about feet.

As a student, I was very prolific! Unfortunately, except for Clarke, most of the UCLA professors were totally indifferent to the work my friends and I were creating. Films were expensive, scholarships were scarce, and somehow it never seemed as though the Black and Chicano film students were getting a fair share of Film Department's funding. For critique and problem solving, we turned to each other, formed a Black Film/Video Association, a Third World (Film) Student Association, and worked with other resources on campus like the Center for Afro-American Studies and the Chicano Studies Center. I remember my amazement when a white student announced one day in class that she had heard about a new way to get money. The strategy, she explained, was making something called a "Third World film." Needless to say, I was not the only Third World student insulted by her ignorance and insensitivity.

By the end of the 1970s I had experienced enough of UCLA and the constant struggle for funding to make the films I wanted to make, so I took a break and went to Europe. Having no idea how long I would be in Europe, I arranged with the director of the still young UCLA Film and Television Archives to store my films and tapes in the UCLA archive vaults. Imagine my horror when I returned ten years later and I was told by the new UCLA archive administration that there is no record of my films and tapes in the archives and that I can't look for them myself! Devastation does not adequately address how I feel about this loss. My only solace at the loss of my work has been my memories and my ability to continue to create new (and hopefully better) work as I carry the legacy of *Black Girl* deep within my heart.

notes

1. In March 1991, Soon Ja Du, a fifty-one year-old Korean grocery store owner, shot and killed fifteen year-old Latasha Harlins, a Black teenager, in a dispute over a bottle of orange juice. A videotape of the shooting revealed that Soon Ja Du shot Latasha Harlins in the back of the head. As punishment, the store owner received a six-month suspended sentence and was ordered to do six months of community service.

2. After the four Los Angeles policemen involved in the beating of Mr. Rodney King were found not guilty by a jury in Simi Valley, California, two officers were later convicted in federal court. Sergeant Stacey Koon and Officer Laurence Powell were sentenced to two and a half years for violating the civil rights of Mr. King. The U.S. Court of Appeals for the Ninth Circuit later revealed that Koon and Powell would be resentenced because their lenient sentences were below the federal guidelines for civil rights offenses. The two other officers involved in the beating, Theodore Briseno and Timothy Wind, although acquitted in both state and federal trials, were dismissed from their jobs in 1994. Powell and Koon were released on parole in December 1995.

love

on

my

e i g h t   **mind**

creating

black women's

love stories

c a r m e n   c o u s t a u t

When I first decided to become a filmmaker, I purposefully wanted to challenge the racist stereotypes that circulate in the media about the Black community. Like many of my colleagues in African American independent cinema, I wanted to offer positive images of Black people that would supplant the negative depictions that riddle mainstream film and television. I wanted to make films that would change the way we are seen and the way we see ourselves. I still want to do that.

This motivation was largely responsible for my first film, *Justifiable Homicide* (1981), a short, five-minute drama I completed in film school at the University of Southern California. *Justifiable Homicide* offers a political critique of police brutality and examines the issue from the perspective of two Black teenagers. The film was not popular with the white community at USC, but I welcomed the enthusiastic response it received from my "revolutionary" counterparts in the Black independent arena. I felt I was well on my way to fulfilling my goal of using film as a political weapon.

But one day I was going through some old files and came across a story entitled "Best Friends" that I wrote while teaching junior high school in Watts. I did not conceive of this short story as a film until I was out of film school. Ironically, at the time, I was desperately searching for ideas for my student projects, but this story just did not surface. As I read through the story, I wondered what it would be like as a film, so I drafted the screenplay while I was still in California and eventually renamed it *Extra Change*. Essentially, the film is about a twelve-year-old Black girl who has a crush on a boy. Rita, the central character, goes through all kinds of extra changes to attract the attention of her classmate, Rodney.

Although I really wanted to shoot the story, I began to feel a bit guilty that the film wasn't "political" enough. There was a girl and there was a boy—no major controversies or issues to wrestle with, as I had originally imagined my calling. In fact, when I read the script to a group of colleagues, they reinforced my fear as many found the plot to be trite, a little girl's story. But not all felt this way; in fact, some women colleagues and students were much more into the plot and identified with the story. I began to realize that one did not have to be confrontational to make a political statement. I began to understand that *Extra Change*, in spite of its simplicity, could make a political statement by representing young Black people in a constructive and wholesome context. This alternative vision of these images would continue to realize my goal of challenging not only racism but sexism as well.

In considering the more subtle ways of challenging social issues, I am reminded of a panel of Black women filmmakers, where a white woman offered a critique of a colleague's film as the introduction to this particular speaker. She ended her remarks by saying the film had not challenged the documentary form (I am paraphrasing here). My colleague graciously dismissed the critique, but I could not sit there and let it go. I very clearly stated that my colleague had challenged every form of filmmaking because she was a Black woman standing behind the camera and she put Black women in front of it! That combination alone defied every form.

And so it is with *Extra Change* (1987). I felt I could satisfy my goal of challenging existing media stereotypes with alternative, more true-to-life images that resemble the people in my community as I know them—not as the larger, external society would like to define them. This is true, especially, with stories about love. They can be constructive, political projects. There are few films from Black women's perspectives about romance, but fortunately, that is beginning to change. In our quests for images of strong, self-reliant, directed women, we have not included romance in our political lexicon. But the time is ripe for us to see ourselves, not only as strong, self sufficient women, but in love and romantic relationships as well. To see Black women and men loving one another, regardless of the inherent difficulties that go hand in hand with love, is an ultimate political statement. It is the fundamental symbol of unity, togetherness—a symbol our community desperately needs.

I seem to be thinking quite a bit about love—this kind of romantic love between Black women and Black men. Although this preoccupation doesn't pervade the surface of my consciousness, I know it's there because it keeps surfacing in my work. There are many reasons for this preoccupation with love. Certainly, my experience as a woman and my observations of women convince me that we concentrate on attaining romantic love, in spite of our successes in other areas of our lives. Of course, romantic love is important to men, but their identity tends to be determined more by their work. It is very different for women, even if they are well-defined in terms of their work.

My particular focus on love in terms of my work is motivated by other aspects as well. As a filmmaker and a film viewer, I long for images that reflect a reality that represents my community. Unfortunately, I rarely see them, and images of romantic love on film tend to reduce Black women to sex objects and male adornment—in other words, he looks good if she looks good hanging off his arm. But I always want to know who she is. I rarely find out in commercial cinema. So I return to my writing and filmmaking once again to capture the images I long to see.

The creative process, however, is rarely that simple. Creativity rarely responds to sociological/political statements one wants to make, although the work ultimately always makes these statements. For me, the work itself comes first, and the statements follow. Several years ago, when the idea for my feature-length, dramatic screenplay, *Harmonica Man*, began to germinate, I had to walk around for months with images dancing in my head. I knew the story would be about a Black professional woman who falls in love with a blues musician, but I had not formulated the specific statement I wanted to make. The idea started when I went to a blues concert (I'm an avid lover of the blues) and listened to this brother play the harmonica. He had such a symbiosis with that instrument; he caressed it, stroked it, licked it, sucked it, blew it, until I was taken up in the sensuality of it all. I'd seen many musicians put that kind of passion into their instruments. I'd been attracted to many musicians (as well as other artists) for the emotion that I felt in their artistry. Although I had never had any romantic involvement with musicians, I had enough experience with other men who displayed a capacity for passion through their work that I made the common mistake of assuming they would have that kind of passion/commitment for me. It never happened.

This is not to say that it never happens at all—just not for me. The more I looked at the situation and the more I talked with women who'd had similar experiences, I began to realize that the brunt of this problem is

141

ours. Often the men make no promises, but we make the assumptions. Just because we see a capacity for emotional connection doesn't mean it's automatically transferable. We just think it is—and therein lie most of our problems with men. Often what we think is going on is not what is happening at all. Instead of looking at the reality of the situation, we get caught up in our fantasies of it—what we imagine it to be, what we want it to be!

We get off really easily. We complain about how this triflin' brother did or did not do this, that, or the other, and so he looks bad. But we rarely look that bad because we don't tell it all. We don't say he never made us any promises. We only talk about what we expected. If he's a doggish brother, we rarely admit that he's doggish because we let him treat us a certain way; we allowed a relationship to progress under negative circumstances. We don't take responsibility for any of that. It's always on the men. This is not to excuse the negative behavior of any individual, but it is to say we have a choice in these matters whether we want that choice or not.

What occurred to me about all these stories I've heard and/or experienced with men is that the women talking were all mature, educated, bright, professional women. How did they get so stupid when it comes to men? Enter Nina Byrd. Nina is the main character in *Harmonica Man*. (I deliberately left the title to focus on the man because essentially that's what Nina does in the story.) Nina is a single, Black, female television producer who is absorbed by her work. Her professional life consumes so much of her time that she has little energy or inclination for a romantic life. In her late thirties, Nina has had her share of experiences with men, and at this point in her life, she is a little too tired to want to bother. Nina is a lot like me, although she is also many other women I know combined into this one character. The relationship is also drawn from my own experiences, from others' experiences, and from my own imagination. In this regard, the story is not autobiographical.

Nina has a close friend from college, Dee Dee. Dee Dee is married to her college boyfriend and is very active in the Washington, DC, social scene. She tries to pull Nina into this scene, and Nina reluctantly participates. Although Dee Dee tries to introduce her to a variety of men, Nina is rarely interested in any of them. Nina and Dee Dee are very different, but they remain good friends.

So, at the point of the story where we meet Nina, she is suffering from a kind of emotional fatigue that is instigated by her limited personal life, which is overshadowed by her professional life. Her fatigue is also physical, of course. Part of her problem when she meets men is that she has little energy to devote to the "games" people play. She's done that already. Most prospects tend to resemble former romances that ended poorly. She's now experienced enough to see the signs before she even gets involved. This efficiency certainly reduces the amount of time one spends searching, but it also reduces the amount of involvement. Nina finds it easier to be alone, and she has come to terms with her "aloneness."

Until she sees Errol play the harmonica. She is completely captivated by his passion, and her subsequent relationship with him interferes with her neat, packaged routine and her easy dismissal of men. Errol is a talented, bright, working-class man whose life sharply contrasts with Nina's. She is well-educated and professionally accomplished, and her social group is comprised of people like Dee Dee, who think Nina's involvement with Errol is beneath her. But Errol and his music remind Nina of home, of a childhood in a working-class community with the blues and jazz as the soundtrack to their lives.

Much to the dismay of a few of my friends who know the story, the relationship with Nina and Errol doesn't work out. It has little to do with class—at least on Nina's part. However, an improvement in Errol's job status would help him work out some problems in his own life. It has more to do, however, with their differing expectations in the relationship. Errol is always honest, though not necessarily clear—mostly because he's not clear within himself. And Nina is unclear—mostly because she relies on her fantasy of the relationship rather than what is actually going on in the relationship.

While much of the story is based on my understanding of myself, much of it is also based on what I see and hear other single, Black women communicate about their relationships with men. One of my biggest frustrations is the degree to which we extend ourselves for romantic relationships, whether they are serious or not. I always want us to be strong and dignified and not stoop to emotional syndromes where we give ourselves away. We not only get tied up in our own fantasies, but we often behave according to pre-established male fantasies of who we should be—the "wait-by-the-phone" syndrome or a distorted form of existence—not for ourselves, but for men.

I find myself wanting to share "rules" with young women—rules that I heard along the path of growing up, rules espoused by the women in my mother's generation, whether they followed them themselves or not. Things like:

Don't wait by the phone.
Don't never lend no man no money.
Don't never let no man hit you.
Keep your drawers up and your dress down. (Fortunately, this
    rule worked well when I was a teenager, but it didn't last!)
Wear it like a loose garment (in the words of my friends' grand-
    mother).

My best lessons came when I saw these women violate their own advice. But their incantations proved valuable, especially when I violated them myself. Although put very bluntly, many admonitions emphasized the need for independence, a clear sense of individuality, self-respect, self-caring, and self-preservation. They warned against abusive relationships (physical or otherwise). These mothers and aunties and grandmothers clearly understood how easily women could lose a "sense" of self when it came to romance. Certainly, this wisdom has withstood the test of time, and it definitely emerges in my work. This insight also provides a pathway of empowerment for women in their individual identities, so that they don't "get lost" in relationships.

This concept is one of the main reasons for creating *Harmonica Man*, but in retrospect, I see traces of it in *Extra Change*. At the time I made the film, I didn't realize I was getting into this love thing and would repeat the theme so much in subsequent works. The film has enjoyed positive response because so many women identify with the struggles of the main character and are reminded of their own adolescence. While Rita is excused because she is only twelve, women of all ages suffer from some of the dubious social codes they have internalized. Regardless of their ages, many women have the tendency to go to extreme lengths in their involvement with men.

I think this motif keeps returning in my work because I don't like to see women considered as victims on a continuous basis. I really don't like to see women victimized in the everyday routines of their intimate relationships. It is not necessary for women to assume a perpetual stance of victimization just because we're women. Women have some say in the matter and have a lot of power over who they are and what type of relationship they will be in. I know many women in very healthy relationships where they are regarded as strong and valuable partners. But there are so many who haven't gotten there yet, and I think this message is directed at them.

The creative process is very difficult to describe and define. A story may emerge from an image, a personal experience, someone else's experience, or from imagination. In my case, it's usually all of the above. As a filmmaker, I tend to see images first, then I code them with descriptive terms. These images appear at unpredictable times, sometimes while driving, showering, sleeping/dreaming. Sometimes something I've read prompts an idea, sometimes something I hear. For me, the story usually metamorphoses in a kind of fast-forward series of images. I do not mean to suggest that I write fast. I don't. But the general sense of an idea comes in individual pictures that get linked together by story details through the writing, then the filming.

I find this process interesting because before I went to film school, I

144

conceived of ideas as literary concepts through words and narrative. Now I conceive of them as images in terms of film language. I am working on another screenplay now, *Listen to the Wind*, and one of the challenges is to link two characters based on their parallel existence before they know each other. I see one character looking out a window, through venetian blinds. The camera follows the gaze and rack focuses on a tree outside the window with the blinds in blurred foreground. Then the tree goes out of focus as a transitional device, and another tree comes into focus, with another set of venetian blinds in blurred foreground. The focus racks in reverse as the second character comes into focus. This kind of parallel cutting is very common in film and is a technique I learned in film school and used in *Justifiable Homicide*. But in this newer script, I'm relying on parallel cutting and transitional devices to intertwine the futures of the two characters while presenting their separate realities before they meet.

When I first went to film school, I was very frustrated and intimidated because I couldn't quite grasp what they kept emphasizing about this "film language." I came from a literary background and knew I could write, but in a way this was a handicap. When I finally broke out of it, I was able to look at the world in different ways—in terms of visual representations. I was able to conceptualize the world from this frame of reference. A funny thing happened to me when I was editing *Extra Change*. I was so accustomed to manipulating images on the Steenbeck (an editing machine), fast-forwarding and reversing, moving the images in slow motion both in forward motion and in reverse and freezing the frame, that I began to impose this mechanical technique on reality. I was walking by a building with a lot of steps. A little girl was jumping down the steps, and in my mind I froze her movements so that her legs were cupped underneath her, and she was suspended in mid-air for longer than she actually was in reality. I had to shake my head to come back to the reality of her continual, uninterrupted movement down the steps.

When I was filming *Extra Change*, I was searching for ways to use film language to reflect a sense of African American culture. We all know that "you really in trouble" when Mama puts her hands on her hips. When Rita's mother discovers her activities and proceeds to scold her, I frame a close shot of the defenseless, guilty Rita framed through her mother's hand/arm on her hip. These are the kinds of shots we search for when trying to communicate in that visual language. I know some filmmakers who see a shot, then develop an entire script around it because the shot is so powerful or so strong in its visual implications.

Clearly, *Harmonica Man* will be a film that has strong reliance on music, especially the blues. Also, jazz, rhythm and blues, and other forms of African American music will greatly inform the text of the film. But the cinematic style is especially critical and is already established through the scripting process. Since Nina relies too much on her fantasies, I will shoot the film, reflecting these fantasies on a visual level, making the distinction between reality and Nina's imagination. The realistic sequences will be shot with normal lenses, using a fairly stationary camera, standard camera speed, and lighting that reflects a naturalistic look with amber overtones. However, the fantasy sequences will use expressionistic lighting, blue gels, fluid camera movement, over cranking, freeze frame, and special sound effects. The fantasy sequences are designed to be seductive to illustrate how Nina's own imagination leads her into a relationship that proves to be less than satisfying—largely because the relationship must function in reality, and not in her imagination. Through this visual style, I intend to create a distinction between the scenes that take place in "real time" and the ones that take place in her imagination.

Finding funding for *Harmonica Man* has been difficult. The hardships of funding for independent filmmakers is standard, but I have had no luck in securing financial support. Part of it in this case, I imagine, is that the film is an ambitious project, calling for substantial resources to produce it as a feature-length project intended for commercial distribution. Also, it relies a great deal on music, which translates into more money. I have been fortunate to have participated in the Squaw Valley screenwriter's workshop, which is a national competition much like Sundance. I received good response for the script with, of course, many suggestions for its improvement. I know there are some story problems to work out, but I also wonder how much of the problem I'm having securing financing has to do with the fact that the lead character is a middle-aged Black woman. Once again, the formula is defied, and there is a lot of reluctance to invest in alternative visions. In fact, at the Squaw Valley workshop, an agent flatly told us that she (also meaning Hollywood) was not interested in stories about grandmothers in Harlem! So much for stories about Black women.

But I continue to come up with ideas about Black women in spite of the disdain for their commercial popularity. I continue because they are stories about me, and I'm not yet ready to give up on myself or on my community. In fact, I can think of nothing else, nor do I want to. Impressions of my people flood my imagination—often at very surprising times.

I traveled to West Africa during the summer of 1993 to begin research for *Listen to the Wind*, a feature-length screenplay currently in progress. I spent five weeks in Senegal and four weeks in Mali because the film will take place in both these countries, as well as in Paris and in the United States. One of the purposes for the research was to gain a familiarity with a cultural environment other than my own. While in Bamako, Mali, I began to think about some of the story problems I was having with *Harmonica Man*. Almost simultaneously, I also began thinking of the way I used to sit on the back porch outside the screen door, listening to my mother and her friends talk about life's trials. I used to love to eavesdrop when they talked because they would tell all the juicy stories that they wouldn't allow me to hear when they knew I was around.

Although I went to Bamako to work on *Listen to the Wind*, something about being so outside myself and my immediate world brought me more in tune with myself. I decided that when I got back home, I would write a background story on Nina in narrative style in hopes of bringing out some of her characteristics that weren't as clear as they needed to be in the screenplay. Before I knew it, I began writing in prose from the perspective of Nina, recounting how she'd eavesdrop on her mother and her mother's friends and how this acquired knowledge affected her relationships later in life. I only wrote a couple of vignettes in Bamako, but when I returned home, I continued by writing Nina's recollections as a little girl, which would then visually segue into an older woman's story (usually one of Nina's mother's friends) about a certain experience—yes, with a man! This recounting would then alternate with a parallel experience of Nina as a young woman, first in college, then in her early professional years.

This visual parallel attests to the value of the wisdom of older women and how younger women listen and learn from the experiences of their elders. It's another way to pay tribute to the historical and cultural link between generations of African American women. Before I knew it, I had a novel-length collection of these stories, and although it is written in prose, it is very visual and can easily be translated into a screenplay. I was surprised myself by how all these projects overlap, while drawing on similar themes. From Washington, DC., USA, to Bamako, Mali, West Africa and back, I managed to address issues in several projects, including *Harmonica Man* and *Listen to the Wind*, and create a completely new piece of work, *Round Table Discussion*, named for the proverbial group of women prophesying around a kitchen table.

Listen to the Wind is a feature-length screenplay that has occupied my imagination for some time. Although I have never had a serious romantic relationship with an African man, I have long had a love for Africa and what Africa means for us as African Americans. I have many African American women friends who are married to African men, but this story is not intended to represent their relationships, although I'm sure there will be many details that they will find familiar.

I have also been very interested in Francophone Africa, and I have studied French off and on for many years without much success until recently. I think my admiration of films from Francophone African countries has also influenced my decision to begin to break down at least one language barrier (French). Also, as Anglophones, I think we as African Americans tend to lean toward the Anglophone African countries, leaving out an important part of West Africa. When I attended the international pan-African film festival, FESPACO, in 1991, I was even more convinced that it was time to take French seriously. The indigenous languages, particularly Bamana and Wolof, will have significant presence in the film, although I have no facility in either of these languages at this time. I will rely on both linguistic and cultural translators during my research.

Enter BeNita LaRue, born and bred in New Orleans (no autobiographical connection; I grew up in San Diego). Nita, as she is called, goes to college during the late 1960s, majors in French, studies at the Sorbonne for a year as an exchange student, meets Demba Kanté from Mali, and falls in love. She comes home, but Demba goes home to marry a girl from his village. Nita marries her high school boyfriend, divorces him, gets a degree in journalism, gets assigned to Senegal and runs into Demba after about ten years.

In this film, I want to emphasize the importance of the historical legacy of Africa for African Americans. Also, I want to look at how a contemporary romantic relationship represents a link between Africans and African Americans. I deliberately use the name BeNita for the central female character because of its similarity to the West African names of Binetou, Binta, etc. Nita's grandmother is named BeNita, as was her grandmother and her grandmother and so on. So there's a connection to West African culture through the survival of a name. Also, I place Nita in New Orleans as an example of French influence on African peoples in the United States, although the parallel is not intended to duplicate that of French colonialism in Africa. And again, her major in French gets her to Paris where there is yet another African connection. We must contend with the historical interventions of Africans in Europe and America. We must contend with our own Americanness, yet ultimately, the connection to Africa binds us across nations and languages and merits jubilant celebration.

Of course, this is a love story. I described the story line to a colleague in Senegal after I described *Extra Change*. His response was "Toujours, une histoire d'amour." Always a love story! It was then that I consciously realized that everything that I was creating was based on a love story.

Although the story line of *Listen to the Wind* is roughly in place, I don't expect it to take root firmly until I finish the research. Fortunately, I received a Fulbright Fellowship and spent the 1994–95 academic year in Mali and Senegal to complete the research and write the screenplay.

My girlfriends who were so disappointed with the unsuccessful relationship in *Harmonica Man* will cheer with the outcome of *Listen to the Wind*. Black women are so anxious to see themselves on screen in constructive roles (see the work done by Jacqueline Bobo and others) and to have their images represented in ways that are true to their experiences. In particular, existing images of Black female/male relationships unfortunately fall

148

into the claws of negative stereotyping. That isn't to say that all representations should be fairytales, but they should portray a sense of identifiable realism. Clearly, there are numerous positive relationships between Black women and Black men. Although much of my work examines the struggles of these relationships from the female perspective, those depictions are still representative. The characters in *Listen to the Wind* are strong with a sense of commitment to their cultural identity. And it is through this identity that their relationship grows, but not without some vulnerability and weak spots.

When they meet, both Nita and Demba are young, idealistic, and committed to their African heritage. Although they acknowledge the similarities of their people (especially political), their idealism does not prepare them for the cultural contrasts. So *Listen to the Wind* will place each character in the other's cultural environment. The result will be the acknowledgment of the similarities, yet also a healthy understanding of the differences. But these distinctions will ultimately undermine the relationship and hinder its development. As they get older, a bit wiser, both a lot more and a lot less tolerant, their initial idealism will survive but mature as a result of their respective experiences. They finally "listen to the wind" and find each other once again.

So many images flash through my mind, and often I can specifically identify the germination of an idea. *Harmonica Man* was conceived in a nightclub, spawned by music and gradually developed into a full-length screenplay. *Extra Change* started as a short story I wrote fifteen years before it was produced. The goals have remained the same throughout—to present and preserve the purity of adolescence. I was struck by my seventh-grade English students and how their age-appropriate behavior defined who they were. They were not exclusively defined by the reputation of their community. In the final analysis, they were just young people very much like any other pre-teens anywhere in the world.

I often get so involved in the writing process that I find I don't consciously think of the resultant goal, essential message, prevalent theme. I see people do things and hear what they say. It's usually after I put it on paper, then on film, that it's clearer to me what the overall premise is. I definitely have one when I start, but I focus more on process, bringing the characters to life, than analyzing why they're doing what they're doing.

Novelists often refer to their characters assuming a life of their own, talking to them, sometimes resisting, oftentimes helping, many times taking the story itself into an unintended direction. This experience happens to filmmakers, also, but on many different levels. Of course, you have the blank page that must be filled, but that's the easy part. Then the idea must be articulated in terms almost alien to the dramatic process—that is, in terms of a proposal to convince a potential sponsor to invest.

If one successfully raises funds, the actual production begins, and every scene must be composed according to a visual language. Each shot must be prepared before the actual production. Also, rehearsal with the cast, meetings with the crew, and every fine detail of the production from location scouting, wardrobe, makeup, food, equipment, stock, to props, sets, scheduling must be planned before any film runs through the camera. No one can adequately describe the aches from a long, arduous day of production, typically lasting anywhere from twelve to eighteen hours. All anyone can think of is getting the shot at any cost.

But the longest part of the process is post-production, when every piece of film shot must be recorded, examined, and filed for ready accessibility. The film comes together in this post-production stage of editing, building sound tracks, composing music, mixing, creating special effects, and so on. Once a filmmaker gets involved in this very detailed process of filmmaking and its many aspects, it is easy to forget the basic point one was trying to make. It's enough just to get through the various stages. Obviously, it's important to have a clear idea from the start, but the nature of the process itself demands continuous change and adjustment. So an idea that is clear at the start of a film may get muddled through the process, but rarely vice versa. I was fortunate that *Extra Change* remained essentially intact, in spite of the many changes along the way. When I came out of the mist and the fog began to clear, I was almost surprised that the original idea of the film was there. During the process, I never thought about whether it would be a good film, whether anyone would like it. I had no idea it would win any awards. I was too busy getting it done to think about all that! It wasn't until later, after the film was done and I received specific responses to the film, that I realized many of my goals for the film were met—that the essence of the film that I conceived in the beginning survived the rigors of actually making the film.

I teach screenwriting, so I am reluctantly admitting the way I develop an idea. I insist that my students do an outline, a synopsis, and a treatment so that they will have a clear idea of the direction of their story. I do have a clear direction for *Listen to the Wind*, for example. But it didn't come until after I drafted a few scenes of Nita and alternated them with Demba during their childhoods. Those images came first. Then I had to sit back and ask myself, "Why am I bringing these two characters together? What are they going to represent? Why do they want my attention? Why do they want to be on film?"

As I mentioned with *Round Table Discussion*, those characters have floated in and out of my imagination for years, certainly from people I already know (although no one character specifically represents a real-life person). And this particular project overlaps *Harmonica Man* specifically, but it draws from the same source the other characters come from. There are

150

many similarities between the different projects because they all come from the same experience, the same culture, the same intention.

And they all seem to operate in some context of romantic love. There's a real sense of protection I have about these characters. I urge them to be careful, "wear it like a loose garment," don't take anything too seriously until you have some solid information, and, most important, be careful of the men you choose. I want my characters (as well as my friends, myself, and other women) to be in charge of their love lives, to recognize their own participation in them, and to acknowledge their choices. I know women are victims of so many things, but in some matters they victimize themselves. I want us to get away from this identity as victims. We do have a say about our lives.

I also want us to find healthy romantic relationships. After all, love is an important component of life. Even the most cynical of us (especially me) understand this fact. Even the most independent, the "I-don't-need-a-man-to-have-a-full-life" of us (especially me), want a partner in love. Even the most weary of us (especially me), who are tired from past disappointments and are reluctant at the thought of trying it again, recognize the void that exists when romantic love does not factor in our lives.

So while "I don't go searching for love," as Patti LaBelle so aptly sings, I admit that it consumes many of us a great deal, whether we have it or not. While I don't complain, worry, or become hysterical about the subject, I acknowledge its importance. I must contend with the fact that as I sit down to write, this yearning comes out whether I want it to or not. It must be the reason I can be so calm about it in my conscious life; it must be the reason I can easily dismiss it in my personal life. But I have to confess that the concern about love is there. My girlfriends (my characters) keep reminding me that I have a lot of love on my mind.

below

the

line

(re)calibrating

the

filmic gaze

c .   a .   g r i f f i t h

between a rock and a hard place

Boston. 1989. I can't shake this chill, and the roar of a second chopper over my head forces me to hunch over and curse under my breath. I watch a ghostly pale Mick Jagger dash out from the helicopter before he is swallowed by a swarm of thick-necked security forces as the crowd screams and lurches forward. I flash my ALL ACCESS stage pass and duck into a side door. The camera room is full of enough equipment to start a small camera rental shop. Eight or ten of the best ACs (Camera Assistants[1]) in the business are setting up for tonight's shoot and trading war stories. The testosterone levels are way past the legal limit for safety, and I have to make sure my kit and all of my operator's (Camera Operator[2]) gear made it off the plane safe and sound. As I work, I whisper a mantra to keep the walls from closing in on me: "Any set is just a set and the camera's just a tool to process film. The camera's just an expensive blender." I introduce myself to the guys, and keep a mental note of the few who are surprised but friendly enough, and the rest who look at me with distrust and perhaps a bit of envy.

We're walking backstage. Anastas (Tass) Michos is about thirty-five with the build and grace of a dancer. He also has one Black woman on each arm. One is me, a woman who has been called attractive or intimidating—it all depends on the context, but one description usually outweighs the other. The other is a stunningly beautiful young woman, his girlfriend, the model. Even backstage among all the jaded paparazzi, fans, and film and music biz people, we cause heads to turn. The director comes up to us, greets Tass warmly, and we all exchange names and niceties. He's busy briefing Tass on the shoot when he stops suddenly and asks, "Tass, where's your man?" "She's right here," Tass responds as we keep walking. "No. Really. Where's your man?" I stop and look at him. "I'm right here." He looks at Tass. Tass smiles. I look him straight in the eye and re-introduce myself. "Crystal Griffith. First AC." He looks uncomfortable. "So what are we talking about here?" Tass says, getting right back to business. "You want the whole concert or just a few cuts?" "At least two cuts, plus the new one—'Rock and a Hard Place.' We'll get you a list for tonight's shoot."

I hadn't really eaten since Tass called me two days ago. He had to convince me why I was the best person for the job before I accepted it: "You do docs, and crazy Rock and Rap videos where there's no time for tape measures, depth of field charts, walk-throughs, or fear." He'd hired me over a long list of others because I pulled focus, stayed calm and easy going, and didn't have time to be afraid. But I was afraid. At dinner, the model, an Australian roadie, and I are the only Blacks in sight. I can't stomach the massive lobster staring at me on my plate. We'll be shooting mostly to playback, except for the live footage tomorrow night at the concert. And the camera we're using is an Arri III.[3] It's lightweight, so it's perfect for steadicam. The only problem is that on an Arri III, if the loop is two or three perfs too long, the emulsion will hit the screw inside the camera body and scratch the emulsion right down the center. If the loop is too short, the camera will jam, or if it's cold enough (this is September in Boston), the film may break. That means the loaders have to be right on the nose. That means that if they're not, I'm in serious trouble for not noticing it, rethreading the mag, and correcting the problem. Of course, AC's make mistakes all the time; the trick is catching them before they're noticed and before they cause any problems—otherwise it's my head.[4] It's Tass's head for hiring an AC that messed up the shoot (but the fact that he trusted a Black woman First AC with their film will be all they'll talk about). And it'll be the director's and DP's[5] nightmare, and the producer's tens of thousands of dollars for film that can't be used.

This is my first big steadicam job as a First and I'm understandably anxious. Fortunately, Tass keeps that magical distance that instills confidence in my ability, yet is close enough to see and alert me to any trouble. Just before we're up, he helps me double-check everything once again, correct problems, and make sure we show no seams and no sweat.

We shoot for hours under incredible stress that night. All eyes are on us. I don't take out my tape measure enough, so they're not sure it's really in focus, although everything looks good in the director and DP's video tape monitor.[6] They ask Tass if it's good for camera and he tells them yes, the composition is good, but they'll have to tell him about focus.[7] The producers do a rush on the film and have it processed and flown back in from New York for screening the next day. Tass calls his friends at the lab for a negative report and we get a message at the hotel a few hours later saying that everything's fine. Still, I don't sleep. I act loose, cool, and copacetic. My jeans are getting looser and my stomach is a tight, tight knot. I exude confidence.

At dusk the next day, during a sound and tech run-through, they throw this amazingly smooth, hot, and impossibly sharp footage up on the giant concert stage screen. Everyone stops what they're doing to watch as the camera holds a long shot on Keith Richards, moves in for a close up, whip pans over to an extreme long shot of Jagger at the edge of the stage, and holds him in sharp, clear focus as he runs directly up to the lens to purse and pucker those famous, thick, juicy lips, all of two inches from the lens. I hear an audible gasp from Tass, from myself, and all around us. I'm thinking, whoever this guy is, he's good. And I'm in trouble. On such a huge screen, the slightest miscalculation, or hesitation in camera movement, the slightest, most trivial loss of focus will look terrible. And they're impossibly flawless. Take after take. I ask Tass if they're going to cut this footage in with what we shot last night and he looks at me, truly stunned. "That's our work up there, Crystal. That's us." I don't recognize it, and I'm not sure how to absorb this information. The reel is over and suddenly, the entire crew, including the roadies who've taken this tour up and down around the world, applaud us. The producer, director, DP, and Tass are pounding my back and shaking my hand. But years later, I still ask this question: what if I'd made a mistake?

adventures in the land of supertech

AC's are expected not to make mistakes, to be machinelike in attention to detail, yet still perform duties machines cannot perform—and, of course, be a "good fellow" throughout. I was very good at what I did. I walked a tightrope called ARROGANT BLACK BITCH SUPERTECH NOIR. The special, limited-engagement show: how to be one of the few professional Black

DP/Camerawomen. The price of the ticket on 15 October 1991: two slipped and herniated disks, a neck that curved the wrong way, and severe nerve damage. I left New York that December. It took my friend and DP, Juan Cobo, over ten excruciating minutes to help me down three flights of stairs, across the treacherous sidewalk, and into a waiting cab. It had rained the night before and the streets were covered with a thin, dangerous coat of ice that told me it really was time to go.

I live in California with my partner of six years. My recovery has been slow, yet somehow, I've been as productive (maybe more) during these five years in California as I was in New York. I'm a published author, I've directed three video narratives, and twice made the finals at Sundance for my first feature-length screenplay. H.T.L. Quan and I are codirecting/producing *The Angela Davis Project* (working title), a documentary series on women of color as cultural workers. We shot the first segment, which includes a conversation between Angela Davis and seventy-five-year-old political activist Yuri Kochiyama, in May 1996. A month later, I completed an MFA at the University of California, Santa Barbara. I've also had the honor and privilege to work and study with leading Black intellectuals like Dr. Cedric J. Robinson and Isaac Julien, who demand excellence and challenge you to excel. Writing this article has meant revisiting what I now refer to as my past life.

I will argue that filmmaking is essentially a blue-collar industry with a glossy but thin veneer of mystique and prestige that makes it appear impenetrable. It is also a highly hierarchical yet collaborative process with artificial boundaries existing above and below the line. By above the line, I mean the producers, directors and lead actors—the handful of people whom audiences, academic cultural critics, and the popular presses reify. Straddling the space between these lines, officially, part of one world, but outside of it in many ways, are the writer and DP. By below the line, I mean the filmmakers that we call the crew, who compose 98 percent of the film production unit, the forgotten, invisible names that roll by in the credits long after the audience have left their seats. I have been a PA, AC, and DP; and the film world looks very different above and below the line.

grand expectations

> At all times, Cameramen ... shall be responsible for doing their work to the utmost of their ability, artistry, and efficiency, and strive to uphold the best traditions of the photographic profession. Bearing in mind that upon their efforts rests the ultimate responsibility for reproducing in artistic and visible form the results of the great expenditures undertaken by the Producer, they shall also strive to per-

form their work efficiently, rapidly, and as excellently as possible, seeking to heighten their efficiency and that of the Production unit with which they work.... Before a person can call himself a Cameraman, he must know and be able to perform the duties of each classification. This knowledge separates the professional from the amateur.[8]

Sexist language aside, this description of the cameraman's responsibilities, a kind of preamble to the responsibilities of the profession, clearly establishes the following: that the producer, and not the director is the site of power and control on set;[9] that the importance of the camera department is critical not only in technical but also artistic terms; and that the profession is intensely exclusive in its pedagogy. By relating a series of experiences—of how I circulated within the independent filmmaking industry/community—and by attempting to analyze critically their meanings, I seek to address the complexity of filmmaking within the framework of race, class, gender, and sexuality. It is critical to our understanding of film theory and film practice to resituate and re-address what happens below the line in order to understand the entirety of the filmmaking process.

As Director of Photography Steven Bernstein points out, "film production is an expensive business and mistakes are not happily tolerated. It is also a high-pressure trade, and pressure naturally leads to mistakes."[10] One might argue that the position called Camera Assistant functions as a kind of gate—the proverbial "weak link" and also the site of a great deal of underexplored power and knowledge. As a professional AC, I not only learned my trade but also that of almost every member of the cast and crew except perhaps the editors, simply by virtue of standing by and working on the camera during shooting or between setups. While a lot of "action" takes place behind closed doors, a great deal happens at and around the camera. Further, the AC is one of few people privy to the conversations, creative machinations and decision-making processes of the producer, writer, director, DP, and the talent. While working in the film industry, I learned firsthand what worked and what didn't, why and why not. It was an invaluable education for which I was paid very generously.

Generally, however, the AC's role is recognized on set as a site of under-explored power, one that demands the utmost professionalism, technical knowledge, and perfection. For example, the AC's job is so important that Bernstein devotes the majority of two chapters to detailing these responsibilities. In *The Professional Cameraman's Handbook*, which is principally used as a technical reference guide (on film stocks, filtration, exposure, and camera equipment, etc.) for filmmakers, the description of the AC's responsibilities exceeds that of the DP's and Camera Operator's combined. It is not an exaggeration to state that the First AC has one of the most critical jobs on set; the best performance and work by the entire cast and crew can be destroyed by small, immediate, or not immediately detectable mistakes by the AC. One of the AC's primary duties is to keep the filmed image in focus. If the image is "soft" (out of focus), off-speed, improperly exposed, or if the film is accidentally "fogged" (exposed to direct light before or after it has left the camera), the image is lost. And if the image is lost, then so is all the time, money, and effort of everyone involved. Such a loss could include irreplaceable or impossibly expensive reshoots of locations and performances. Because the First AC is so important, this site of power is closely and very jealously guarded with signs that read "no mistakes," "no women," and "no people of color allowed."

From the beginning of film production in this country, and still today, filmmakers recruited from the dominant society employed biological essentialist arguments to justify their exclusive, nondemocratic practices. It is, of course, highly problematic to argue that only a certain race (white) and gender (male) is capable of performing certain duties, or that directing and producing a so-called Black film must be done only by blacks themselves. In the case of a woman doing "a man's job," it is generally argued and believed that women cannot take the pressure and long hours involved with filmmaking. Women are presumed to be too small and too weak to carry heavy camera equipment for the usual 12+-hour-day. It is also argued that more Blacks and women are needed to challenge or subvert racist or sexist film images and ideologies. To all of this, I respond with the following, greatly abbreviated list of insights as a counter-intuitive challenge to such problematic claims :

A small toddler who insists upon being carried (30–60 lbs.).

A Panavision with a loaded 400 foot rear-slung mag (film magazine), 50mm lens, follow focus attachments, video tap, hand-held brace (about 40 lb.).

The stress of working full time and raising two children as a single parent.

The stress of a 5-day, 14–16 hours per day production schedule with not enough turn around and a switch to shooting nights at mid-week.

White/Male filmmaker John Sayles's *Brother from Another Planet*.

Black/Male filmmaker Mario Van Peebles's *New Jack City*.

Black/Female filmmaker Julie Dash's *Daughters of the Dust*.

White/Female filmmaker Martha Coolidge's *Fast Times at Ridgemont High*.

Black/Female filmmaker Leslie Harris's *Just Another Girl on the IRT*.

Black/Male filmmaker Charles Burnett's *To Sleep With Anger*.

Black/Male filmmaker Bill Duke's *The Cemetery Club* and *Deep Cover*.

c. a. griffith

158

A backpack full of textbooks for a research paper on a crowded bus (15–30 lb.).

A case full of Panavision prime lenses (20–35 lb.).

PMS.

Male ego (masked insecurities).

A full-time career and intimate relationship, perhaps with a few sexist assumptions that women should cook, clean, and raise children (14–16 hours per day).

A 6-day-week of 12–14-hour-days on a low budget feature under high stress in a remote location with the only other woman/gay/person of color as your nemesis and a director who can't make up their mind.

Living, working, and giving 110+ percent for only 60 percent of the salary as compared to equally qualified men.

Down-loading, loading, and threading a Panavision (under 1 minute).

Threading a spool and bobbin on a sewing machine (about 1 minute).

Excelling in your career of choice and being dismissed or devalued as an oversensitive minority or unqualified affirmative action hire.

Five hundred years of resistance.

The erosion and erasure of thirty years of civil rights gains.

The bag of cotton my grandmother Lily James picked and carried alone to the scale when she was 24 years old (100 lbs.).

The Arri BL IV with a loaded 1,000 foot mag, 10–1 zoom lens and attachments, mini Worral geared head, matte box, filter, follow focus, video tap, extended extended eye-piece and tripod that I moved by myself—there was no grip available to carry it for me so I squatted underneath the tripod legs, set the shoulder pad at the curve of my neck, held onto the rods and the legs, and in correct form, lifted the entire camera smoothly, with absolute confidence and relative ease across the room because the DP and director kept barking for the camera—and inadvertently won the respect and awe of most every man and woman on set (100 lb.).

And finally, when compared to even the most convincing biological essentialist argument, I do not know what compares to living, working, surviving, resisting, and ABOVE ALL, MAINTAINING YOUR SANITY AND SENSE OF HUMOR in an amerika.

redefining the lines

Most cultural scholarship tends to focus on film content through an analysis of how meaning is conveyed by the above-the-line personnel and how ideology and emotion are perceived by the audience. This assumes a myopic and problematic binary of film production: that only the above-the-line filmmakers are worthy of analysis, and that an audience is definable. Completely absent from this academic and popular discourse are the below-the-line personnel. I believe this discussion needs to include, and more thoroughly examine, the physical, intellectual, and artistic contributions of these filmmakers generally marginalized by the strict borderlines of film theory and film practice, above and below the lines.

Regarding the analysis of the audience and the filmmaker, as much as individual, group, and cultural identity politics do play a role in audience and filmmaker perspectives, audience and demographic analysis will always be problematic. A "Black audience perspective" or a "female audience perspective" and perhaps even a "Black film aesthetic" do not exist except within an all too conveniently narrowed scope that does not approach or reflect the complex realities of those existences. Such diverse and conflicting groups should not be so easily categorized. I will use these terms and group designations with full awareness that they are contested terrains. Therefore, it is with some hesitation that I begin this investigation into New York's independent filmmaking industry and community during the late 1980s to early 1990s.

Many of the cultural critics who research and write on film have attempted to define the Black aesthetic and the role of film as art and ideology, but remain focused solely on the actors and directors (auteur theory), or producers and film costs (production, marketing, and distribution). Such analysis overlooks the highly collaborative nature of filmmaking and remains stuck above the line. Film genre, technical and creative innovation or reproduction, aesthetics and film as art, and ideological formation also remain stuck on the above-the-line film practitioners.

We must interrogate why academic film criticism and the popular press are so heavily invested in reporting on how a handful of directors, actors, and producers[11] create a body of work over time, how they communicate their artistic vision, and how that vision is infused with traceable intellectual and political agendas. Such hierarchical and exclusive approaches to a medium that is so influential and multifaceted beg a more thorough and democratic analysis—particularly given the hierarchical and nondemocratic nature of filmmaking itself. And while cultural scholars Manthia Diawara, Tommy Lott, and others have attempted to bridge the gap between film theory and film praxis, I believe that it is equally critical to expand the scope of what it means to be a filmmaker to include and more accurately represent the reality of the filmmaking process. The process is highly stratified yet collaborative, and it is embedded with mystique and prestige. Films are achieved by a highly specialized elite core of what I call "neon blue-collar workers." Finally, it is a process where both above- and below-the-line personnel are filmmakers, making artistic interventions and contributing skill and labor to the film.

More important perhaps, the usual Marxist thinking that differentiates mental labor from physical labor and posits that the "real" work in society is the result of manual laborers does and does not hold true here. For example, on any given film set, one is likely to find enough electricians (lighting department), carpenters (set builders), riggers (grip department), painters and draftspersons (art department/production designers), specialized technicians (special effects, sound and camera departments), construction supervisors (assistant directors, production managers, and continuity/script supervisors), jacks of all trades (production assistants, a.k.a. PAs), real-estate specialists (location scouts), developers and architects (directors and producers), to design and construct a small apartment complex. Interestingly, when film work slows down, many grips and electrics moonlight doing construction work.

That most filmmakers who are defined as film technicians do not describe themselves or understand themselves to be blue-collar workers is due to the mystique and prestige of working in the film industry. This makes class conflict unusual in that the worker is not envisioned as part of a mass unionization effort, but as an elite core. For example, in 1990, union membership for a First AC cost $3,500 and did not guarantee rights for all. Rather, it guaranteed rights for a highly selective (read: generally nepotistic, racist, sexist, homophobic) few. Union membership is a perk obtained through apprenticeship and seniority, criteria that have systematically excluded anyone not part of the inner circle. This could mean other white males, but principally it means excluding women and people of color. In the early 1970s, Alicia Weber became the first woman camera operator in New York's IATSE.[12] The man who sponsored her membership refused to yield to threats and intimidation. In 1991, I became an IATSE First AC while doing *Juice* (1992) and became the first Black woman focus puller in the union, and one of the few Black people to enter the union as a First AC.[13] In addition to learning from the top AC's in the business and receiving my training at General Camera Corporation,[14] which at the time was the top camera rental house on the East Coast, it took the intervention of Larry Banks, Robert Shepard (African American DPs), Bruce MacCallum (an Irish American First AC), Alicia Weber (a British Cameraperson), and others to help get me in at IATSE

The intersections of race and gender within a profession that is almost exclusively white and male were often the cause of tension and conflict. It was frustrating to challenge constantly bigots and sexists and still function professionally with my character and will intact—day after day. It was also confusing and exhausting to counteract the weight of negative stereotypes about women and people of color, weather the abuse, and then find myself fiercely supported by many of those who had made working so difficult. For example, some white men who initially gave me absolute hell (initiation by fire) sometimes became my staunchest allies or fiercest protectors. The same guys that hurled every racist, sexist joke and jab to see how much I could take, then chastised me for not being able to "take it like a man" and fit in with the guys, or who dismissed the pain they inflicted as part of "paying dues, just like the rest of the guys," later got me hired on top jobs. They also shared with me the benefits of their experience and mistakes.

Ironically, some women and men who initially responded warmly to me when I was a "lowly PA" became predatory and threatened when I expressed interest in working in the camera department. Some Black independent filmmakers who espoused more open and inclusive hiring practices seemed resistant to hiring a Black woman as their First AC until they learned that I'd AC'd first for white filmmakers and production companies such as MGMM, Mark (MTV) Pellington, or Pennebaker and Associates. Black and white directors, producers, and DPs alike hesitated entrusting their film to a woman—who also happened to be Black—until they doublechecked my rep, or learned that the crew and talent responded well or more favorably to me as a person and film professional.

Most interesting, however, were the cases where Black women directors and actors dismissed me by nature of my position as a film technician. Overall, however, significantly more Black women mentored, challenged, and helped me to reach my goal of becoming a top-notch documentary DP/Cameraperson. They also encouraged me to find whatever it was that would intrigue me emotionally, artistically, and financially. Grace Blake, Ada Gay Griffin, Michelle Parkerson, and Kathe Sandler were among the Black women who gave me my first and best breaks. In sum, manifestations of paternalism and institutional racism and sexism at times blurred with more manageable rites of passage such as mainstream society coming face to face with "the other," who happened to be me.

In addition to the complex intersections of race and gender, I must add class (formerly upper middle, but during college and on my own in Manhattan, I barely made rent), education (elite and private), and sexuality (gay). I moved to New York in 1991, having been blessed by finding a share in a huge, rent-controlled, raggedy three-bedroom apartment with a living room, dining room, foyer, two bathrooms, and a magnificent view of the river and bridge. It was in Washington Heights, on Haven Avenue between 174th and 175th Streets, and I shared it with two other women. We split the $560-a-month rent three ways. The reason I mention all of this is that had it not been for this unheard of rent, I would never have survived on the $6K I made doing film work as a PA that first year. This is very important. New York is an expensive city and because, like most cultural work, film work is freelance, there is no job security. Very few can consider, let alone attempt and overcome such obstacles.

It is ironic that most perceive filmmakers as wealthy and glamorous. I had moved to New York with literally only one connection—producer Grace Blake—$200 for the next month's rent and utilities, and only $50 to spare for food and transportation (often, I couldn't afford subway fare and had to jump the turnstiles, risking a $50 fine). A "good daughter" is not supposed to graduate from Stanford University and then turn down a full ride for graduate school at Howard University (and lose an opportunity to work with Haile Gerima), only to move to one of the highest crime rate areas of New York in order to try and do camera work in the film business. It was "critical" that I succeed without any help from home.

In 1987, at the age of twenty-three, I didn't know that I had chosen a career in which very few women, few Blacks, and perhaps no other Black woman at that time had achieved "success." I was in a field dominated by neon blue-collar white males who might have gone to college, but few had attended top institutions because it was not a priority when being an "A-list" AC or DP was the "family business." I was a curiosity and a threat. And I learned quickly that I had to hide my educational background, my parents' class status and professions, my sexuality, and to try to be as asexual as possible. This was not easy.

I am the child of a first-generation American whose parents emigrated from Panama, and a Southerner who grew up in Jim Crow amerika. Both were raised in extreme poverty, excelled in their careers, and raised the three of us children never to forget where they, or we, had come from, what it would take to move on, and, most of all, that we must always "reach back" to help others along. They saw this as one of the best ways to move forward as individuals, as a society, and as a people. In New York, I was fortunate to meet people who "reached back" for me: complete strangers, new friends, and colleagues looked out for me, trained me, and hired me. With dedication, skill, finesse, and perhaps the odd luck of being the "wrong" color and sex at the "right" time (resistance to Reagan and Bush's destructive and divisive policies), I found allies in the strangest of places. Most people spend almost five years in each subfield before moving on to the next career step. However, an odd combination of timing, education, people, values, apprenticeships, and luck made it possible for me to move incredibly rapidly from PA, to Second AC, to First AC, to Camera Operator and DP—in five short years.

By interning at General Camera Corporation, I was able to network with some of the top AC's in the business while learning how to prepare, operate, troubleshoot, and, if needed, do on-the-set repairs of almost every type of motion picture camera, lens, or accessory. With General

Camera credentials, and excellent mentors, I not only became a "top-notch" film professional but also someone able to "reach back" for others as well.

I brought in, hired, and trained as many "outsiders"—women, people of color, and poor whites—as possible. Sometimes, this meant bringing someone along on a camera check out, going by Spike Lee's office and talking to Monty Ross or the Production Office Coordinators (POCs) to lobby for someone. Sometimes this meant introducing people at parties, getting someone on set as a PA and then helping them move up or over to where they really wanted to be, and once, it meant telling a little lie to a director.[15] These are some of the same things others did for me. And I returned "the favor" in the way they requested, my parents expected, and the only way I knew how: by doing the same for someone else.

a neon blue-collar artist?

We're in Washington, DC, filming Billy Jackson's *Didn't We Ramble On: The Roots of Black Marching Bands.* The crew is ready to go and the talent has fallen asleep in the middle of his interview. Nobody moves. We look at each other, afraid to wake him. The man is seventy-two years old and still on the road. He's one of the greatest living musicians in the world. Right now, with his chin tucked down on his chest like a large, beautiful owl, he could be my grandfather, or father to any one of the men on the crew. He's now a weary old man, but he once took Miles Davis under his wing. He helped to invent bebop. Mr. Dizzy Gillespie snores gently and we watch him sleep. After almost ten minutes, he startles awake, embarrassed.

> "Was I out long? Damn."
> "I don't know," Billy says as we all take our places, pretending that
>   we just now got ready. "Camera ready? Sound ready?" We nod.
>   Gillespie yawns through most of the interview. When we pause
>   to change mags, he gets up from the chair.
> "Billy. I'm beat. We'll do this another time, okay. No more. I'm
>   tired."

The director is crushed. There is no more time. It's got to happen. He tries everything he can to convince him. "Fifteen, twenty minutes max," he promises. But Gillespie isn't hearing him. He's shaking hands with the crew. I look to Bobby Shepard, my DP, not sure what to do. Billy tells him to turn off the lights. That's as good as calling it a wrap.

I'm one of the last to say good-bye to Gillespie. I cup his hand in mine and tell him what a pleasure it was to meet him after listening to him since I was "this high." He doesn't believe me so I tell him how I found all these moldy 78s while cleaning my parent's house the summer I turned thirteen. I had discovered a whole new world—Ray Charles, Dinah Washington, Billie Holiday, Harry Belafonte, Sarah Vaughan, and Dizzy Gillespie.

"And your favorite?" he asked. I've never had much of a poker face so I had to tell him the truth. At thirteen, with a major case of adolescent blues, it had to be Lady Day. He tells me little stories about her as the rest of the crew packs up. And I tell him what wonderful stories he told today, during the breaks, and how much I'd enjoyed them. I tell him it's a shame that touring keeps him so busy and so exhausted. I tell him that there are so many people who would love to just sit and listen to him talk, hear his stories, and learn about the history of jazz and its roots.

> "It's been so wonderful today I have to pinch myself. I feel really
> honored to be here and learn from you."
> He grins like a school boy, flattered, incredulous.
> "Really, now?"
> "Yeah. Really."
> "Oh, I'm just full of air."
> "Oh, no you're not Mr. Gillespie."
> "Call me Diz, child."

Somehow, he's sitting back in the interview chair. I kneel beside him, chatting, and being my mother's child. I have to tell you that my mother possesses a good old, genuine, Southern charm, and is a beautiful, big-boned, heavy-hipped, preacher's daughter, whose warmth is irresistible. And that same charm, when used sparingly and potently by me, her daughter, got Dizzy Gillespie to do what no one in that room could do— get him to feel a little younger, a little more bold, and more like the distinguished older gentleman of the world that he was.

He knew what an awkward spot the director was in. He knew this tour was packed and the chances of Billy catching up with him on the East Coast were slim to none. He knew that we were a tight crew and it would be hard to find a better one. He knew that the history of the Black marching bands and their Mardi Gras and African roots were a crucial and underexplored link to the development of jazz and blues as cultural art forms. Independently produced documentaries can take years, sometimes a decade or more, to complete. And he knew that a little more of his time, right here and now, would make all the difference in the world. But as he straightened his clothes and cleared his voice, he said, "Okay. I'll do it for Crystal."

Obviously, this is not a story about how charming I am. Rather, this story demonstrates how respect for the subject, collaborative work, and a nonvoyeuristic, nonsensationalist approach is critical to filmmaking. This story also makes the case that interventions by film technicians can not only make or break a shoot but also can and do have real artistic impact. This example is not an exception, and more attention needs to be devoted to studying the roles of film technicians as filmmakers.

(re)calibrating the filmic gaze

Like most women of color, I have not had the luxury to be mono-issued. My sexual orientation was a "nonissue" compared to proving myself as a Black woman technician and filmmaker in a white, hyper-heterosexual, male-dominated field. My larger concern was subverting the sexual tension and sexual harassment that appeared to be an occupational hazard of being the only woman in the camera department, often with zero female representation or support in the sound, lighting, and grip departments.

Having and maintaining a comfortable professional and social relationship with the majority of the men I worked with for a minimum of twelve hours a day, under extreme stress and pressure, was difficult on many levels. My identity as a Black, gay, female, college-educated, middle-class woman working with both Black and white independent filmmakers raised eyebrows and caused tension that had to be constantly renegotiated and dissipated. The fact that my job as First AC often required me literally to be responsible for keeping the image focused on women and people of color in a very male/objectified gaze was problematic. What was most troubling, however, was that in order to keep the images focused and perform my job well, I had to participate in creating these same problematic constructions of race and gender identities, rehearse and anticipate the "action." At times, I was at liberty to discuss or even challenge these constructions. These were rare pleasures.

However, having to remain silent as I helped maintain a problematic gaze was all too often the norm. For example, while working with DP/Operator Bill Dill during a music video for Guy's hit song, "I Like," I had to mount the camera on a dolly with a jib arm which Bill swept over the lingerie-clad bodies of several beautiful women laying on satin sheets. Cinematically, I learned that pale rose satin (awful) looked marvelous under deep chocolate (surprise) gelled lights. But as one of the few women on the crew, it was difficult for me to take part in a production which totally objectified these women as interchangeable sexual toys and morsels of flesh to be admired, revealed, and consumed for the camera and male gaze.

These women were quite literally made delicious. The women were told to seduce the camera, and Bill hovered above them, one knee resting on the "bed" or straddling them in order to sweep the camera over the landscape of their bodies. The sensual music guided his movements. And my job required absolute concentration on seminude body parts so that I could determine that the lenses, which seemed more phallic than usual, did not accidentally hit these women in the Camera Operator's zeal for a close shot. I had to make sure that the full, moist cleavage of their breasts (it's hot under the lights) was kept in sharp focus from about 7'1" to 6.3" from the film plane (which is behind the lens, an inch or so into the camera body). I have helped shoot love scenes also. My embarrassment for the talent and for myself was acute on a closed or open set—either way, it was claustrophobic, voyeuristic, sexy, and mechanical at the same time. It was very difficult to turn off my raging mind to do what I must do: lose myself in the moment, abandon myself to the sensual, and stay focused.

As a woman, and as a filmmaker who wishes to resist issues of power/dominance implicit to the male gaze, I find myself perplexed as to how I will communicate the erotic scenes and sensuality embedded in my writing, films, and videos. For example, my MFA project, a video installation entitled *Border Line . . . Family Pictures*, is the first of a four-part series on the contested terrain of biography and history in four urban cities: East Palo Alto, Los Angeles, Washington, DC, and New York City. Like much of my recent work, the story on which the installation is based addresses issues of agency and resistance, but it also explores the sensual and non-traditional modes of filmmaking. The video juxtaposes a fictionalized story about a poor Black woman within an elite university and her experiences of loss, and secrecy regarding her sexuality, with memories of her grandfather, who was a member of the Brotherhood of Sleeping Car Porters. The video incorporates original footage, historical footage, and images from the bloody history of the California Railroads and Stanford University. Most importantly, by having four diverse women of color portray a single main character, the project challenges essentialized identity while creating a democratic space for shared experience.

In my own work, and in the films that I seek out as a member of the audience, I value films that destabilize the dominance and power of a gaze that devalues gender, sexuality, and race. How I will evoke the erotic as powerful and woman centered without the visual and theoretical baggage of oppression, voyeurism, and objectification is still something with which I am grappling. But I will use the sensual, inclusive, democratic lens of Julie Dash's and Arthur Jafa (A. J.) Fielder's *Daughters of the Dust* (1991) as a guide. In this film, lighting and movement caressed and elevated the multifaceted nature of Black female identity and form like no film I have seen before or since.

How do we situate the works of established and upcoming independent filmmakers who are attempting to innovate and redefine the so-called Black film aesthetic in a creative manner? Where are the voices and perspectives of women?

My experiences working on *Juice* demonstrate some of the concerns regarding how to define the Black aesthetic, and the limitations of identity politics or biological essentialist arguments. This was an independently produced film, written, directed and performed by Black men, and coedited by a Puerto Rican American woman. Yet however much the film attempted to challenge mainstream constructions of public enemy number one, the Black male youth, it instead reproduced a genre that ghettoized, demonized, and pitted young Black and Puerto Rican men against each other. It failed to address faithfully the real enemies: poverty, police brutality, economic apartheid, and poor education. Further, *Juice* ended up replicating the archetypal, dangerously narrow, male gaze of *Boyz 'N the Hood* (1991), where the lives and struggles of Blacks were reduced to a typical mainstream construction of Black life through Black boys who saw most women as oppositional to their "homies," caretakers, or sex objects. Unfortunately, the interventions of the women on set, in the cutting room, and the women in these Black men's lives did little to alter this nonliberating cinematic construction. *Juice*, like many films situated in the "hood" by Black male or Black female directors, sacrificed or devalued women for the "larger good" of the race/class/culture/nation. This is a serious problem that permeates government policies, personal politics, spectacles like the Million Man March, and films.

As a filmmaker and film consumer, I look forward to the creation and distribution of more positive, liberational films. However, I do not think that only Blacks can make these films. Like many, I believe that such biological essentialist arguments are ahistorical and inherently flawed. My thinking is more in line with cultural critic Tommy Lott, who argues for a "no-theory theory" of Black film, which addresses the "complexity of meanings we presently associate with the political aspirations of Black people ... a theory which is designed to be discarded when those meanings are no longer applicable."[16] Lott's theory suggests some hope that we will see an end to this most recent wave of blaxploitation films by bad Black boyz and girlz in the director's chair. It also suggests that, like filmmaking, film criticism may also take on a different form. Lott maintains that "when a film contributes ideologically to the advancement of Black people, within a context of systematic denial, the achievement of this political objective ought to count as a criterion of evaluation on a par with any essentialist criterion."[17] Lott seeks to disrupt Hollywood's "master narrative" of Black self-hate and oppression while recognizing that films have tremendous power.

Political scientist and film critic Cedric Robinson concurs with Lott's call for a pluralistic, liberational "political theory of Black cinema"[18] and insists that we need "oppositional voices and images which are redemptive of Black images on film and the society in which they are made."[19]

Such models of film culture are instructive, necessary, and attainable. For Robinson, the film that best fits his model for redemptive, democratic, and liberational filmmaking is *Daughters of the Dust*. For me, it is seeing and wishing to emulate *Daughters of the Dust* and being a part of making *A Litany for Survival: The Life and Work of Audre Lorde* (1995).

There is always a moment of transition between the lines of one path and the lines of the next. In this case, the line from AC to DP/Operator took an unexpected detour and became the line that led to directing, writing, and academic life. I had begun turning down AC jobs because the only way to move into the next stage was to begin doing it and not look back. If finances demanded it, or a friend needed me, I'd AC. Twice, I was ready to AC for people I would do anything for, and was stunned and honored when they reached back and brought me up to the next stage. The first was D. A. Pennebaker, who asked me to be a Cameraperson for a documentary on Branford Marsalis. The second, and the last, were Ada Gay Griffin and Michelle Parkerson, who asked me to DP/Operate *A Litany for Survival*. I DP/Operated for this documentary not knowing exactly what was wrong with me, only knowing that I was in too much pain. I shot the Barbara Smith interview and Audre's New York State Poet Laureate awards ceremony, with Michelle and Ada refusing to let me carry anything, even my own bags. They took the camera off my shoulder as soon as the shot was over.

My experience filming Smith's interview was challenging on many levels. The decisions I made in terms of lighting and composition were the sum of my own aesthetic, heavily influenced by Bobby Shepard, Larry Banks, and A. J. Fielder. We were filming in the tiny, ground-floor apartment of her home. It was so small that she had to step through a simple lighting set-up that turned into an obstacle course in the claustrophobic space we shot in: the Kitchen Table Press office. I was stunned by what had been before my eyes all along: literally, a kitchen and a few tables. This is the only women of color press in the United States and it's been around for almost thirty years. That this small organization had made such an impact on the world from such a modest and tiny space was indeed mind-boggling.

Ada and Michelle have always made every member of the crew feel valued for their skill, expertise, and artistry. Audre's opinion, their opinion, the PA's opinion, the DP's opinion, were all critical to their process. Their's was the most truly democratic, warm, and affirming set I have ever had the privilege to be a part of. When Ada called and asked me to go with her and Michelle to St. Croix to film Audre, probably for the last time before she died, I was touched and honored, but my body and spirit were still too broken. That I could not join my sisters, and say good-bye to Audre, is one of my great regrets. And although I worked on the film, when I finally saw it I found myself so moved, I was unable to restrain my tears. I was unprepared for the emotional force of this film that took them almost a decade to complete. I was utterly devastated by this film on Audre's life—its poignancy, grief, indomitable spirit, and life-affirming joy. For a change, no one moved from their seats until the last of the credits rolled by. And for a long moment afterwards, there was absolute silence, then the deafening thunder of applause. Ada and Michelle could not be there to present it at the Los Angeles International Gay and Lesbian Film Festival. They asked filmmaker Dawn Suggs and me to introduce it for them. We did, and tried our best to answer audience questions, to accept thanks for everyone who made the film possible. After the Q & A, as my partner and I were leaving, a woman came up to me and shook my hand. But she didn't thank me. She said, "Thank you all."

Above and below the line may always need to exist in film credits—it's a way for filmmakers to get known and get work, and it's how the popular media and cultural critics site and track films and filmmakers. But as soon as you separate the tasks of some of the filmmakers with the tiny little word "by"—as in "directed by ..." or "cinematography by ..." and then list the rest of the crew without this distinction, a clear line is drawn. Ideally, I would like to do a film and have the credits make no distinction between above and below the line. But this is not entirely possible and perhaps it is not really important. My goal is to blur these artificial boundaries in the credits and to eradicate them on the set. This is the way we worked on Litany. On the set, above and below the line didn't really exist. But what about the artistic temperament and all of the tender egos, you ask? Perhaps my friend has the answer: "I see big egos every day. Humility is more grand."

checking the gate[20]

We need to make more and clearer connections between film scholars in the academy and filmmakers in the industry. Open dialogues between these parties at every stage of film production—writing, filming, and editing—would benefit both sides. Filmmakers would benefit from years of research by scholars, from an opportunity to receive critical feedback, and from having the platform and time to make important changes if needed. Film scholars would benefit from seeing and learning firsthand the many-faceted issues, concerns, and limitations of the filmmaking process. They would also provide more informed knowledge on the meaning and realities of the entirety of film production.

In sum, before calling a wrap to this discussion I must stress that I have barely explored the surface of a complex and profound subject. I have suggested that a "clearer" vision is critical to our understanding of film culture, and this article is really just a beginning. On set, a long lens is often used to capture images up close. Unfortunately, many film historians and theorists have thus far mimicked, reified, and adapted to viewing film culture through this same lens. Let us not mimic the hierarchical traditions of dominant film culture. Let us recalibrate the filmic gaze by employing a more democratic lens. Let us now pan, tilt, and track with a long lens, and intercut the scene with a wide-angle lens as well. In that way, we can interrogate and capture the complexities and spaces above and below the line.

In order to begin this task of recalibrating the cinematic gaze, more integrative and critical writing and research on a whole set of crucial problems needs to be explored. The complex dynamics that reside above and below the line need to be explored in academia, the film industry, and the film community. Problems of power need to be explored as well. In particular, we need to reconsider the problematics of "show biz mystique" and the reification of cinematic and cultural icons. Filmmaking and the prestigious/mystical world it creates for itself are already hierarchical. As cultural critics, filmmakers, and audiences, we must consider what roles we play in perpetuating the power and mystique of an industry and medium of socialization that systematically excludes and demonizes women, people of color, and oppositional/liberational independent filmmakers who reside in the tenuous boundaries above and below the line.

FADE TO BLACK
ROLL END CREDITS
"THE BEGINNING"

Notes

1. According to *The Professional Cameraman's Handbook*, "the Assistant Cameraman must be familiar with and able to: check camera equipment and accessories to determine they are in working order and that no items are missing; inventory and record all raw stocks assigned him; load magazines; assemble and prepare the camera at the photographic site; make hand tests; run the tape, set marks; check parallax, handle the slate; make camera reports; set lens aperture; regulate all focus changes; record meter readings; execute use of filters, gauzes, mattes, and diffusion discs; change lenses; check gate; change magazines; thread camera; disassemble and store camera equipment and accessories; charge batteries; unload and reload magazines; label, pack, and ship exposed stock to the laboratory; re inventory film supply; present duplicate camera, raw stock, and exposed stock reports to the Production Manager; any further necessary and incidental duties that may be required." However, in my experience, AC's were also required to perform the following duties, those designated in this "industry bible" as the Camera Operator's responsibilities, such as to "set the groundglass focus; ascertain the parallax, regulate all shutter changes, note footage count; and assure the

security of the mounted camera." Verne and Sylvia Carson, *The Professional Cameraman's Handbook* (London and Boston: Focal Press, 1981), 17–18.

2. According to the same text, "the Camera Operator (Second Cameraman) must be completely familiar with and able to: execute smooth and efficient camera movements; maintain the composition(s) prescribed by the Director of Photography; and certify each 'take' as it relates to camera operation" (ibid., 17).

3. "Arri" is short for "Arriflex," a German camera.

4. An AC cannot, under any circumstances, even utter the word "OOPS" anywhere on set, and particularly near the camera. One of the best AC's in the business had told me this. He'd said the dangerous word when he dropped a pen and suddenly, ten sets of panicked eyes were upon him. "If you make people nervous, you don't get called again," he said. "Your rep is everything."

5. Also according to *The Professional Cameraman's Handbook*, "the Director of Photography (First Cameraman) must be completely familiar with and able to: light studio and location settings; compose scenes; take [light] meter readings; select lenses; determine the use of filters, gauzes, mattes, and diffusion discs; call attention to and solve any photographic problem pertaining to the production which may arise. Whenever requested by the Producer, he shall advise the Producer; attend story conferences, give advice and suggestions in connection to the designs and selection of sets, costumes, and locations as they relate to photography; and generally render assistance in simplifying production, in heightening production values, and affecting economies" (Carson and Carson, *Cameraman's Handbook*, 17).

6. The First AC pulls focus directly on the lens barrel without looking through the camera by judging the distance between the object filmed and the film plane — except with steadicams, where a remote control unit is used to adjust the focus, adjust zoom, and aperture settings, and even to turn the camera off and on.

7. When you shoot steadicam, the eyepiece is dead weight, so it's removed if possible. If not, it's closed and taped over to prevent light leaks. The operator looks at a small, on-board monitor.

8. Carson and Carson, *Cameraman's Handbook*, 17.

9. After all, in most film festivals, it is the Producer, not the Director, who receives the award for Best Picture.

10. Steven Bernstein, *Film Production* (Oxford: Focal Press, 1994), 76. Bernstein was the DP for *Like Water for Chocolate* (1993).

11. Missing from this "short list" is the writer, who must begin with the blank page. S/he is rarely credited with originating this vision, or made central to the critical discourse.

12. The International Association of Theatrical Stage Employees.

13. I was hurt while working on a feature and did not have the opportunity to pay off the balance of my membership and receive my official union card. Fortunately, as a union member, I was eligible for disability payments for a full year. Had it not been for IATSE coverage, the first sixteen to twenty months I spent literally on my back would have landed me in the poorhouse. Workman's Compensation is insufficient and is in many ways a contradiction in terms.

14. Film equipment is prohibitively expensive. Thus, filmmakers usually rent the cameras, lighting, and grip equipment. Also, there are essentially three

routes to becoming a DP: being a DP's child, working in the electric/lighting department, or working in the camera department. Like everything, it takes connections to get on set and through the door of a rental house. There are simply too many people ahead of and behind you. I used connections, incessant but friendly phone calls, and one day of sitting in the lobby with a copy of Richard Wright's *The Outsider* (1953) for company until someone would see me. I'd just finished working in Spike's New York production office while they were in Atlanta shooting *School Daze* (1988) and was feeling bold. After several hours, the West Indian receptionist who'd had to tell me that the person I needed to see "was in a meeting" for the past three months picked up her phone and said (and I still can't believe it), "I don't care what you tell me. I'm sending her up right now." Thank you, sister! I must add that there were perhaps five women, all clericals, that worked there. The only other woman to work on the camera-rental floor had sued for sexual harassment and discrimination. I got in the door and was told they'd try it out with me there for a week. I stayed six months.

15. I am proud to say that I told a littey bittey lie to St. Clair Bourne. St. had asked me to recommend a DP and I suggested several. He chose Juan Cobo, but seemed a little anxious that Juan seemed a little young. St. said that it didn't matter, because Juan's reel was fantastic, but he ended his sentence with an inarticulate "but ..." So I looked him in the eye and said that Juan just had a baby face but he was really in his mid-thirties. Actually Juan was my age, about twenty-four. We did *The Making of Do the Right Thing* (1989) with St. Clair. His producer, Dolores Elliot, was so impressed that she hired him to DP *Portrait of Max Roach* (still unreleased). I often wonder if some of the people who got me on jobs "forgot" to mention that I was Black or female, because I certainly got some surprised expressions on people's faces.

16. Tommy Lott, "The No-Theory Theory of Contemporary Black Cinema," *Black American Literature Forum* 25, 2 (September 1991): 223.

17. Ibid., 231.

18. Ibid., 232.

19. Author's interview with Dr. Cedric Robinson, Chair of the Department of Black Studies (UC Santa Barbara) and author of *Terms of Order: Political Science and the Myth of Leadership* (Albany: SUNY Press, 1980), and *Black Marxism: The Making of the Black Radical Tradition* (London: Zed, 1983).

20. Before filming ends for the day and we call it a wrap, the film gate is checked one last time to insure that the film emulsion has not been scratched, or that a "hair" (dust, or other debris) is not caught in the gate — which could render the image shot unusable.

part three   **in their**

own words

michelle

a visionary

risk taker

gloria j. gibson

There was a time, not so long ago, when Black lesbian filmmaking was a one-woman show. Even today as Hollywood slowly begins to acknowledge the substantial communities of lesbian and gay people in America, most film aficionados would be hard pressed to name one Black lesbian surviving the "good ol' boy" network of the film industry. But Michelle Parkerson, armed with courage, creativity, and an unshakable tenacity, has established herself as a trailblazer with a cadre of new, younger artists following her lead. Through her rich portraits of American character, whether it is the jazz vocalist Betty Carter or male impersonator Storme De Larverie (a performer and emcee of the Jewel Box Revue), Parkerson insightfully and candidly illuminates aspects of race and gender relations that are usually neglected or ignored in more mainstream productions. While she never claims to have all the answers, Parkerson tackles difficult social issues with relish and the zeal of one truly commited. I have been fortunate to talk with Parkerson on a number of occasions, some formal and others just as friends. In this interview we talked extensively about the struggles of Black women filmmakers, and the emerging homoerotic cinematic aesthetic. Parkerson also expressed her concerns about the schisms that seemed to further alienate a sometimes divided homosexual community, the increase of homophobia in the Black community, and the prolific legacies of the late poet/warrior, Audre Lorde.

Like Lorde and numerous other Black women writers and video/film makers, Parkerson strives to use "difference" as a mechanism to educate and to enlighten. Moreover, she subscribes to Lorde's mandate that one should use their various identities as power bases to communicate and to stimulate other communities. The challenge becomes at what cost does one "step out" or "come out." Certainly as Black women artists, be they filmmakers, writers, painters, or musicians, many take "risks" by creatively expressing Black women's triumphs and struggles. For Parkerson and many others, "risk" is the only option, because complicity and silence are ultimately self-destructive.

As a pioneer of the Black lesbian film and video genre, Parkerson's work spans a vast spectrum of themes and issues. As a student at Temple University, Parkerson codirected *Sojourn* (1974) with a friend, Jimi Lyons Jr. The film won a Student Academy Award from the Academy of Motion Picture Arts and Science in 1974. Her next two films document the creative contributions of Black women artists.... *But Then She's Betty Carter* (1980) provides an unforgettable portrait of the jazz legend who founded her own recording company and has since maintained a dedicated independence from the intrusions of commercialism. *Gotta Make This Journey: Sweet Honey in the Rock* (1983) is the broadcast record of the politically active singing ensemble, Sweet Honey in the Rock, a vocal group organized by Bernice Johnson Reagon in the 1970s.

A lead performer and at times stage manager of the Jewel Box Revue (an integrated traveling show featuring male impersonators from the 1940s to the 1960s), Storme De Larverie is the subject of Parkerson's *Storme: The Lady of the Jewel Box* (1987). In this interview, Parkerson insightfully contextualizes the eight-year project (unfinished at the time of this interview but currently in distribution) that culminated in the poignant and powerful documentary *A Litany for Survival: The Life and Work of Audre Lorde* (1995). Parkerson codirected the film with Ada Gay Griffin, director of Third World Newsreel, an independent distribution organization based in New York. Audre Lorde (1934–1992) was an award-winning poet, writer, and lesbian political activist. Lorde's prolific work spans more than fifty years and includes *Uses of the Erotic: The Erotic as Power* (1978), *The Cancer Journals* (1980), *Zami: A New Spelling of My Name* (1982), and *Sister Outsider: Essays and Speeches* (1984), among others. In 1991, New York's governor, Mario

Cuomo, consigned Lorde the honorary position of New York State Poet for 1991–1993. She died of breast cancer in 1992.

Parkerson's other works include *Odds and Ends* (1993), a Black Amazon science fiction video set in the year 2086. Parkerson completed this project as part of her stint in the American Film Institute Directing Workshop. In 1984, she published a short volume of fiction and poetry entitled *Waiting Room* with Common Ground Press. In addition to her film, video, and literary projects, Parkerson recently completed a multimedia performance piece, *The Amazon Papers*, which premiered in Minneapolis at the Intermedia Arts Galleria. The work is a mosaic of poetry, short fiction, character sketches and music that Parkerson describes as a document of Black lesbian desire, homoerotic satire, and survival on the eve of the new world order.

Gloria J. Gibson: The last time we talked in 1987 you had just finished *Storme*. What was the response to that film?

Michelle Parkerson: *Storme* received a great response. It premiered at Filmfest DC, the Washington, DC, International Film Festival, which I think is now in its sixth year. It had a great reception there. Storme herself was present to field questions from the audience. This was a great moment because people got to see her, to be in her presence, to hear words come out of her own mouth, and to respond not vicariously through the filmmaker's perceptions of Storme, but to Storme herself. That was a great thing. The film has gone on to various venues from there, however no television venues. One of the things that was prohibitive about *Storme* was its length. It is a twenty-one minute piece. It's done very well on the Gay and Lesbian Film Festival circuit, and at schools and universities.

GJG: At one time I thought you were thinking of expanding it.

MP: We had talked about extending it to a fuller length experience, but the money ran out. I'm sure you've heard a lot of "when the money ran out" stories, especially when you're talking to Black women filmmakers. There are sometimes success stories that come even after "the money's run out" and you still make it happen somehow.

179

GJG: Have you done any other films between *Storme* and *Odds and Ends*?

MP: I completed a video for a television series called *Urban Odyssey*, which was a seven-part series of half-hour dramas highlighting ethnic leaders from Washington, DC Some of the historical figures were: Nanny Helen Burroughs, Sterling Brown, and Reverend Chung, who was a religious leader in the Chinese American community. Some of the leaders are still alive. They were all portrayed by Washington, DC actors from within those various ethnic communities. The series was produced for WHMM TV, Channel 32, the Howard University Public Television Station in Washington. It was funded by the DC Humanities Council.

GJG: What was the year span? When did you start that project and when did it air?

MP: We started casting and rehearsal during the mid-summer of 1990 through the Christmas holiday. The shows aired in February of 1991. WHMM TV began airing them during Black History Month, and that led into March, Women's History Month, and then they rebroadcast them in June of 1991.

GJG: Did you serve as producer?

MP: I was producer and director, woman of many hats. It was kind of a one-woman band. Dr. Joseph Jordan of the Humanities Council oversaw the program. In some ways my serving as producer/director worked. I think if there had been other directors, the series would have had many more "colors" than just my perception of the input from the writers who did the scripts and the Humanities scholars who helped shape it. It was great to go through an entire process in terms of working with the writers on rewrites, getting the scripts down to a television reality in terms of the dialogue, blocking, and set design, and also working with the actors who were very, very hard-working people committed to the series' intent. They had a lot to factor into a half-hour program, a lot to memorize.

GJG: Can you explain *Odds and Ends*, its form, and the ideas behind it?

MP: *Odds and Ends* is a half-hour video science fiction. I call it a Black Amazon science fiction. It's based on a short story I wrote many, many years ago that I always wanted to see on the screen. It was my project for the Directing Workshop for Women, which is now an AFI program. I think the DWW started in the mid-'70s, and it's been a consistent workshop for women who have emerged as major directors including Martha Coolidge, Randa Haines, and Neema Barnette. A lot of people have gone through it, some are now celebrities, and others of us are yet unknown. It was great training. I wanted to reach for something that I don't usually do in terms of the format.

GJG: Tell me a little about it.

MP: It's an all-Black cast. The clones are white—white men. The enemy figures are white men, although there's the suggestion that the enemy is not all male and not all white. The production staff was predominately Black women, a good percentage of them were Black lesbians. The production crew was a great mixture of people with some working professionals in Hollywood. The producer, director, associate producer, first AD, and second AD, were all Black women. The DP/videographer was Michelle Crenshaw. The sound recordist Veda Campbell is also a Black woman, as was the editor, and so on.

GJG: In the meantime you're putting the finishing touches on the Audre Lorde film. When did you start with this project?

MP: Let me stress, first of all, that I came into the project through Ada's invitation. Ada Gay Griffin is the codirector/producer of the project. It's a collaboration and she began the project in 1986, originally shooting lots of the footage in video. In 1987 she invited me into the mix to "direct" it. I say these titles with quotes around the positions because Ada has directed several of the interviews, and I have brought in some money to the project. However, Ada is primarily responsible for the big money that keeps the project going some eight years later. It is also her dream, her carrying of the torch that has kept the project moving over eight years when people have remarked "Why isn't it finished? It should be shorter. Just cut a video of it, make it a half-hour film." All these suggestions came from the need to see Audre Lorde's work and her biography in some form that could be shared with people in a media format. Unfortunately, we were not able to complete the film during Audre's lifetime. She passed in November of 1992, but we certainly feel she has been with us and has had input in the process through what she left us in terms of taped interviews and phone conversations. We talked candidly off-camera about what was missing in the film and who should be in it. And certainly with the accessibility to her through her estate, we still feel we have her input, alive and well in the process.

GJG: She has two children.

MP: She has a daughter and a son, Elizabeth Lorde Rollins and Jonathan Lorde Rollins. Jonathan works in banking and her daughter is a doctor. Gloria Joseph was Audre's last companion. They form the hub of her estate.

181

GJG: What is Audre Lorde's legacy?

MP: I think Audre leaves legacies to various communities not necessarily Black, not necessarily women, not necessarily gay or lesbian, not necessarily adults, not necessarily feminists. One of Audre's operating tenets was to use one's differences and the many different parts of ourselves in the service of other people, the humanity of who we all are, and in the environment that sustains us. She was about the use of one's identities as a base of power, be that identification, as she called herself, a Black, lesbian, warrior, poet, mother. She was also a teacher. She was a professor of English at Hunter College. For many people she was one of the primary voices of the Black literary movement during the mid-'60s. She came to public recognition in several waves. Langston Hughes published her in *New Black Voices* in the 1960s and in *Anthology of New Black Poets*. She subsequently began to be published by Broadside Press which was one of the major autonomous Black presses of the '60s and '70s. It was Dudley Randall's operation, which was based in Chicago. Broadside Press, published people like Don L. Lee, as Haki Mahabuti was known then, Nikki Giovanni, Sonia Sanchez, and Lance Jeffers. Many of the enduring voices of the new Black power, Black nationalist, and pan-Africanist movements of the late '60s, '70s were published by Broadside Press.

In terms of her coming out as a lesbian, that dynamic brought many more audiences to her, and in some cases, in terms of the Black nationalist and Black arts movement of the time, alienated many people from her, although she had always been a lesbian in her own name and out and about. She taught at Tougaloo College in Mississippi in 1968 when the Jackson State insurrections and political uprisings were happening. She had a lot of connections with the Black nationalist and liberation movements. As she began to be published by feminist presses, she became one of the foundational figures in the feminist literary canon that continues to this day. She was also a founding member of Kitchen Table: Women of Color Press with Barbara Smith and many other women of color, which remains to this day the only autonomous women-of-color publishing house in this country. Internationally their books are distributed not only in the terms of the voices of Black women but also in terms of the African Diaspora. Women writers of the Latino community, Asian Pacific Islanders community, Native American community, and other indigenous international communities are represented. Audre had a wide reach as a writer, and as a founding light for those publishing houses that have a political underpinning, primary to people of color and women. She was also a prolific speaker.

182

Audre Lorde was a teacher whose work has had international impact. She supported the autonomy of the Maori women of New Zealand, and led writing workshops in Germany. She encouraged the Afro-German community, particularly the women, to publish their own history and contemporary reality in a book called *Farberbekennen*. She also worked with her companion Gloria Joseph in helping to further the work of SISA, Sisters in Solidarity with Sisters in South Africa, an organization supporting women's self-help groups in South Africa. She wrote several books of poetry, several books of essays, she even documented her own struggles with cancer, which took form in essentially one bout in the late '70s and a second bout in the mid-'80s. She survived cancer for fifteen years because she had support and perhaps the privilege of having access to alternative therapies and homeopathic responses to having cancer. So on many levels—health, politics, as a mother, as a Black lesbian voice—Audre Lorde is important to many people. She used her privileges in the service of others who did not have that access.

GJG: I think that is an excellent synopsis of Audre Lorde's contributions. I want to shift gears here. I recently read a statement in which Barbara Smith suggested that some Black feminist critics do not embrace Black lesbians in their work, and by not doing so, are really leaving out an essential component of who we are as Black women. I wanted to start off by asking you in general about stereotypes of Black lesbians.

MP: I am a Black lesbian, so therefore these things are really fascinating to me. I think there are predominate stereotypes of lesbians being man haters, of not having children, being separatists, and not even wanting to interact with men. Within our own African American community, there is a reticent acknowledgment that gay and lesbian people exist whether they've been teachers, folks in the church choir, or leaders in political movements. Stereotypes have not allowed us our humanity or diversity within the community. I think within the African American community there has been a complicity of silence that says, "We know you're around. You're in our families. You're in our institutions, but we don't talk about it. As long as we don't talk about it, it's okay." I think people reach for the broad strokes of how we can point out and name people, like for example, the bent wrist or the snap queens in our community.

I think this attitude has allowed heterosexual people an easy out not to explore the fact that the straight-looking person next to you may be gay or lesbian, or in fact, if you looked at yourself, you may see that you are homo- or bisexual. It denies a larger humanity. Within us all, there is maleness and femaleness. These are socially imposed paradigms. Stereotypes deny people humanity. We get a brief glimpse of a Black bulldagger in *The Emperor Jones*, the Paul Robeson film of 1933, when he goes in a sporting house to meet Fredi Washington. The madam of the sporting house is, of course, replete with double-breasted suit, a rough and tumble girl, big, fat, Black, a dark, dark Black woman, not a light Black person. We can also get into the color differentiation of what "bulldagger" means. It's a color stereotype as well, including current manifestations of it, such as the Black gay men as snap queens in *Living Color* or Eddie Murphy's spoofs of them, or even Spike Lee's lesbian vamp in *She's Gotta' Have It*, the lesbian vamp who didn't appear at that Thanksgiving table with the guys (but anyway, that's another topic). There's a void there, and what I'm saying is that there's an ever larger void of humanity when we speak of Black lesbians. I knew all along that I was not the only "out" lesbian among Black women filmmakers. There's a younger generation of sisters like Cheryl Dunye, Jocelyn Taylor, Dawn Suggs, Sylvia Rhue, and Aarin Burch. See, I can call them by name! And they've got a whole body of work that's a part of a new homoerotic thrust in Black imagery as we cycle this process called Black filmmaking. More well known are Black gay men like Isaac Julien on the Afro-European set, the late Marlon Riggs here at home, Jack Waters, and Thomas Harris. You see, I can call names and that means there is a significant change in the politics, the temper and the bravery of this generation of film/videomakers who are willing to make images in their own name.

GJG: Do you feel a woman's sexual preference influences the way she writes a script?

MP: I can't answer in general. I certainly would say that it has influenced my own choices of subjects in films, even though, until *Storme*, the sexual preference subtext of the subjects in my films were not part of what ended up on the screen. It was discussed but didn't make the cut for various reasons, which would probably take too much time to explain and maybe has no bearing because the products end up being what they are and people see the films for what they are in terms of *Sweet Honey in the Rock*, and *. . . But Then, She's Betty Carter*. I hesitate to say that only Black lesbians include Black lesbians in their films. When I look at the coupling of Yellow Mary and Trula in *Daughters of the Dust*, it's there. A lot of people have a critique about Mary's lover, her partner, her "suggested" lover never speaking. But that too has its power and metaphor, because perhaps Yellow Mary's own voice was speaking for them both. Who knows? I'm saying that it's not just Black lesbian filmmakers and videomakers who are including gay and lesbian imagery in their films. I don't think it's that essentialist. I certainly think Ayoka Chenzira's work is reaching in that direction. I can point to things that I feel have a wider swing in terms of sexual preference in the imagery. Zeinabu irene Davis's work as well, *A Powerful Thang*, is a good example of lesbian imagery. I don't think it's as essentialist as, "You're a lesbian so therefore you're the only one who puts it in your films."

GJG: What about Black women scholars?

MP: I certainly look to the works of, say, bell hooks, who frequently references Audre Lorde in many of her writings, to open up the range of sources that we can look to when it comes to feminist critical analysis of African work, Black work, whatever you want to call it.

GJG: I guess what I'm asking is how can nonlesbian feminist critics become more sensitized?

MP: If there's anything I can suggest, I think it's to reach beyond a certain comfort zone in terms of the references you pull from. Look at the range of references you use when you are structuring paradigms or pedagogical tools of comparative analysis in your work. It need not always be heterosexual referenced, or white referenced, or male referenced. That's a great question for bell hooks and I'd like to hear her answer. How do scholars make that reach, because there is a lot to lose. There's a lot to lose. Silence can sometimes pay off if you don't bring certain things up. I think that's been a shelter for a lot of people. You can lose a lot if people know that you are a lesbian. I don't know what the particular cost has been in my own career. I can't even estimate it. But I don't have time to even think about it. I've never even looked at the reductive side of it. I only see what it's done for me. I know that I couldn't be were it not for being all of my selves and being out about that.

GJG: Most recently there's been some discussion about Black gay aesthetics especially in regards to Isaac Julien and his work. Do you feel there's a critical mass of work and we can start trying to analyze components of a Black gay aesthetic, or perhaps a Black lesbian aesthetic?

MP: I think one of the great things the body of the work by Black gay and lesbian film- and videomakers has produced is a redefining of what homoeroticism is, by first of all introducing Black homoerotic images.

GJG: What do you mean by that?

MP: Homoerotic describes images that are sexually charged, images of sexuality between Black men and Black men, Black women and Black women. These images are present in Isaac's work, Pratibha Parmar's work, and the works of African American lesbian film/videomakers. I think the erotic aesthetic in Black films and videos has been dominated by a heterosexual reference. There has been a further stereotyping within that of only heterosexual images in Black films and videos. Those windows of homoerotic imagery were initially opened up by Black gay men. It has established a certain reference, in terms of same-sex stories, same-sex documentaries, and, in the case of Isaac Julien and

Marlon Riggs, feature length products. I think that there has yet to be a definable Black lesbian aesthetic, but it's emerging and I hope to be a part of its establishment, whether documentary or narrative, and hopefully feature length. Most of our work has been short form structured in a variety of genres. It has been animation, documentary, autobiographic, and AIDS media. AIDS media have been responsible, in a large measure, I think, for people getting access to information about AIDS and AIDS education. AIDS media have allowed a window for gay and lesbian imagery to get a toe-hold and open up the window. People are a little more willing to engage gay imagery when it comes to AIDS and health. It has also done a great deal to dispel the myth that it's only a gay epidemic. I think what you're going to see in the 1990s is a push toward Black lesbian imagery. It began in the late 1980s. Sisters got access to enough funding, certainly there was never a lack of ideas. Getting access to enough money to put those ideas on a screen is difficult. I think we've had a taste of a developing aesthetic through Isaac Julien's and Marlon Riggs's work, which has been exemplary. Their work has broken down barriers for all of us, lesbians or gay men. I think sisters have a unique take on the gay experience. I don't have a list of characteristics other than they bring homoerotic images of Black women together as opposed to the heterosexual vision of Black women that is objectified or more "politically correct." Black lesbian film/videomakers consider the dynamics of women loving and the fact that eroticism can be more than just sex. It is more than just sexual. Spectatorship, or the gaze of these kinds of references, had their theoretical basis in feminist film theory. However, it has moved far beyond a white reference, far beyond a patriarchal reference, far beyond a white feminist reference. It's moved far beyond those kinds of early definitions that people began to use as their stock and trade lexicon of how you talk about film. I think Black lesbian imagery and aesthetics are in process.

GJG: Are there other issues or concerns?

MP: Yes, formats. There's a natural bias—against, first of all, documentaries. They're not perceived as real movies. The only real movies are feature-length, blockbuster, epic narratives. Those are "movies" to most people—to your everyday audience, to those who are not cineastes, film scholars, or filmmakers. So when you are talking about sisters who have produced several programs but they're in video, or they're eight to thirty minutes in length, there's already a natural second-class status that's applied, which is also complicated by the fact the subject matter is lesbian or is Black. For example, one thing that helped put Julie Dash on the map in many people's minds was that she produced a feature-length film. Many people ignored her earlier work, the beauty of it, and the genius of her shorter pieces. It was when she did a feature-length film that she gained wider attention.

GJG: How are relations between Black gays and lesbians?

MP: Just because we're all gay and lesbian people doesn't mean that misogyny doesn't operate between gay men and women. It's very alive and well. Sexism is very alive and well. Moreover, the distributors of gay and lesbian media have primarily been white gay men, as well as many of the funders. We faced it with the Audre Lorde film project. And it's also how "Black" a film can be. I think the "Africanness" of our opinions and perhaps our imagery is off-putting and scares some of the funders.

GJG: I think the whole notion of racism within the gay community is a very important issue, and it's one that people don't necessarily think about.

MP: Julie Dash has a quote and I'm going to do a bad paraphrasing of it. When folks asked her about the difficulty of bringing *Daughters of the Dust* to theatrical release, she talked about the fact that people are willing to role play, to engage in what's going on in the screen. To play a yo' boy for two and a half hours and then know you're really a white man who is getting ready to jump into his Mercedes, you can live it vicariously. And she said, "Nobody wants to be a Black woman for even two and a half hours." So these are the barriers, further complicated by being a Black lesbian. What audiences will engage that? The complicity of these kinds of oppression is like a chain-link.

GJG: Let's talk about gay/lesbian films in the classroom. Students may be put off or offended by some of the images that they see in a film such as *She Don't Fade*. How does an instructor deal with that sort of resistance?

MP: I think that you show it and you find out why, and what it is, that is offensive. You try to understand why students don't want to see it, why they can't stand it. Which means that, of course, the class discussion leaps out of the realm of film studies and lands into areas of psychology and other political levels of discussion. But where better for it to happen than within a safe space. It's happening in the street in so many other kinds of destructive ways, with people being murdered or being called names. At least in a classroom it is a supposedly safe space, a forum, for this kind of discussion to be aired and for everyone's point of view at least to be heard. I think not to show gay/lesbian films is to further affirm, and by complicity to, in fact, endorse certain attitudes.

Of course, if it means your job, that's another consideration. I don't know how to weigh that. But if you're a filmmaker, you love risk anyway. You're not in this because it's a safe thing and there's a steady income. All of us are a little out and a little on the edge. We love the whip of wind as we step off a cliff, not knowing where we'll land—on a cushion or on the jagged rocks below.

GJG: Do you think homophobia is lessening in the Black community?

MP: No. I don't think it's lessening in any community. I think homosexuality is kind of the last frontier. I don't think racism is lessening either. It just takes on new permutations. The tragedy is that who you love can still certainly get you killed.

an

intimate talk

with

ntozake

shange

an intererview

p. j a n e   s p l a w n

Although she is most often known as the author of the award-winning play *for colored girls who have considered suicide/when the rainbow is enuf*, poet, playwright, and novelist Ntozake Shange (née Paulette Williams) has been one of the most prolific figures in contemporary African American and feminist literature. Her interests are wide-ranging and diverse; her political views global, often centering on issues affecting people of color throughout the world. Her work has been available in print for more than two decades and includes several major poetry collections: *nappy edges* (1978), *Bocas: A Daughter's Geography* (1983), and *The Love Space Demands* (1991), along with *Ridin' the Moon in Texas* (1987), a collection of poetry and prose. Her work in theater consists of *for colored girls* (1976), *A Photograph, Spell # 7*, and *Boogie Woogie Landscapes*, all contained in the collection *Three Pieces* (1981). Her novels include *Sassafrass, Cypress & Indigo* (1982), *Betsey Brown* (1985), and *Liliane: Resurrection of the Daughter* (1994). The number of Shange's nonpublished theater productions is vast, and the following are notable among them: an adaptation of Bertolt Brecht's *Mother Courage and Her Children* (1980), a play; *Three Views of Mt. Fuji* (1987); and *Nomathemba* (1995), a play written in collaboration with the South African a cappella group Ladysmith Black Mambazo. Despite her impressive vitae and the diverse political issues her work engages, Shange's role as a novelist, poet, and playwright has yet to receive the critical attention it deserves.

p. jane splawn

Shange's contribution to African American artistic production makes her an appropriate addition to this volume on Black women independent film- and videomakers. As she explains in this interview, the distinction between theater and film is not so definitive. Months after I spoke with Shange, she presented for the first time "Crack Annie," a performance piece later published as part of the piece "I Heard Eric Dolphy in His Eyes" in *The Love Space Demands: (A Continuing Saga)*, her latest volume of poetry. *The Love Space Demands* was subsequently transformed into a performance piece and has been presented at various theaters on the East Coast, notably Crossroads Theater in New Brunswick, New Jersey, and the Painted Bride Arts Center in Philadelphia. Additionally, at the time of this interview, Shange was also busy at work on her recently published novel *Liliane: Resurrection of the Daughter* (1994). In her discussion of her own creative process, Shange delineates the vital similarities in all facets of creative expression.

The shared connection between drama and film has for some time been noted, though it is not often examined in the literature. Many screenwriters nurtured their professional roots in writing for the theater. Lorraine Hansberry, Ed Bullins, Kathleen Collins, and Judi Ann Mason each wrote plays before they began writing for television and film. The organic connection between theater and film has perhaps been best expressed by Mason, an acclaimed writer for the television series *I'll Fly Away*, who explains that the camera eye of film allows the spectator a view that can be likened to the perspective of a peephole, while theater provides the audience with a full, panoramic view. Moreover, because theaters are largely dependent on public donations, grants, and endowments, many writers have been forced to write for television and for commercial cinema out of financial necessity. Indeed, a number of writers for mainstream cinema still consider themselves to be primarily playwrights though they may not have produced a work for the stage in years. Some playwright-filmmakers such as Kathleen Collins, for example, created highly artistic, independent films that might have been more difficult to finance as theater pieces.

In this interview, perhaps more so than in previously published interviews, Shange speaks candidly about her relationship to feminism and her position on gender and race. We discussed the creative process, feminism, and Third World issues during an extended dialogue at the author's former home in Houston, Texas, on October 30–31, 1987. The following is an edited, condensed version of that discussion.

the creative process

P. Jane Splawn: Tell me about your first poetry reading.

Ntozake Shange: It was at a fundraiser in 1968 and Pedro Pietre, who did the first Puerto Rican anthology of poetry for Doubleday, was the MC. Everybody else there were Latins, Black, and white. We were all Black people, but some of us were Latin, some were not. But you couldn't tell by looking at them; you had to wait until they opened their mouths. And it turned out that I was the last English-speaking person in the room, and I was also the only one who didn't read. So Pedro told me, "Go ahead and read. You can only talk what you know. And if they don't like it, fuck them. If they can't deal with you speaking English the hell with them." So I did it. But I got a lot of support from the Puerto Rican community. A lot. Not just Pedro, but from a lot of people. And not just because I was predisposed to it. I think it was also a point we could make. Which is to say that, when you look at us you can't tell what country we come from, so don't make any stupid mistakes.

PJS: Is it difficult for you to move from poetry to drama to novel? How do you decide which form is best suited for a particular character, idea, or theme?

NS: I used to think that the characters were the theme. In that way I didn't have to figure out whether a work would be a poem or a novel or what. The work would just come out the way it was supposed to come out. Initially it wasn't as scary for me to switch genres because I felt that I wasn't necessarily switching genres but, rather, that the material was presenting itself the way it was supposed to be presented. I also discovered that when I read short stories I read a lot of dialog. So I don't have to do a lot to a short story in order to make it into a piece for the theater because they have different purposes. Novels are explorations and short stories are much more like poems to me. By that I mean that when I write a poem, I am looking for an emotional reaction, whereas with novels or theater pieces there's more space to fool around with. Everything doesn't have to be pushing toward a function. There can be more allusive elements in novels. I can be more leisurely in a novel than I can afford to be on the stage.

PJS: Do you see connections between the genres music, poetry, and dance?

NS: There is a connection. I don't know how to make it make sense, but I love being a dancer. Being a dancer for me was like the ultimate activity in life because to reach people with simply the force of one's body is such a grand and lovely idea. Black people were valued for our physical labor—our bodies' labor during slavery—we were valued for our bodies when they were having the infant syndrome during the '20s. We were valued for our labor during the '30s when they were breaking unions with Black labor. Our bodies, our physical presence, has been a political ploy for the last four hundred years, if you include slavery. And yet we haven't taken advantage of that for ourselves. What was it about our bodies that made us so desirable? What was it that we could do that nobody else could get from themselves? When we ask those questions, we always end up with it's our culture. Our culture is what has made American music what American music is. It's what's made American dance what American dance is. And to a large extent, it's what has influenced the language spoken by Americans. And to me that's a very significant thing that we don't take credit for. And we should get it. We have determined how these people talk. They use all kinds of Black idiomatic expressions to express themselves, and I know as well as I'm standing here that they are not me. But they don't feel any kind of inhibition about appropriating my language to explain how they feel. And to me that means that we have won a lot of battles without even having been in any war . . . which I think is a war. I use the colloquialisms that I use on purpose because I have a right to deify the language of my people. This is where I come from. This is sacred to me. I don't care what white people think about it.

PJS: That comes across in your work.

NS: It does. I hope so because this is how we talk. I want to make it sound like the way we talk. And if you don't like it, then don't read it. Read something else. Because I can't do that for them; I can't give them something that they don't desire. And the only time I really feel vicious and nasty is when I know I'm playing intellectual games with white people, when I feel I am stealing back something they had no right to in the first place.

PJS: *Word Paintings*, the subtitle of *Ridin' the Moon in Texas*, seems a very appropriate phrase to describe your work since you're skillful at creating visual images, and your novels, plays, and poetry are very lyrical.

NS: Yes, I think that may be correct. Words are not just phenomenological constructs. They are like nourishment to me. They are real things. So that if you have rocks or skies or rodeo lassos you have to be able to feel the texture of the thing, in addition to presenting its dictionary meaning. The writer must be able to show the reader what a thing smells like and feels like. I respond to beautiful language the way some people respond to flowers. Words are like rhapsodies to me. And I like to approach language with a sort of dizzying and weightless experience in my writing because then I know that I've seduced the reader. That we're having our own affair.

PJS: Do you still feel that the material presents its own shape, or now, after all these years of writing are you more conscientious about form?

NS: Yes, I am. Now I decide that I'm going to write a novel or that I'm going to write a story. The different process has more to do with having a family. I don't have as much time as I used to, nor the privacy to explore ideas the way I'd like to. So I have to be more demanding of myself when I get a chance to work. I have to say, "This is what I'm going to do." I don't have as much time to discover. I'm going to try to change that this year by using my time more wisely.

PJS: It would seem that you would have to take advantage of any available moment to get your ideas down.

NS: Exactly. But that's a problem that women and minority writers have always had. Unless you just didn't have any children, and you didn't have a lover, then you could just do what you wanted. But even when Savannah [Shange's daughter] is not here—like when she's gone to school in the daytime—I'm still aware of her presence and I don't feel like I am alone. I used to have a lot of luxuries when I was younger. I had two whole floors just to myself (laughter). I could wander around and confront myself. I could confront myself at all hours of the day, but I can't do that anymore.

PJS: How important is it to confront yourself in the process of writing?

NS: I think writing is a very lonely career. It's also very primitive and that's one of the reasons why I used to dance so much because I would see people. If I didn't teach school and dance, I would never have seen anybody. There was nothing in my career that made it necessary for me to see anybody. I would just be here by myself day in and day out.

PJS: In *Momma*, Alta talks about the unique problems women writers have when they are confined to a limited space at home, a space that they share with their children who have to be fed, etc., so that finding time for creativity becomes a real challenge.

NS: Yes. Children have to eat every day. They have to have a normal life schedule. I can't just feed my daughter, and then decide that after 6:30, I don't have to talk to her anymore (laughter). It can be a draining experience in that sense. But it's equally important to me to keep it balanced so that I don't begin to resent my child. I think that's a real danger. I try to keep my relationship with her on the up-and-up so that it's rewarding for both of us. I don't feel that it's her fault. I had the baby; she did not have the mother. It's my responsibility that I gladly take. It just means that I have to rearrange some other things.

PJS: To what extent is *Betsey Brown* autobiographical?

NS: To the extent that it allowed me to fix things that weren't fixed for me in my childhood. I gave myself a lot of things in *Betsey Brown* that I didn't get—a lot of emotional things that didn't happen. So I relived *Betsey Brown* in a way, fixing for myself things that I would have liked to have had.

PJS: Is there a connection between magic and writing?

NS: Writing is submission to real impulses that might be overlooked if you suppress them. The thing that is most dangerous for me as a writer is that I can't resist any impulses that I have. So then for me, if I'm really trying to be honest in what I write, then the magic in that is I really can't allow anything any other human being has ever said to me to deter me from acknowledging the feelings that I'm having. And I think that magic, for the most part, is manifested for us in moments of fervor and abandonment to joy or fear, to incidents where it doesn't matter what anybody thinks about us. And that's what writing is for me. It's when it doesn't matter what they think I'm writing. What matters is that I could get it on paper. That I was free enough at that point in time to expose all this. Because that's what it is. Exposure is revelation. And revelation itself is magic. And when these things get revealed to you, one becomes vulnerable. And the only unfortunate thing about being vulnerable in the twentieth century is that it's looked upon as a weakness. As if you haven't taken control of your world; you have succumbed to it. However, I think that strength is revealed by the ability to be vulnerable and still be able to go back and be vulnerable again and make some more decisions. It's not the lack of vulnerability that makes us strong; it's the willingness to sustain it.

ii. feminism

PJS: How do you see women of color's role in the feminist movement? Is womanism—and/or even "Black feminism"—a more appropriate way to approach Black women's experiences?

NS: I can't make a distinction, and this does not make me very popular. I know we all have to look at our specific worlds and design a strategy that helps us in our specific situations. But I don't particularly hold that women of color have to have some separate feminism. That doesn't make any sense to me. If there's a women's culture, then that's what it is. It's not a Black women's culture or a white women's culture and a Latina women's culture. There's women's culture and then in our own ethnic groups we have particular ways of manifesting this. I don't think the feminist movement can afford to be so divided. Also I think of my womanness as primary. I don't go out in the street and get mugged because I'm Black; I get mugged because I'm a woman. I take my femaleness as a primary priority, then we'll talk about being a Black person.

PJS: But in Cypress's dream segment in *Sassafrass, Cypress & Indigo* there does seem to be a warning against women of color blindly joining white feminist movements. Were you making a statement about the need for the feminist movement to include issues that affect women of color?

NS: I think so, but I think that's being done. That part of *Sassafrass, Cypress & Indigo* was written, what . . . ten years ago? Nine or ten years ago? But there's a really substantial movement that has been taking place in women's perceptions of one another. What I was getting at then is that we will be victims, and we will continue to be victims until we take some responsibility for ourselves. I resent women of color telling me that feminism is for white women when we rely on feminists to make sure that abortion laws are enforced, and that there are safe houses and shelters, and that there are crisis centers for us to use. And I don't understand how we can take advantage of something and share in facilities offered to us by other women without our being on the front line of this movement as well. And that's why I like June Jordan's and Ai's work so much because neither of them has ever suggested that they were not going to be responsible for themselves nor that there wasn't a fighting woman in them. That's what I was trying to get at in that section. Somebody is always going to take advantage of you if you allow them to do it. And the only way you can have control of yourself and influence what is going to happen to you is by putting your neck on the line. Not by waiting for somebody else to do it. Not by saying you have other priorities. It doesn't make sense to me for a woman of color who has been battered and needs a place to stay to decide she can't go to the shelter because it's run by white women. Also most women who are in the prisons are Black and Latin women. Who's going to help them? If we as Black people say that the jails were full of political prisoners during the Black Power Movement, what do we call women in prison right now? Aren't they political prisoners? Isn't that what they are? The

195

women who have really been screwed around by the patriarchy—
prostitutes, women who write bad checks because they don't get child
support—are our political prisoners in terms of what sexism has done
to our families and to our sisters. So, I believe in activism. The Kitchen
Table Press is a Black lesbian press. I'm very excited about them being in
existence. I want them to do that. But that means to me that that was a
perfectly reasonable way to say, "OK, I'm not represented in the correct
way by women's presses because I'm Black and lesbian; therefore, I
need my own." Great, that's the ultimate conclusion of your oppression. In order to stop oppression, you must do something about it
yourself. If you have women who are finding that their needs aren't
being met by a feminist community, then they have to create institutions that will meet them for themselves. But that's not white women
doing anything to us, that's our responsibility.

PJS: What impact did *Caught Looking*[1] have on you?

NS: I used to belong to Women Against Pornography and to Women
Against Violence Against Women and Children. I have very strong
feelings about pornography. I think it objectifies women and contributes to the humiliation and the oppression of women. On the
other hand, I was also disturbed by the kinds of alliances feminists were
making with evangelicals and conservatives to defeat pornography.
The alliances they were making were with the same people who were
against abortion. The same people who were antibusing. And these
were strange, uncomfortable alliances for me. One of the points in
Caught Looking is that there has to be a possibility of eroticism without
the possibility of misogyny. The editors had documented 100 years of
what they had considered to be erotic art by various men and women,
and there were ten scholarly articles examining the antipornography
movement. And I thought it was an unique concept because there
were absolutely titillating images throughout the collection (laughter), and yet there were arguments for preserving the rights for the
dignity of women. And I felt that that was a real breakthrough because
I am antipornography, but I'm not anti–First Amendment. I think the
other thing is that true erotic art isn't designed so that one person is
the victim and the other is the master. I think what makes erotic art
more challenging is that it's two people out of control; it's not just that
one is out of control and the other isn't.

PJS: What comes across well in *Sassafrass, Cypress & Indigo*, in that there is
much emphasis on African retentions in the Americas.

NS: For me there's a difference between having William Styron doing Nat
Turner and having in *Sassafrass* people who are the ghost slaves.

William Styron comes to Nat Turner as an outsider and there's something that marks that work for me as exploitation. I can't find the same kind of discrepancy, the same kind of intellectual rape, when I'm involved in digging through my own past and my own past lives and the cultures of neighboring peoples who share with me the denial of our reality. So that if we don't do it for ourselves correctly then, our cultures are stolen from us. Even when Alice Adams wrote *Thinking of Billie*, she took our greatest blues singer, our greatest jazz singer, and made her a leitmotif in a novel about white women. This is not to say that they shouldn't be able to engage these historical figures. But we should be very aware that it's different. It's not the same thing as what Alice Walker would do with Billie Holiday. It's a totally different relationship.

PJS: Why is it important to have a woman spirit—particularly Billie Holiday—come to Sassafrass's aid in *Sassafrass, Cypress & Indigo*?

NS: When Billie Holiday comes to see her, I think it's the spirit of women who have a little more self-confidence and determination than Sassafrass has at that time. They offer to share that with her. She will have the capacity later on in the novel—when Mamie Smith comes to her, for instance—to bring that out of herself.

There is an army of women's spirits who will come to your assistance when you're in a time of need. I think that's what I was trying to get at more as opposed to perennially calling on Jesus. You can call on other women or the memories of other women, or what they've done in their lifetimes. A few years ago I started collecting Virgin Marys because, of all the people in the history of the world, she's the one who gave people their savior. So if anyone could interdict for you, she should be it (laughter). Savannah and I have all these Virgin Mary statues in my house. And of Ogun. So Savannah knows that if you want something and it's not exactly something you want everybody in the world to know about, you can go talk to one of these female statues who embody the spirit of women who have great power. And I think that's an important thing for girls to have. They need to know that they can get things from other women who are not necessarily their mothers. You don't have to get things from men all the time—from the male patriarchal deity, or from the male patriarch himself—you can bypass them.

PJS: How important is being in touch with our spiritual selves?

NS: Adrienne Rich talks about the wild unmothered daughter. And I think that one way to assuage the wild unmothered daughter is by offering her spiritual guidance and gifts from other females because

197

that's where you get nurturance from. So all these stories that grand-mother used to tell us, and aunties used to tell us, or our mothers used to tell us are in some way taking the place of the kind of advice we might get from women if it weren't for the domination of the patri-archy. There is a kind of surreptitious way to heal wounds that are often unavoidable.

I chose the women who appear before Sassafrass very purposefully because I didn't want her to be a woman who had had no experience. I didn't want her to be a woman who had been given a "triple A" rating by the patriarchy. I wanted her to be a woman that men would hold in disdain or with contempt because they were not making the virgin and the whore separations. So I deliberately picked women who might have tainted reputations. Because what is a tainted reputation except the real oppression of the patriarchy? Women are called sluts and trol-lops and all those words that are used to define women's relationships to men. These words are used to define and immobilize us. I wanted those women to come along and be the freeing forces in the story because I think it's important to keep track of who we respect and why we respect them. This helps us to understand whether we're doing the most healthy thing for ourselves.

PJS: What is the significance of the sexually assertive women in your work?

NS: I think women need to be able to say what it is they want. I think that unless women are allowed to say what it is they want, then we really are objects in the sexual act. We're not getting anything ourselves, we're just giving things. So it's important that they have a sexual per-sonality. That they have something very specific that they're trying to get to. And as a human being it's important, because ecstacy has to be something that you know about. In order to know what ordinary is you also have to know what ecstacy is. We have a right to that. Yet when we talk about women who are in ecstacy, we're never talking about women we respect. And I think we need to talk about women we respect. We need to be able to use the same words for women we respect when we say worldly. He's a very worldly man, that means he's experienced in savoir-faire. If we say she's a worldly woman, that often implies that she's some sort of jackass.

PJS: Many of the women characters you create are in the process of self-actualization, especially so at the beginning of the work. What do you think a fully self-actualized woman would be like?

NS: I know some women who are self-actualized. They are productive, loving, warm, very strong, and very articulate. They're able to function without necessarily having lovers or without having children. They're not into thinking of themselves as failures or successes because they have children, or they don't have children. They have a husband, or they don't have a husband. Their self-love comes from their interaction with the planet and with their work. Yes, I do know some.

PJS: Strong spiritually, intellectually, and sexually?

NS: Yes, but intellectually, we have to be careful that the way we devise feminist scholarship is done in a way that is as threatening as feminism is. We have to question all the rules. Every single rule that can contribute to our misunderstanding of ourselves has got to be questioned. Academic scholarship and methodological strategies have been used against us. Then we have to question using those same rules on ourselves and our own stories, which is not to say that we throw everything out, but I do think that women like Shere Hite, who devise new methodologies, are very courageous because that is exactly what we have to do. We're talking about things that haven't been talked about before because there was no language for them, and because the standards that they're being set up against are designed to destroy those things. It's very important that we set up whole new methodologies and new texts, and new mythologies as well because that's what we've got to do.

PJS: Does it bother you that some critics only focus on one aspect of your work, without delving fully into what you have to say?

NS: Yes. I know I'm not a racist because I have a lot of friends who are not Black. They never have been, and they never will be. And I think that's part of what's missing with the feminist movement in terms of trying to get us to be women together, as opposed to white women and Black women and Asian women and Native American women. I know we all have different things we have to try to clarify. Native American women have reservations and all those laws. That's a whole different thing from what I have to deal with. But they have to figure that out. I can't figure that out for them. They have to do that.

PJS: Just as women who live in societies where clitorectomies, etc., are performed have to handle that themselves?

NS: Exactly. They have to do that. I can write pieces about it and make it sound as terrible as I think it is, but it's only going to be the women who live there who can actually make a change. I can't make a change. And that's why I think we all have a specific kind of power. And coming to terms with the powers that we have is what's going to make us be successful or not successful.

PJS: An anthropologist like Maria Cutrufelli would argue that the purpose of African initiation rites is to make pubescent girls ready for sexuality.[2]

NS: Yes, but they had no clitorises left, nothing. It's as bizarre as hanging a sheet outside with blood on it. That's crazy. Every virgin does not bleed. You don't have to bleed to be a virgin. Yet there were women who were castigated for years because they didn't have blood on their sheets! And that to me is bizarre.

I really feel very strongly that my primary oppression has been as a female person; it has not been as a Black person. And I don't like that. And I would like to say that all my life I've worked for the Black people, and I want the Black people to survive and sustain themselves, which is true. But I sure would like to work for my rights as a woman too as opposed to [for] some Black male who I can't be. I get tired of that. I get tired of being asked to support the entire culture, because who will support me?

A clitorectomy is major surgery that is related to the defamation of women's sexuality. That's why I chose the so-called slovenly women to be the heroines in my books because I want those women to get the recognition that they deserve. They were determined that they were going to defy everything that was against them to be who they were. And if they were sluts, they were sluts. But what does it mean to be a slut? Does it mean that you have slept with the man you want? How can that be a crime? What's wrong about that? A man has you because you wanted to have him? What's wrong with that? Nothing's wrong with that. But we have been so bashed in the head and in the spirit by men's definitions of appropriate and inappropriate behavior that a lot of times we deny ourselves a lot of things that might even be good for us. There's nothing wrong with living out a healthy sexual appetite. If that healthy sexual appetite has to do with several men, that does not make you a slut. It makes you a healthy woman. And yet if we deal with the way they record history, these women are labeled "sluts." So then it becomes very important to decide how you read history—how you perceive yourself. You cannot accept definitions from the other; they don't know about us. They are trying to destroy us. They do not want us to survive as we are. They want us to be who they want us to be and not who we are. And it's very dangerous.

I've got to figure out a way for myself to help my daughter make these distinctions so that she doesn't get caught up in their definitions of realities that don't make sense. And I don't know how to do that yet, but I'm going to try very hard to figure that out. If I owe her anything at all, I owe her a life that is not marked for death before she's had a chance to live it. She has a right to live her life, and she has a right to feel the things she wants to feel. And these men can't take that away from her by curbing her own healthy sexual desires. We sell what we've got because we've got nothing else to sell. And if all we are valued for is for having vaginas, that makes it a very low bottom market, because half the people in the world have vaginas. So that doesn't make a lot of sense to me. It's very sad to me. And it makes my life harder. It's a big problem.

third world connections

PJS: What does it mean to be a person of color in the world right now?

NS: The best thing about being a person of color in the world right now is having the opportunity to be a kind of archaeologist. I have the opportunity to draw upon mythologies that have been suppressed and make them come alive in contemporary literature and theater. It means having a stunning sort of reunion with our past, because if I step aside from western civilization—because there is nothing there for me . . . nothing I can use that would validate or make legitimate my experiences—then I would have opened up all the resources. One hundred years of all the skills and crafts of all the people of color that went into the making of American and African mythologies and deities. That's why it was so important in my development that I studied Afro-American dance, and Cuban dance, and Brazilian dance, and Hindu dance—as opposed to solely ballet and modern dance—because the movements and the inclinations of an African American dancer are much more related to jazz than they are to classical music. There are parallels and similarities in all these art forms that reinforce a sense of otherness that is not an alienating otherness.

PJS: Is there a dialectical exchange between yourself and other Third World writers in your work?

NS: Yes. Ishmael Reed is doing that right now. He's working on this piece that includes working-class white people, Native Americans, Afro-Americans, Asian Americans, and Latin Americans. I think that's an important community. It's particularly important for us as we approach the year 2000 because by then two-thirds of the state of California will be people of color. This means that we are going to have the opportunity to dominate culture in some places. In some parts of Manhattan you can feel that already. Because of that, we don't want to repeat the processes we've been through before. We don't want to experience imperialism. We don't want to practice exploitation. The only way we can avoid these things is to share with one another. That's why it's so important to communicate with all writers of color, not just the ones that are English-speaking or who are writing about the South, because we don't want to have cultural hegemony by default. We should pursue this goal actively. We should be able to teach one another's works without having a special course title saying, "Latin American Writers" or "African American Writers." We need to approach a period of time when, if we are going read contemporary literature, we will automatically find those texts there. I think connecting with other Third World writers is important.

There are revolutionary movements going on in other parts of the hemisphere and in other parts of the world that we should be relating to because, "there but for the grace of God go we." We need to be much more knowledgeable about South African literature and South African music and dance and about Nicaraguan literature and El Salvadorian literature. I know when I was at the International Black Book Conference this past year in London, it was the most invigorating and heady experience because there were Black and Latin authors from all over the world, and we could talk to each other. The thing that was so exciting is that we were all struggling with the same issues even though some of us were in exile, some of us were American nationals and some were Puerto Rican, some of us were from Honduras, some from Guatemala, some were from Nigeria, and yet all of us had things to say to one another that were enlightening about our own experiences. I think that it is very important for us to be bilingual or trilingual because I think that's how white society controls us by isolating us from other people of color because we don't speak the language. And so it's very important to see another Black person and not see a foreigner, but instead to see a compatriate.

The thing I really try to work on in most of my work—not in everything—is to try to make sure that we don't forget that there are other Black people who have legitimate concerns that are very much like ours. And we will be a stronger people, a politically more effective people, the more we take advantage of natural alliances we have with other independent people of color. We should be a much more powerful lobby against apartheid. If we took being Black seriously, we would be. If we took it seriously in an international sense, we'd have much more impact on American policies in South Africa, and Angola, and Mozambique.

PJS: Who are some of the Latin American authors who have influenced your work?

NS: Neruda, Asturias, Carpentier, Cabrera Infante, and Lydia Fagundes Telles. I think what is amazing about Latin American writers is that they are also able to be involved as officials and diplomats, with international relationships. One of the things I think Black and Latin people here have a terrible problem with is being able to have opinions that supersede white English-speaking politics. In other words, whites get very upset with Jesse Jackson when he gets involved with foreign affairs. When he talks about poverty and minimum wage, and about Black people who are poor and English speaking in the United States, that's fine. But no Black and Latin people can say anything that has international implications. But in Latin American countries and in the French-speaking Caribbean, for instance, in Martinique, Aime Cesaire and Leon Damas were poets who were also diplomats. So were Neruda and Carpentier. Carpentier was Mexico's Ambassador to France, and Asturias was an Ambassador. There are precedents outside the English-speaking world for people of color who have international status. That for me is very important because we don't live here just with white people. We live with all the people. All people aren't white and English-speaking.

PJS: Your work also emphasizes connections between an individual and her ancestors. What do you think homage to one's ancestors entails?

NS: Well, you don't have to go back as far as to our ancestors. When I think of all the struggles that Black people in my own family endured, I recognize that I can't be less than they were. I think I'm just trying to plod ahead and follow the thoughts my grandfather had and my grandmother had, and just follow through the ideas very simple people had. I can't work any less than they did, or it would make them look foolish for having struggled to be free, or to put meat on the table, or to change the Jim Crow laws. Their bloodshed and all the lynchings become unsubstantial if we don't take up the struggle ourselves. And I think that there is a lot of contempt for racism now because it's unfashionable. But what's unfashionable is that you admit that racism is unfashionable. In other words, you can be Black as long as you don't act Black. But if you want to wear corn-rows, or a nose-ring, or if you listen to John Coltrane or the Art Ensemble of Chicago, then you're being too colored and too threatening to get a job at IBM.

I think before the Civil Rights Movement there was this idea in white peoples' heads. It is an image of Black people that Tom Wolfe described as the scariest thing in the world for white people is to be out at night and see a Black youth with sneakers on. That terrifies them. Today I think what terrifies white people is the force of our culture. That's why I was so incensed when they put the signs up on the subway that say you can't listen to boomboxes on the subway. White people found our music offensive. So now it's against the law to play music in the street. And that to me is really insidious. And those are the kinds of things we have to watch. Those are the kinds of reasons

203

why we really have to make an effort to keep our culture alive. We can do that by having historical research. We can do that by re-invigorating old customs and mythologies, and we can also do that by continuing to create because part of the dynamic of the art of people of color is that the art was not meant to be saved. It was meant to be used and to make one's life function in a smoother and more beautiful way. So we still have an art that is expendable, but it's expendable because we are continually creating. We're continually in process.

PJS: Do you think the converse can also be true, that some white people are only interested in Black people who wear rasta braids and kente cloth?

NS: Yes, they're looking for the old "noble savage" syndrome. Here is the noble savage aspect of it: I've been working on a biography of Josephine Baker, and one of the things I've been amazed by is that when she first moved to Paris at nineteen and did the famous banana dance, all the reviews of the show went on and on about this beautiful native creature who had all this African animalism and energy! Josephine Baker is from a major American midwestern city. She knew about as much about Africa as an Abidjan trader in Alaska. But they perceived her that way in order to make her innocent, gentle, and exotic. They exoticized a midwestern dance-hall girl into a kind of African goddess. That was solely a European need, not something Josephine Baker invented. She couldn't believe some of the things that white people thought about her because they were so unlike her true reality.

PJS: Why do you think white people like your work?

NS: All species have the instinct for survival. I think when they look at our writing, they see us as something that is impossible. I couldn't have happened. How can they have thought these thoughts? And that I think is really disgraceful for the American intelligentsia.

PJS: What is your vision of a pedagogy for Afro-American studies?

NS: We have to change the methodology of investigating our past. The methodology has to be changed from the perspective of the owners down to the perspectives of the people who were once owned. We need to tell our side of history, not their side of history. What history looks like to us. And I don't think it's the same thing at all. One of the reasons I had to leave the university was that I was tired of apologizing for myself. I just got to where I couldn't do it anymore. I would have people coming up to me saying, "I have a poem by a Black writer about a stairwell." And I'd say, "Yeah, 'life for me ain't been no crystal stair.'"[3]

And they'd say, "Yeah, how'd you know that." And I'd say, "Because I was raised on it, that's why I know it." I was so infuriated at that point that I could know all the significant myths and leitmotifs of western civilization and they could lightly mention someone who was amazing for all the Black people as though their finding him was some sort of happenstance. I was furious about that. And yet we would call them the most liberal people of the United States. It was denigrating to me; it humiliated me, so I left.

PJS: Is it a problem when critics tend to want to look at you categorically as Ntozake Shange, Black woman writer?

NS: Yes. I've always felt that I was a part of a movement of people. I wasn't doing this by myself; this is not my personal crusade. I'm not going to be made empress of the United States when I finish my life. What I would like to have happen is to have a truly pluralistic, integrated society that I can leave to my daughter. That's what I'd like to be fighting for. I don't know that we can do that. I'm not even sure that literature is the way to start. But it's all I can do, so I've got to do what I can.

notes

1. Kate Ellis, Nan D. Hunter, Beth Jaker, Barbara O'Dair and Abby Tallmer, eds., *Caught Looking: Feminism Pornography & Censorship* (New York: Caught Looking, Inc., 1986).
2. Maria Rosa Cutrufelli, *Women of Africa: Roots of Oppression* (London, Zed Press, 1986).
3. Langston Hughes, "Mother to Son," *Selected Poems of Langston Hughes* (New York: Vintage, 1974), 187.

selected bibliography

works by the author

Fiction

Betsey Brown. New York: St. Martin's Press, 1985.
Liliane: Resurrection of the Daughter. New York: St. Martin's Press, 1994.
Sassafrass, Cypress & Indigo. New York: St. Martin's Press, 1982.

Theater   205

"Daddy Says." In *New Plays for the Black Theatre*, ed. Woodie King Jr. Chicago: Third World Press, 1989.
for colored girls who have considered suicide/when the rainbow is enuf. New York, Macmillan, 1976.
Liliane in Moon Marked & Touched by Sun. Ed. Sydne Mahone. New York: Theatre Communications Group, 1994.
Three Pieces: Spell # 7, A Photograph: Lovers in Motion; Boogie Woogie Landscapes. New York: St. Martin's Press, 1981.

POETRY

A Daughter's Geography. New York: St. Martin's Press, 1983.
nappy edges. New York: St. Martin's Press, 1978.
Ridin' the Moon in Texas. New York: St. Martin's Press, 1987.
The Love Space Demands. New York: St. Martin's Press, 1991.

critical studies

BOOKS

Lester, Neal A. *Ntozake Shange: A Critical Study of the Plays*. New York: Garland Press, 1995.

ARTICLES

Flowers, Sandra Hollin. "Colored Girls: Textbook for the Eighties." *Black American Literature Forum* 15: 2 (1981): 51—54.

Geis, Deborah R. "Distraught Laughter: Monologue in Ntozake Shange's Theater Pieces." In Enoch Brater, ed., *Feminine Focus: The New Women Playwrights*. New York: Oxford University Press, 1989.

Richards, Sandra. "Conflicting Impulses in the Plays of Ntozake Shange." *Black American Literature Forum* 17: 2 (1983): 73—78.

Timpane, John. "'The Poetry of a Moment': Politics and the Open Form in the Drama of Ntozake Shange." In June Schlueter, ed. *Modern-American Drama: The Female Canon*. Rutherford, NJ: Farleigh Dickinson University Press, 1990.

INTERVIEWS

Blackwell, Henry. "An Interview with Ntozake Shange." *Black American Literature Forum* 13 (1979): 134—38.

Brown, Edward K., II. "Ntozake Shange: An Interview by Edward K. Brown, II." *Poets & Writers* 2421: 3 (May/June 1993): 38—47.

Lester, Neal A. "An Interview with Ntozake Shange," *Studies in American Drama, 1945—Present* 5 (1990): 42—66.

DISSERTATIONS

Lester, Neal A. "Ntozake Shange's Development of the Choreopoem." Dissertation, Vanderbilt University, 1987.

Splawn, P. Jane. "Rites of Passage in the Writing of Ntozake Shange: The Poetry, Drama, and Novels." Dissertation, University of Wisconsin, 1988.

Judi Ann Mason. Dialogue with Audience. Ohio State University, Conference on Images of Race in the American Theater, May 1, 1993.

p. jane splawn

suggested

course

design

black women film

and video artists

jacqueline bobo

The course can be taught either on the quarter or semester system. Three meetings per week, two for lectures and one for screening films/videos, are the general pattern for film studies courses. These suggested materials can also be used effectively in courses not designed exclusively around Black women's films/videos. Portions can be extrapolated for use as part of course material for classes in Black studies, women's studies, literature, sociology, history, as well as film and media courses devoted to other topics. Many of the films, especially the shorter ones, can be shown during the class meetings, rather than in a separate showing as is usually done for film studies. The readings have been selected to complement the films and to provide sufficient background about the specific subject and/or about the filmmaker, the works' production history, critical reception, and audience responses.

The film/videography has been included in this volume to assist faculty in placing the works within the structure of the class. When it is available, full descriptions about format, length, and whether it is in color or black and white are given. Information is also provided about where to locate the films/videos, with distributors' addresses and telephone numbers listed.

course overview

Black women filmmakers have been active since the early part of this century. Currently, there are scores of Black women who consistently produce film and video products as well as commercial television programs. Films made by Black women are constructed in a variety of forms, such as animation, documentary, experimental, and narrative. The women also bring a unique perspective to the stories they choose to record. This course will give students an opportunity to view the films, examine the specifics of film/video production in general, compare the various works produced by Black women, and acquire the skills necessary for film/video and cultural criticism. The requirements for the course will be to view the films, complete the assigned readings, write short analysis papers, as well as complete a longer research/analytical project, and take a final exam.

required readings

Jacqueline Bobo, ed. *Black Women Film and Video Artists* (New York: Routledge, 1998).

Timothy Corrigan. *A Short Guide to Writing About Film.* 2d ed. (Glenview, Illinois: Scott, Foresman and Co., 1994). This book is helpful for those trained in film analysis and also for those who are not. It gives a basic understanding of films, is well written, and is easy to comprehend for those who are unfamiliar with film criticism.

Course reading packet (usually available at the university copy center, or the readings can be placed on reserve at the university library).

assignments

Reaction paper: This can be just a brief (two pages) paper that students write about their reactions to the course material. The assignment is useful as many of the students, including those who are film and television majors, are usually unfamiliar with the works of Black women film/videomakers. The reaction papers (or sometimes students are asked to keep a journal of the films viewed) aid students to recall the works over the duration of the course. It will assist them in writing the longer analysis projects.

Textual analysis paper: After the students have read the book by Timothy Corrigan they should have a general understanding of the rudimentary elements of film/video criticism. Film concepts are explained and relevant examples are given by the author, illustrating elements such as mise-en-scène, editing, the function of sound, narrative, character, and point of view.

This assignment should be a brief paper (three to five pages) that concentrates on the specific elements involved in film/video creation and criticism. The purpose of the assignment is to broaden students' capacities for critical engagement with a range of cultural forms, thus incorporating film analysis into their repertoire, along with literature and other disciplines. It introduces them to the specific language of film analysis and prods them toward watching films critically, rather than simply for entertainment. The assignment should be due about the middle of the term for courses conducted on the quarter system, or about five to six weeks into the term for those on the semester system.

Research paper: An academic paper eight–ten pages in length, with standard notes and bibliography, is recommended because it gives students an opportunity to learn how to do research in film and video. Students can become familiar with the sources and reference materials in film and television. Students should also be able to use the readings in the required course packet, because the specific topic of Black women filmmakers has not been explored a great deal in traditional academic research.

If at all possible, the films and videos should be available for students to review the works several times outside of class. If the university has a media center, the films/videos can be housed there so students can schedule their viewings through the media center.

Exams: Some form of examination, either in the middle or at the end of the term, can be required. This depends on the discretion of the instructor. For exams and analysis papers, it is useful to point out the parts of the films and videos of which students should take careful note. This can usually be done in lectures or discussion sections, either as a preview of the programs or through discussing the works in depth with the class.

course schedule

Week 1

SCREENINGS

I Am Somebody (1970) by Madeline Anderson.

A Minor Altercation (1977) by Jacqueline Shearer.

Valerie: A Woman, An Artist, A Philosophy of Life (1975); *A Sense of Pride: Hamilton Heights in Harlem* (1977); *Learning through the Arts: The Children's Art Carnival* (1979); all by Monica Freeman.

READINGS

Jacqueline Bobo, "Black Women's Films: Genesis of a Tradition," Chapter 1 in *Black Women Film and Video Artists.*

Spencer Moon, "Behind the Scenes: A Pioneer in Public Television," *Black Film Review* 6: 4 (1991): 27–28 (on Madeline Anderson).

J. H. O'Dell, "Charleston's Legacy to the Poor People's Campaign," *Freedomways*, Third Qtr. (Summer 1969): 197–221.

Jacqueline Bobo, "Conclusion," in *Black Women as Cultural Readers* (New York: Columbia University Press, 1995), 197–205.

Timothy Corrigan, "Writing About the Movies," Chapter 1 in *Writing About Films.*

Week 2

SCREENINGS

Fundi: The Story of Ella Baker (1981) by Joanne Grant.
Gotta Make This Journey: Sweet Honey in the Rock (1983) by Michelle Parkerson.

READINGS

Carol Mueller, "Ella Baker and the Origins of 'Participatory Democracy'," in Vicki L. Crawford et al., eds., *Women in the Civil Rights Movement: Trailblazers and Torchbearers 1941–1965* (Bloomington: Indiana University Press, 1993), 51–70.

Ella Baker, "Developing Community Leadership," in Gerda Lerner, ed., *Black Women in White America: A Documentary History* (New York: Vintage, 1973): 345–52.

Bernice Johnson Reagon, "Let Your Light Shine: Historical Notes," in Bernice Johnson Reagon et al., eds., *We Who Believe in Freedom: Sweet Honey in the Rock . . . Still on the Journey* (New York: Anchor Books, 1993), 13–69.

Timothy Corrigan, "Preparing to Watch and Preparing to Write," Chapter 2 in *Writing About Film.*

Week 3

SCREENINGS

The Cruz Brothers and Miss Malloy (1980); *Losing Ground* (1982); both by Kathleen Collins.

READINGS

Oliver Franklin, "An Interview: Kathleen Collins," in *Independent Black American Cinema* (conference program brochure published by Third World Newsreel, February 1981), 22–24.

David Nicholson, "A Commitment to Writing: A Conversation with Kathleen Collins Prettyman," *Black Film Review* 5: 1 (Winter 1988/1989): 6–15.

Gloria J. Gibson-Hudson, "Aspects of Black Feminist Cultural Ideology in Films by Black Women Independent Artists," in Diane Carson et al., eds., *Multiple Voices in Feminist Film Criticism* (Minneapolis: University of Minnesota Press, 1994), 380–90.

Timothy Corrigan, "Film Terms and Topics," Chapter 3 in *Writing About Film*.

Week 4

Sports Profile (featuring the first Black woman Olympic Gold Medal Winner Alice Coachman) (1981); *The Days When the Animals Talked* (1982); both by Carol Munday Lawrence.

Dreadlocks and the Three Bears (1991) by Alile Sharon Larkin.

Readings

Carol Munday Lawrence, "Carol Munday Lawrence: Producer, Director, Writer," Chapter 5 in *Black Women Film and Video Artists*.

Barbara Christian, "The Race for Theory," *Feminist Studies* 14: 1 (Spring 1989): 67–79.

Michele Wallace, "Negative Images: Towards a Black Feminist Cultural Criticism," in Lawrence Grossberg et al., eds., *Cultural Studies* (New York: Routledge, 1992): 654–71.

Timothy Corrigan, "Six Approaches to Writing About Film," Chapter 4 in *Writing About Film*.

Week 5

Screenings

Varnette's World: A Study of a Young Artist (1979); *Conversations with Roy Decarava* (1983); *Smithsonian World: "Nigerian Art—Kindred Spirits"* (1990); all by Carroll Parrott Blue.

Readings

Ntongela Masilela, "Women Directors of the Los Angeles School" Chapter 2 in *Black Women Film and Video Artists*.

Gloria J. Gibson-Hudson, "The Ties That Bind: Cinematic Representations by Black Women Filmmakers," Chapter 3 in *Black Women Film and Video Artists*.

Timothy Corrigan, "Researching the Movies," Chapter 6 in *Writing About Film*.

Week 6

Screenings

Your Children Come Back to You (1979); *A Different Image* (1982); both by Alile Sharon Larkin.

Alile Sharon Larkin, "Black Women Filmmakers Defining Ourselves: Feminism in Our Own Voice," in E. Deidre Pribram, ed., *Female Spectators Looking at Film and Television* (New York: Verso, 1988), 157–73.

Kwasi Harris, "New Images: An Interview with Julie Dash and Alile Sharon Larkin," *Independent* (December 1986): 16–20.

Pearl Bowser, "Sexual Imagery and the Black Woman in American Cinema," in Gladstone L. Yearwood, ed., *Black Cinema Aesthetics: Issues in Black Independent Filmmaking* (Athens, OH: Ohio University Center for Afro-American Studies, 1982), 42–51.

Edward Mapp, "Black Women in Films: A Mixed Bag of Tricks," in Lindsay Patterson, ed., *Black Films and Filmmakers: A Comprehensive Anthology from Stereotype to Superhero* (New York: Dodd, Mead & Co, 1975), 196–205.

Felly Nkweto Simmonds, "*She's Gotta Have It*: The Representation of Black Female Sexuality in Film," *Feminist Review* 29 (Spring 1988): 10–29.

Week 7

SCREENINGS

Cinematic Jazz of Julie Dash (1992) by Yvonne Welbon.
Four Women (1975); *Illusions* (1983); and *Praise House* (1991); all by Julie Dash.

READINGS

Valerie Smith, "Julie Dash: Filmmaker," in James V. Hatch et al, eds., *Artists and Influence 1990*, vol. 9 (New York: Hatch–Billops Collection, 1990), 27–35.

S.V. Hartman and Farah Jasmine Griffin, "Are You as Colored as That Negro?: The Politics of Being Seen in Julie Dash's *Illusions*," *Black American Literature Forum* 25: 2 (Summer 1991): 361–73.

Gloria J. Gibson-Hudson, "African American Literary Criticism as a Model for the Analysis of Films by African American Women," *Wide Angle* 13: 3, 4 (July–October 1991): 44–54.

Week 8

SCREENING

Daughters of the Dust (1991) by Julie Dash.

212

READINGS

Jacqueline Bobo, "*Daughters of the Dust*" and "Black Women Reading *Daughters of the Dust*," Chapters 4 and 5 in Bobo, *Black Women as Cultural Readers* (New York: Columbia University Press, 1995), 133–96.

Zeinabu irene Davis, "*Daughters of the Dust*," *Black Film Review* 6: 1, 12–17, 20–21.

Screenings

The Massachusetts 54th Colored Infantry (1991) by Jacqueline Shearer.
Mother of the River (1995) by Zeinabu irene Davis.

Readings

Jacqueline Shearer, "How Deep, How Wide? Perspectives on the Making of
  The Massachusetts 54th Colored Infantry," Chapter 6 in *Black Women Film and
  Video Artists*.
Phyllis R. Klotman and Janet K. Cutler, "Keys to the Kingdom: A Final Inter-
  view with Jacqueline Shearer," *Black Film Review* 8: 2 (1995): 16–17, 32–33.
Ted Shen, "Reel Life: New Lessons From African Folklore," *Chicago Reader*,
  July 7, 1995: sect. 1, p.1.
Nell Irvin Painter, "Soul Murder and Slavery: Toward a Fully Loaded Cost
  Accounting," in Linda K. Kerber et al., eds., *U.S. History and Women's His-
  tory: New Feminist Essays* (Chapel Hill, NC: University of North Carolina
  Press, 1995), 125–46.

Week 10

Screenings

Suzanne, Suzanne (1982); *Finding Christa* (1991); *The KKK Boutique Ain't Just Rednecks* (1994); all by Camille Billops and James V. Hatch.

Readings

Monique Guillory, "The Functional Family of Camille Billops," Chapter 4
  in *Black Women Film and Video Artists*.
Valerie Smith, "Telling Family Secrets: Narrative and Ideology in *Suzanne,
  Suzanne*," in Diane Carson et al., eds., *Multiple Voices in Feminist Film Criticism*
  (Minneapolis: University of Minnesota Press, 1994), 380–90.

Week 11

Screening

A Litany for Survival: The Life and Work of Audre Lorde (1995) by Ada Gay Griffin
  and Michelle Parkerson.

Readings

Gloria J. Gibson, "Michelle Parkerson: A Visionary Risk Taker," Chapter
  10 in *Black Women Film and Video Artists*.
Audre Lorde, "The Uses of the Erotic: The Erotic as Power," in *Sister/Out-
  sider* (Freedom, CA: The Crossing Press, 1984), 53–59.
June Jordan, "Many Rivers to Cross," in *On Call: Political Essays* (Boston:
  South End Press, 1985), 19–26.

Barbara Smith, "The Truth That Never Hurts: Black Lesbians in Fiction in the 1980s," in Joanne M. Braxton and Andree Nicola McLaughlin, eds., *Wild Women in the Whirlwind: Afra-American Culture and the Contemporary Literary Renaissance* (New Brunswick, NJ: Rutgers University Press, 1990), 213–45.

Week 12

SCREENINGS

Remembering Wei Yi-Fang, Remembering Myself (1995); and *Sisters in the Life: First Love* (1993); both by Yvonne Welbon.
She Don't Fade (1991); *The Potluck and the Passion* (1992); both by Cheryl Dunye.
Spin Cycle (1991) by Aarin Burch.
I Never Danced the Way Girls Were Supposed To (1992) by Dawn Suggs.

READINGS

Yvonne Welbon, "Black Lesbian Film and Video Art: Feminism Studies, Performance Studies," *P-Form* (Spring 1995): 12–15.
C.A. Griffith, "Below the Line: (Re)Calibrating the Filmic Gaze," Chapter 9 in *Black Women Film and Video Artists*.

Week 13

SCREENINGS

Extra Change (1987) by Carmen Coustaut.
Land Where My Fathers Died (1991) by Daresha Kyi.
A Question of Color (1992) by Kathe Sandler.

READINGS

Carmen Coustaut, "Love on My Mind: Creating Black Women's Love Stories," Chapter 8 in *Black Women Film and Video Artists*.
Patricia Ferreira, "The Triple Duty of a Black Woman Filmmaker: An Interview with Carmen Coustaut," *African American Review* 27: 3 (1993): 433–42.
Jesse Rhines, "Stimulating a Dialogue Among African-American Viewers: An Interview with Daresha Kyi," *Cineaste* 20: 3 (April 1994): 43–44.
Kathe Sandler, "Finding a Space for Myself in My Film About Color Consciousness," in Deborah Willis, ed., *Picturing Us: African American Identity in Photography* (New York: The New Press, 1994): 105–112.

Week 14

SCREENINGS

Fired Up! (1992) by O.Funmilayo Makarah.
Cycles (1989) by Zeinabu irene Davis.

O.Funmilayo Makarah, "Fired-Up!" Chapter 7 in *Black Women Film and Video Artists*.

Davis, Zeinabu irene, "Daunting Inferno," *Afterimage* 21 (Summer 1993): 20.

Christina Springer, "Waiting and Dreaming, Praying and Cleaning," *Sojourner: The Women's Forum* 15: 8 (April 1990): np.

Ann Filemyr, "Zeinabu irene Davis: Filmmaker, Teacher With a Powerful Mission," *Angles* (Winter 1992): 6–9, 22.

Week 15

SCREENING

Alma's Rainbow (1993) by Ayoka Chenzira.

READINGS

Dorothy Thigpen, "A Conversation with Ayoka Chenzira," in *Take Two Quarterly* (Columbus, OH: National Black Programming Consortium, 1995): 21–28.

Keith Boseman, "Ayoka Chenzira: Sharing the Empowerment of Women," *Black Film Review* 2: 3 (Summer 1986): 18–19, 25.

P. Jane Splawn, "An Intimate Talk with Ntozake Shange: An Interview," Chapter 11 in *Black Women Film and Video Artists*.

suggested course design

selected

video/

filmography

black women

video/filmmakers

Ajalon, Jamika
 Introduction to Cultural Skit-zo-frenia. Video, color, 10 min. 1993 (Third
   World Newsreel).
 Shades. Video, color, 13 min. 1994 (Third World Newsreel)

Anderson, Madeline
 Tribute to Malcolm X. Video, b/w, 14 min. 1969 (William Greaves Produc-
   tions, Inc.).
 I am Somebody. 16mm, color, 28 min. 1970 (First Run/Icarus Films).
 Andrade-Watkins, Claire
 Espiritode Cabo Verde (The Spirit of Cape Verde). Video, color, 28 min. 1986
   (Eclipse).

Ballenger, Melvonna
 Rain. 16mm, color, 12 min. 1978.
 Nappy-Headed Lady. 16mm, 30 min. 1983.

Barnette, Neema
 Sky Captain. 65 min. 1985.
 My Name is Zora. Color, 60 min. 1989. (PBS).
 Different Worlds: An Interracial Love Story. 1992. (CBS School Break).
 Better Off Dead. 1993 (Lifetime Cable Movie).

Billops, Camille
> *Suzanne, Suzanne.* 16mm, b/w, 26 min. 1982 (Third World Newsreel).
> *Older Women and Love.* 16mm, color, 26 min. 1987 (Third World Newsreel).
> *Finding Christa.* 16mm, color, 60 min. 1991 (Third World Newsreel).
> *The KKK Boutique Ain't Just Rednecks.* 16mm, color, 77 min. 1994 (Camille Billops and Third World Newsreel).

Blue, Carroll Parrott
> *Varnette's World: A Study of a Young Artist.* 16mm, color, 26 min. 1979
> *Conversations with Roy DeCarava.* 16mm, color, 28 min. 1983 (First Run/Icarus).
> *Smithsonian World:* "Nigerian Art: Kindred Spirits." Video, color, 60 min. 1990 (PBS Video).
> *Nova:* "Mystery of the Senses: Visions." Video, color, 60 min. 1995 (PBS Video).

Bowser, Pearl
> *Namibia: Independence Now!* 16mm, color, 55 min. 1985 (Third World Newsreel).

Brand, Diane, and Ginny Strikeman
> *Sisters in the Struggle* (National Film Board of Canada).

Burch, Aarin
> *Dreams of Passion.* 16mm, color, 5 min. 1989 (Women Make Movies).
> *Spin Cycle.* 16mm, color, 5 min. 1991 (Women Make Movies).
> *Club Q.* Video, color, 8 min. 1991.

Chenzira, Ayoka
> *Syvilla: They Dance to Her Drum.* 16mm, color, 25 min. 1979 (Red Carnelian Home Video).
> *Hair Piece: A Film for Nappyheaded People.* 16mm animated, color, 10 min. 1984 (Red Carnelian Home Video).
> *Secret Sounds Screaming: The Sexual Abuse of Children.* Video, color, 30 min. 1986 (Women Make Movies).
> *The Lure and the Lore.* Video, color, 15 min. 1988 (Third World Newsreel).
> *Zajota and the Boogie Spirit.* 16mm animated, color, 20 min. 1989 (Red Carnelian Home Video).
> *Alma's Rainbow.* 35mm, color, 85 min. 1993 (Red Carnelian Home Video).

Chisholm, Cheryl
> *On Becoming a Woman.* 16mm, color, 90 min. 1987 (Women Make Movies).

Cobb, Portia
> *No Justice . . . No Peace/Black, Male ImMediate.* Video, 15 min. 1991 (O.Funmilayo Makarah).

Collins, Kathleen
> *The Cruz Brothers and Miss Malloy.* 16mm, color, 54 min. 1980 (Mypheduh).
> *Losing Ground.* 16mm, color, 86 min. 1982 (Mypheduh).
> *Gouldtown: A Mulatto Settlement.* 1986.

Coustaut, Carmen
> *Justifiable Homicide.* 16mm, b/w, 5 min. 1981 (Carmen Coustaut).
> *Extra Change.* 16mm, color, 28 min. 1987 (Third World Newsreel).

Dash, Julie
> *Diary of an African Nun.* 16mm, b/w, 13 ½ min. 1977.
> *Four Women.* 16mm, b/w, 7 min. 1975 (Third World Newsreel).
> *Illusions.* 16mm, b/w, 34 min. 1982 (Third World Newsreel).
> *Praise House.* Video, color, 27 min. 1991 (Third World Newsreel).
> *Daughters of the Dust.* 35mm, color, 2 hrs. 1991 (Kino—also available in 16mm and videocassette).

Davis, Zeinabu irene
> *Filmstatement.* b/w, 13 min. 1982.
> *Re-creating Black Women's Media Image.* Video, color, 30 min. 1983 (Circles–London, England).
> *Crocodile Conspiracy.* 16mm, color, 13 min. 1986 (Third World Newsreel).
> *Sweet Bird of Youth.* Video, color, 5 min. 1987
> *Cycles.* 16mm, b/w, 17 min. 1989 (Women Make Movies).
> *A Period Piece.* Video, color, 4 min. 1991 (Women Make Movies).
> *A Powerful Thang.* 16mm, color, 51 min. 1991 (Women Make Movies).
> *Mother of the River.* 16mm, b/w, 30 min. 1995 (Wimmin With a Mission Productions).

Dunye, Cheryl
> *Janine.* Video, color, 9 min. 1990 (Third World Newsreel).
> *She Don't Fade.* Video, b/w, 23 min. 1991 (Third World Newsreel).
> *Vanilla Sex.* Video, b/w, 5 min., 1992 (Video Data Bank).
> *The Potluck and the Passion.* Video, color, 22 min. 1992 (Third World Newsreel).
> *Untitled Portrait.* Video, b/w, 5 min. 1993 (Third World Newsreel).
> *Greetings From Africa.* 16mm, color, 10 min. 1994 (Women Make Movies).
> *Watermelon Woman.* 16mm feature film, color & b/w. 1996. (First Run Features).

Fabio-Bradford, Cheryl
> *Rainbow Black: Poet Sarah Webster Fabio.* 16mm, color, 31 min. 1976.

Featherston, Elena
> *Visions of the Spirit: A Portrait of Alice Walker.* 16mm, color, 58 min. 1989 (Women Make Movies).

Frazier, Jacqueline
Shipley Street. 16mm, 30 min. 1981.

Freeman, Monica
Valerie: A Woman, an Artist, a Philosophy of Life. 16mm, color, 15 min. 1975 (Phoenix Films).
A Sense of Pride: Hamilton Heights in Harlem. 16mm, color, 15 min. 1977 (Atlanta African Film Society).
Learning Through the Arts: The Children's Art Carnival. 16mm, color, 17 min. 1979 (The Children's Art Carnival).

Frilot, Shari
A Cosmic Demonstration of Sexuality. Video, color, 15 min. 1993 (Third World Newsreel).
What is a Line. Video, color, 10 min. 1994 (Third World Newsreel).
Black Nations/Queer Nations. Video, color, 50 min. 1995 (Third World Newsreel).

Gerima, Shirikiana
Brick by Brick. 16mm, color, 37 min. 1982 (Mypheduh).

Gibson, Linda
Flag. Video, color, 26 min. 1989 (Women Make Movies).

Gilliam, Leah
Now Pretend. 16mm, b/w, 10 min. 1991 (Third World Newsreel).
Sapphire and the Slave Girl. Video, color & b/w, 18 min. 1995 (Third World Newsreel).

Grant, Joanne
Fundi: The Story of Ella Baker. 16mm, color, 63 min. 1981 (New Day Films).

Griffith, C. A.
Shock Treatment. Video, b/w, 35 min. 1994.
So I Didn't Believe Her. Video, b/w, 10 min. 1995.
Border Line . . . Family Pictures. Video, color, 30 min. 1996.

Hilliard, Tricia
I Remain. 16mm, b/w, 15 min. 1989.
Jackson, Muriel
The Maids! Video, color, 28 min. 1985 (Women Make Movies).

Jennings, Pamela
I've Never. Video, b/w, 5 min. 1992 (Video Data Bank).

Kyi, Daresha
The Thinnest Line. 16mm, color, 10 min. 1988 (Women Make Movies).
Land Where My Fathers Died. 16mm, color, 23 min. 1991 (Women Make Movies).

Larkin, Alile Sharon
> *Your Children Come Back to You.* 16mm, b/w, 27 min. 1979 (Women Make Movies).
> *A Different Image.* 16mm, color, 51 min. 1982 (Women Make Movies).
> *Miss Fluci Moses.* Video, color, 22 min. 1987 (Women Make Movies).
> *Dreadlocks and the Three Bears.* Animation, color. 1991 (Inter-Image Video).

Lawrence, Carol Munday
> ### Nguzo Saba Folklore Series of Animated Films
> *Unity: The Tiger and the Big Wind* (Umoja). 16mm animation, color, 8 min. 1972.
> *Responsibility: Modupe and the Flood* (Ujima). 16mm animation, color, 5 min. 1975.
> *Faith: Beegie and the Egg* (Imani). 16mm animation, color, 8 min. 1976.
> *Creativity: Simon's New Sound* (Kuumba). 16mm animation, color, 8 min. 1978.
> *Self-Determination: The Kangaroos Who Forgot* (Kujichagulia). 16mm animation, color, 6 min. 1979.
> *Purpose: Mary Jean and the Green Stone* (Nia). 16mm animation, color, 5 min. 1980 (based on a short story by Alice Walker).
> *Economic Cooperation: Noel's Lemonade Stand* (Ujamaa). 16mm animation, 9 min. 1981 (screenplay by Kathleen Collins; story concept by Henry H. Roth).

> ### Were You There Film Series
> "When the Animals Talked." 16mm, color, 28 min. 1975.
> "The Black West." 16mm, color, 30 min. 1979.
> "The Facts of Life." 16mm, color, 28 min. 1981 (directed by Gilbert Moses).
> "Sports Profile." 16mm, color, 29 min. 1981.
> "Oscar Micheaux, Film Pioneer." 16mm, color, 29 min. 1981 (starring Danny Glover).
> "Portraits of Two Artists." 16mm, color, 29 min. 1981.
> "The Cotton Club." 16mm, color, 29 min. 1982 (directed by Stan Lathan).
> The films of Carol Munday Lawrence are all available in video and are distributed by The Altschul Group Corporation Educational Media.

McCullough, Barbara
> *Water Ritual #1: An Urban Rite of Purification.* 16mm, color, 4 min. 1979 (Third World Newsreel).
> *Shopping Bag Spirits and Freeway Fetishes: Reflections on Ritual Space.* Video, color, 60 min. 1981 (Third World Newsreel).

Makarah, O.Funmilayo
> *Fired Up!* Video, color, 60 min. 1992 (O.Funmilayo Makarah).
> *Grandma Willey.* Video, color. 1977 (O.Funmilayo Makarah).

Survival: The Black South African Theatre Project '77. Video, b/w 1977 (O.Funmilayo Makarah).

Ritual for Third World Women Artists. Video, color. 1978 (O.Funmilayo-Makarah).

. . . Just Names . . . Just Names. Video, color. 1988 (O.Funmilayo Makarah).

Define. Video, color. 1988 (O.Funmilayo Makarah).

Creating a Different Image: Portrait of Alile Sharon Larkin. Video, color, 5 min. 1989 (O.Funmilayo Makarah).

Maple, Jessie

Will. 16mm, color, 80 min. 1981 (20 West).

Twice as Nice. 16mm, color, 70 min. 1989 (20 West).

Materre, Michelle

Muhammad and Larry. 16mm, color, 30 min. 1982.

Don't Drive Drunk (music video for Stevie Wonder). 35mm, color, 6 min. 1985.

Lou, Pat, and Joe D. 16mm, b/w, 85 min. 1986.

Think (public service music video for Aretha Franklin). 35mm, color, 4 min. 1988.

Mekuria, Salem

As I Remember It: A Portrait of Dorothy West. Video, color, 56 min. 1991 (Salem Mekuria).

Sidet: Forced Exile. Video, color, 60 min. 1991 (Salem Mekuria).

Onwurah, Ngozi

And Still I Rise. 16mm/video, color, 30 min. 1991 (Women Make Movies).

The Body Beautiful. 16mm/video, color, 23 min. 1991 (Women Make Movies).

Coffee Colored Children. 16mm/video, color, 15 min. 1988 (Women Make Movies).

Parkerson, Michelle

Sojourn. 16mm, b/w & color, 10 min. 1973 (Eye of the Storm Productions).

. . . But Then, She's Betty Carter. 16mm, color, 53 min. 1980 (Women Make Movies).

Gotta Make This Journey: Sweet Honey in the Rock. Video, color, 58 min. 1983 (Women Make Movies).

Storme: The Lady of the Jewel Box. 16mm, color, 21 min. 1987 (Women Make Movies).

Odds and Ends. Video, color, 30 min. 1993 (American Film Institute).

A Litany for Survival: The Life and Work of Audre Lorde (co-director with Ada Gay Griffin). 16mm, color, 88 min. 1995 (Third World Newsreel).

Phipps, Cyrille

Respect is Due. Video, color, 10 min. 1991 (Third World Newsreel).

Our House: Gays and Lesbians in the Hood (and Not Channel Zero). Video, color, 21 min. 1992 (Third World Newsreel).

Black Women, Sexual Politics and the Revolution (and Not Channel Zero). Video, color, 30 min. 1992 (Third World Newsreel).

Sacred Lives, Civil Truths (with Catherine Saalfield). Video, color, 58 min. 1993 (Third World Newsreel).

Mumia Abu-Jamal: Facing the Death Penalty (with Paper Tiger TV). Video, color, 30 min. 1995 (Third World Newsreel).

Robinson, Debra

I Be Done Been Was Is. 16mm, color, 58 min. 1984 (Women Make Movies).

Kiss Grandmama Goodbye. 16mm, b/w, 70 min. 1992 (Women Make Movies).

Royals, Demetria and Louise Diamond

Mama's Pushcart. Video, color, 54 min. 1988 (Women Make Movies).

Sandler, Kathe

Remembering Thelma. 16mm, 15 min. 1981 (Women Make Movies).

A Question of Color. 16mm, 58 min. 1992 (California Newsreel).

Sharp, Saundra

Back Inside Herself. 16mm, b/w, 5 min. 1984 (Women Make Movies).

Picking Tribes. 16mm, color, 7 min. 1988 (Women Make Movies).

Shearer, Jacqueline

A Minor Altercation. 16mm, color, 30 min. 1977 (Women Make Movies).

Eyes on the Prize II: The Keys to the Kingdom. Video, color & b/w, 60 min. 1990 (PBS Video).

Eyes on the Prize II: The Promised Land. Video, color & b/w, 60 min. 1990 (PBS Video).

The Massachusetts 54th Colored Infantry. Video, color, 58 min. 1991 (PBS Video).

Simmons, Aishah Shahidah

Silence . . . Broken. Video, color, 7:40 min. 1993 (Third World Newsreel).

Smith, Cauleen

Chronicles of a Lying Spirit (by Kelly Gabron). 16mm, color, 6 min. 1992 (Canyon Cinema).

Smith, Vejan Lee

Mother's Hands. Video, color, 10 min. 1992 (Third World Newsreel).

Human Touch: Power and Pain. Video, color, 30 min. 1993 (Third World Newsreel).

Springer, Christina

Creation of Destiny. 16mm, color, 57 min. 1993

Suggs, Dawn
  Chasing the Moon. 16mm, b/w, 3:30 min. 1990 (Third World Newsreel).
  I Never Danced the Way Girls Were Supposed To. Video, color, 7 min. 1992
    (Third World Newsreel).

Sumter, Ellen
  Rags and Old Love. 16mm, b/w, 55 min. 1986.

Taylor, Jocelyn
  24 Hours a Day. Video, color, 18 min. 1993 (Third World Newsreel).
  Frankie & Jocie. Video, color, 18 min. 1994 (Third World Newsreel).
  Bodily Functions. Video, color & b/w, 20 min. 1995 (Third World News-
    reel).

Udongo, Ayanna
  Edges. Video, color, 5 min. 1992 (O.Funmilayo Makarah).

Welbon, Yvonne
  Monique. 16mm, color, 3 min. 1991 (Third World Newsreel).
  Cinematic Jazz of Julie Dash. Video, color, 26 min. 1992–93 (Third World
    Newsreel).
  Sisters in the Life: First Love. Video, color, 23 min. 1993 (Third World News-
    reel).
  Missing Relations. 16mm to video, 13 min. 1994 (Third World Newsreel).
  Remembering Wei Yi-fang, Remembering Myself. Video, color & b/w, 30 min.
    1995 (Third World Newsreel).

Woods, Fronza
  Killing Time. 16mm, 8 1/2 min. 1978.
  Fannie's Film. 16mm, b/w, 15 min. 1981.

Woodson, Jacqueline and Catherine Saalfield
  Among Good Christian People. Video, color & b/w, 24 min. 1990 (Third
    World Newsreel).

directory

of distributors

Altschul Group Corporation
Educational Media
1560 Sherman Avenue, Suite 100
Evanston, IL 60201
(800) 421–2363
FAX (847) 328–6706
E-MAIL agcmedia@starnetinc.com

American Film Institute
P.O. Box 27429
2021 N. Western Avenue
Los Angeles, CA 90027
(800) 774–4234

Atlanta African Film Society
P.O. Box 50319
Atlanta, GA 30302
(404) 525–1136

California Newsreel
149 Ninth Street #420
San Francisco, CA 94103
(415) 621–6196

Camille Billops
491 Broadway
New York, NY 10003
(212) 966–3231

Canyon Cinema
2325 Third Street, Suite 338
San Francisco, CA 94107
(415) 626–2255

Carmen Coustaut
P.O. Box 41272
Washington, DC 20018
(202) 269–0364

The Children's Art Carnival
62 Hamilton Terrace
New York, NY 10031
(212) 234–4093

Eclipse
P.O. Box 2053
Astor Station
Boston, MA 02123

Eye of the Storm Productions
P.O. Box 21568
Washington, DC 20009
(202) 332–7977

Filmmakers Library
124 East 40th Street
New York, NY 10016
(212) 808–4980

First Run/Icarus Films
153 Waverly Place, 6th Floor
New York, NY 10014
(212) 727–1711
(800) 876–1710

Inter-Image Video
P.O. Box 47501
Los Angeles, CA 90047–0501
(800) 843–9448

Kino International Corporation
333 West 39th Street
New York, NY 10018
(800) 562–3330

Mypheduh Film, Inc.
48 Q Street, NE
Washington, DC 20002
(202) 289–6677

National Film Board of Canada
1251 Avenue of the Americas
New York, NY 10020
(212) 586–5131
FAX (212) 246 7404

New Day Films
121 West 27th Street
Room 902
New York, NY 10001
(212) 645–8210

O.Funmilayo Makarah
P.O. Box 48561
Los Angeles, CA 90048

PBS Video
1320 Braddock Place
Alexandria, VA 22314–1698
(800) 344–3337

Phoenix Films
468 Park Avenue South 10th Floor
New York, NY 10016
(800) 221–1274

Red Carnelian Home Video
Black Indie Classics Collection
107 Lexington Avenue
Brooklyn, NY 11238–1401
(718) 622–5092
FAX (718) 622–1174
E-MAIL RCarnelian@aol.com

Salem Mekuria
19 Glade Avenue
Jamaica Plain, MA 02130

Third World Newsreel
335 West 38th Street, 5th Floor
New York, NY 10018
(212) 947–9277

20 West: Home of Black Cinema
20 West Twentieth Street
New York, NY 10018

Video Data Bank
School of the Art Institute of Chicago
280 South Columbus Drive
Chicago, IL 60603
(312) 443–3793

William Greaves Productions, Inc.
230 West 55th Street, 26th Floor
New York, NY 10019
(800) 874—8314

Wimmin With a Mission Productions
7727 N. Marshfield Ave, #7
Chicago, IL 60626—1107
(708) 467—1164
FAX (708) 467—2389
E-MAIL:
z-davis@merle.acns.nwu.edu

Women Make Movies, Inc.
225 Lafayette Street, Suite 206
New York, NY 10012
(212) 925—0606
FAX (212) 926—2052
E-MAIL DISTDEPT@WMM.COM

selected

bibliography

"Ada Griffin: 'What's Mine is Not Mine/What's Mine is Ours/What's Mine is Yours/What's Yours is Yours/(Power Sharing in America)'." *Felix: A Journal of Media Arts & Communication* 1: 2 (Spring 1992): 14.

"Africentric: Ayoka Chenzira." *Felix: A Journal of Media Arts & Communication* 1: 2 (Spring 1992): 45.

Andrade-Watkins, Claire. "La Force du Vodu." (On Elsie Haas.) *Black Film Review* 6: 1: 18–20.

Attille, Martina and Maureen Blackwood. "Black Women and Representation." In Charlotte Brunsdon, ed., *Films for Women*. London: BFI, 1986. 202–208.

Baker, Ella. "Developing Community Leadership." In Gerda Lerner, ed., *Black Women in White America: A Documentary History*. New York: Vintage, 1973, 345–52.

Baker, Houston A., Jr. "Not Without My Daughters: Interview with Julie Dash." *Transition: An International Review*, Issue 57 (1992): 150–66.

Blue, Carroll Parrott. "Sometimes a Poem is Twenty Years of Memory: 1967–1987." *Sage: A Scholarly Journal on Black Women* 4: 1 (Spring 1987): 37–38.

Bobo, Jacqueline. *Black Women as Cultural Readers*. New York: Columbia University Press, 1995.

———. "Black Women in Fiction and Nonfiction: Images of Power and Powerlessness." *Wide Angle* 13: 3&4 (July–October 1991): 72–81.

———. "The Politics of Interpretation: Black Critics, Filmmakers, Audiences." In Gina C. Dent, ed., *Black Popular Culture: A Project by Michele Wallace*. Seattle, WA: Bay Press, 1992, 65–74.

———. "'The Subject is Money': Reconsidering the Black Film Audience as a Theoretical Paradigm." *Black American Literature Forum* 25: 2 (Summer 1991): 421–32.

———, ed., *Available Visions: Improving Distribution of African American Independent Film and Video Conference Proceedings*. San Francisco: California Newsreel, 1993.

Bobo, Jacqueline, and Ellen Seiter. "Black Feminism and Media Criticism: *The Women of Brewster Place*. *Screen* 32: 3 (Autumn 1991): 286–302.

Boseman, Keith. "Ayoka Chenzira: Sharing the Empowerment of Women." *Black Film Review* 2: 3 (Summer 1986): 18–19, 25.

Bowser, Pearl. "Sexual Imagery and the Black Woman in American Cinema." In Gladstone L. Yearwood, ed., *Black Cinema Aesthetics: Issues in Independent Black Filmmaking*. Athens, OH: Ohio University Center for Afro-American Studies, 1982, 10–29.

———. "The Existence of Black Theatres." *Take Two Quarterly*. Columbus, OH: National Black Programming Consortium, 1995, 19–21.

Campbell, Loretta. "Reinventing Our Image: Eleven Black Women Filmmakers." *Heresies* 4: 4 (1983): 58–62.

Cham, Mbye B., and Claire Andrade-Watkins, eds., *Blackframes: Critical Perspectives on Black Independent Cinema*. Cambridge, MA: MIT Press, 1988.

Christian, Barbara. "The Race for Theory." *Feminist Studies* 14: 1 (Spring 1988): 67–79.

Collins, Patricia Hill. *Black Feminist Thought: Knowledge, Consciousness, and the Politics of Empowerment*. London: HarperCollins Academic, 1990.

———. "The Social Construction of Black Feminist Thought." *Signs* 14: 4 (1989): 1–30.

Corrigan, Timothy. *A Short Guide to Writing About Film*. 2d ed., Glenview, IL: Scott, Foresman and Co., 1994.

Darling, Lynn. "*Daughters of the Dust*." *New York Newsday*, January 13, 1992: 46–47.

Dash, Julie. *Daughters of the Dust: The Making of an African American Woman's Film*. New York: The New Press, 1992.

Davis, Zeinabu irene. "*Daughters of the Dust*." *Black Film Review* 6: 1: 12–17, 20–21.

———. "The Future of Black Film: The Debate Continues." *Black Film Review* 5: 3 (1990): 6, 8, 26, 28.

———. "Daunting Inferno." *Afterimage* 21 (Summer 1993): 20.

Day, Barbara. "Black Woman Makes 'the kind of film I've always wanted to see'." *Guardian*, January 22, 1992, 20, 19. (On *Daughters of the Dust*.)

Dent, Gina C., ed., *Black Popular Culture: A Project by Michele Wallace*. Seattle, WA: Bay Press, 1992.

Diawara, Manthia, ed., *Black American Cinema*. New York: Routledge, 1993.

Ferreira, Patricia. "The Triple Duty of a Black Woman Filmmaker: An Interview with Carmen Coustaut." *African American Review* 27: 3 (1993): 433–42.

Filemyr, Ann. "Zeinabu irene Davis: Filmmaker, Teacher with a Powerful Mission." *Angles* (Winter 1992): 6–9, 22.

Foner, Philip. *Women and the American Labor Movement*. New York: The Free Press, 1980.

Franklin, Oliver. "An Interview: Kathleen Collins." *Independent Black American Cinema* (program pamphlet). New York: Theater Program of Third World Newsreel, 1981, 22–24.

Gibson, Gloria J. "Moving Pictures to Move People: Michelle Parkerson Is the Eye of the Storm." *Black Film Review* 3: 3 (Summer 1987): 16–17.

Gibson-Hudson, Gloria J. "A Different Image: Integrating Films by African-American Women into the Classroom." In Diane Carson and Lester D. Friedman, eds., *Shared Differences: Multicultural Media and Practical Pedagogy*. Urbana-Champaign: University of Illinois Press, 1995, 127–48.

————. "African-American Literary Criticism as a Model for the Analysis of Films by African-American Women." *Wide Angle* 13: 3, 4 (July–October 1991): 44–54.

————. "Aspects of Black Feminist Cultural Ideology in Films by Black Women Independent Artists." In Diane Carson, Linda Dittmar, and Janice Welsch, eds., Multiple *Voices in Feminist Film Criticism*. Minneapolis: University of Minnesota Press, 1994, 365–79.

————. "Through Women's Eyes: The Films of Women in Africa and the African Diaspora." *Western Journal of Black Studies* 15: 2 (1991): 79–86.

————. "The Ties that Bind: Cinematic Representations by Black Women Filmmakers." *Quarterly Review of Film and Video* 15: 2 (1994): 25–44.

————. "Recall and Recollect: Excavating the Life History of Eloyce King Patrick Gist." *Black Film Review* 8: 2 (1995): 20–21.

Giddings, Paula. *When and Where I Enter: The Impact of Black Women on Race and Sex in America*. New York: Bantam Books, 1984.

Gossage, Leslie. "Black Women Independent Filmmakers: Changing Images of Black Women." *Iris: A Journal About Women* (Spring–Summer 1987): 4–11.

Guerrero, Ed. *Framing Blackness: The African American Image in Film*. Philadelphia: Temple University Press, 1993.

Harris, Kwasi. "New Images: An Interview with Julie Dash and Alile Sharon Larkin." *Independent* (December 1986): 16–20.

Hartman, S. V., and Farah Jasmine Griffin. "Are You as Colored as That Negro? The Politics of Being Seen in Julie Dash's *Illusions*." *Black American Literature Forum* 25: 2 (Summer 1991): 361–73.

hooks, bell. "Black Women Filmmakers Break the Silence." *Black Film Review* 2: 3 (Summer 1986): 14–15.

————. "Dialogue Between Bell Hooks and Julie Dash." In Julie Dash, *Daughters of the Dust: The Making of an African American Woman's Film*. New York: The New Press, 1992, 27–67.

Jones, Jacquie. "The New Ghetto Aesthetic." *Wide Angle* 13: 3, 4 (July–October 1991): 32–43.

Jordan, June. *Civil Wars*. Boston, MA: Beacon Press, 1981.

————. *On Call: Political Essays*. Boston, MA: South End Press, 1985.

Kafi-Akua, Afua. "Ayoka Chenzira, Filmmaker." *Sage: A Scholarly Journal on Black Women* 4: 1 (Spring 1987): 69–72.

Kempley, Rita. "'Daughters of the Dust': Spirit of a Time Past." *Washington Post*, February 28, 1992, C1, C3.

King, Deborah K. "Multiple Jeopardy, Multiple Consciousness: The Context of a Black Feminist Ideology." *Signs* 14: 1 (Autumn 1988): 42–72.

King, Karen. "Black Films in the Festival of Festivals: *A Powerful Thang*." *The Metro Word: Toronto's Black Culture Magazine*, September 10–October 7, 1992, 15.

Klotman, Phyllis Rauch, ed., *Screenplays of the African American Experience*. Bloomington: Indiana University Press, 1991. (Contains overviews and complete scripts of *Losing Ground*, by Kathleen Collins; *Illusions*, by Julie Dash; and, *A Different Image*, by Alile Sharon Larkin).

Klotman, Phyllis Rauch and Janet K. Cutler. "Keys to the Kingdom: A Final Interview with Jacqueline Shearer," *Black Film Review* 8: 2 (1995): 16–17, 32–33.

Larkin, Alile Sharon. "Black Women Filmmakers Defining Ourselves: Feminism in Our Own Voice." In E. Deidre Pribram, ed., *Female Spectators Looking at Film and Television*. New York: Verso, 1988. 157–73.

Lekatsas, Barbara. "Encounters: The Film Odyssey of Camille Billops." *Black American Literature Forum* 25: 2 (Summer 1991): 395–408.

Lorde, Audre. "The Uses of the Erotic: The Erotic as Power." *Sister Outsider*. Trumansburg, NY: Crossing Press, 1984, 53–59.

Lubiano, Wahneema. "Black Ladies, Welfare Queens, and State Minstrels: Ideological War by Narrative Means." In Toni Morrison, ed., *Race-ing Justice, Engendering Power: Essays on Anita Hill, Clarence Thomas, and the Construction of Social Reality*. New York: Pantheon Books, 1992, 323–63.

Maple, Jessie. *How to Become a Union Camerawoman: Film-Videotape*. New York: L. J. Film Productions, Inc., 1977.

Mapp, Edward. "Black Women in Films: A Mixed Bag of Tricks." In Lindsay Patterson, ed., *Black Films and Filmmakers: A Comprehensive Anthology from Stereotype to Superhero*. New York: Dodd, Mead & Co., 1975, 196–205.

Martin, Sharon Stockard. "The Invisible Reflection: Images and Self-Images of Black Women on Stage and Screen." *The Black Collegian* 9 (May–June 1979): 74–81.

Moon, Spencer. "Behind the Scenes: A Pioneer in Public TV." (On Madeline Anderson.) *Black Film Review* 6: 4 (1991): 27–28.

Morrison, Toni. *Playing in the Dark: Whiteness and the Literary Imagination*. Cambridge: Harvard University Press, 1992.

Mueller, Carol. "Ella Baker and the Origins of 'Participatory Democracy'." In Vicki L. Crawford et al., eds., *Women in the Civil Rights Movement: Trailblazers and Torchbearers 1941–1965*. Bloomington: Indiana University Press, 1993, 51–70.

Nakvasil, Lynn. "Video Production Brings Out Multi-Minority Performers." *The Wave* 73: 23.

Nicholson, David. "A Commitment to Writing: A Conversation with Kathleen Collins Prettyman." *Black Film Review* 5: 1 (Winter 1988/1989): 6–15.

———. "Conflict and Complexity: Filmmaker Kathleen Collins." *Black Film Review* 2: 3 (Summer 1986): 16–17.

———. "Which Way the Black Film Movement?" *Black Film Review* 5: 2 (Spring 1989): 4–5, 16–17.

O'Dell, J. H. "Charleston's Legacy to the Poor People's Campaign." *Freedomways*, 3d qtr. (Summer 1969): 197–221.

"O.Funmilayo Makarah: Traditions, the Black Experience at Smith." *Felix: A Journal of Media Arts & Communication*. 1: 2 (Spring 1992): 20–22.

Okazawa-Rey, Margo. "Viewpoint: In Hollywood, Black Men are In: Black Women are Still Out." *Black Film Review* 6: 1: 25.

Painter, Nell Irvin. "Soul Murder and Slavery: Toward a Fully Loaded Cost Accounting." In Linda K. Kerber et al., eds., *U.S. History and Women's History: New Feminist Essays*. Chapel Hill: University of North Carolina Press, 1995, 125–46.

Parkerson, Michelle. "Did You Say the Mirror Talks?" In Lisa Albrecht and Rose M. Brewer, eds., *Bridges of Power: Women's Multicultural Alliances*. Santa Cruz, CA: New Society Publishers, 1990, 108–117.

———. "Women Throughout the Disapora Tackle Their Firsts." *Black Film Review* 6: 1: 10–11.

Perreten, Dan. "Finding Christa." *Windy City Times*, March 5, 1992, 30.

Petrakis, John. "Women in the Director's Chair Film and Video Festival: *Finding Christa, Land Where My Fathers Died*." *NewCity*, March 5, 1992, 11.

Reagon, Bernice Johnson et al., eds., *We Who Believe in Freedom: Sweet Honey in the Rock . . . Still On the Journey*. New York: Anchor Books, 1993.

Reid, Mark A. "Dialogic Modes of Representing Africa(s): Womanist Film." *Black American Literature Forum* 25: 2 (Summer 1991): 375–88.

"(Re)positions, or, Permission for My Motives: Cheryl Dunye." *Felix: A Journal of Media Arts* 1: 2 (Spring 1992): 24.

Rhines, Jesse. "Stimulating a Dialogue Among African-American Viewers: An Interview with Daresha Kyi." *Cineaste* 20: 3 (April 1994): 43–44.

Rich, B. Ruby. "In the Eyes of the Beholder." (On *Daughters of the Dust*.) *Village Voice*, January 28, 1992, 60, 65.

Rule, Sheila. "Director Defies Odds with First Feature, *Daughters of the Dust*." *New York Times*, February 12, 1992, C15, C17.

Sandler, Kathe. "Finding a Space for Myself in My Film About Color

Consciousness." In Deborah Willis, ed., *Picturing Us: African American Identity in Film*. New York: The Free Press, 1994, 105–112.

Shen, Ted., "Reel Life: New Lessons From African Folklore," *Chicago Reader*, July 7, 1995, Sect. 1, p.1.

Simmonds, Felly Nkweto. "*She's Gotta Have It*: The Representation of Black Female Sexuality on Film." *Feminist Review* 29 (Spring 1988): 10–29.

Smith, Barbara. "The Truth that Never Hurts: Black Lesbians in Fiction in the 1980s." In Joanne M. Braxton and Andree Nicola McLaughlin, eds., *Wild Women in the Whirlwind: Afra-American Culture and the Contemporary Literary Renaissance*. New Brunswick, NJ: Rutgers, 1990, 213–45.

Smith, Patricia. "Recasting the Stereotypes." (On numerous Black women filmmakers.) *San Jose Mercury News*, September 9, 1991, 7B.

Smith, Valerie. "Reconstituting the Image: The Emergent Black Woman Director." *Callaloo: A Journal of Afro-American and African Arts and Letters* 11: 4 (Fall 1988): 710–19.

———. "Telling Family Secrets: Narrative and Ideology in *Suzanne, Suzanne*." In Diane Carson et al., eds., *Multiple Voices in Feminist Film Criticism*. Minneapolis: University of Minnesota Press, 1994, 380–90.

———. "Julie Dash: Filmmaker." In James V. Hatch et al., eds., *Artists and Influence 1990*, Vol 9. New York: Hatch-Billops Collection, 1990, 27–35.

Snead, James. "Images of Blacks in Black Independent Films: A Brief Survey." In Mbye B. Cham and Claire Andrade-Watkins, eds., *Blackframes: Critical Perspectives on Black Independent Cinema*. Cambridge, MA: MIT Press, 1988, 16–25.

Springer, Christina. "Waiting and Dreaming, Praying and Cleaning." (On Zeinabu irene Davis.) *Sojourner: The Women's Forum* 15: 8 (April 1990).

Springer, Claudia. "Black Women Filmmakers." *Jump Cut* 29 (1984): 34–37.

Suderburg, Erika. "Guerrilla Video: LA Freewaves—Grassroots & Messy." *ArtWeek* 20: 41: 22.

Tate, Greg. "Cinematic Sisterhood." (On numerous Black women filmmakers.) *Village Voice*, June 1991, 73, 76, 78.

Taylor, Clyde. "The Future of Black Film: The Debate Continues." *Black Film Review* 5: 3 (1990): 7, 9, 27–28.

———. "The Paradox of Black Independent Film." *Black Film Review* 4: 4 (Fall 1988): 2–3, 17–19.

Thigpen, Dorothy. "A Conversation with Ayoka Chenzira." *Take Two Quarterly*. Columbus, OH: National Black Programming Consortium, 1995, 21–28.

Thomas, Deborah, and Catherine Saalfield. "Geechee Girl Goes Home: Julie Dash on *Daughters of the Dust*." *Independent* (July 1991): 25–27.

Thomas, Kevin. "Salute Set for Black Women in Film." *Los Angeles Times*, January 29, 1982, pt. 6, p. 15.

Wallace, Michele. "Negative Images: Towards a Black Feminist Cultural Criticism." In Lawrence Grossberg, Cary Nelson, Paula Treichler, eds., *Cultural Studies*. New York: Routledge, 1992, 654–71.

Welbon, Yvonne. "Calling the Shots: Black Women Directors Take the Helm." *Independent* (March 1992): 18–22.

———. "Black Lesbian Film and Video Art: Feminism studies, performance studies," *P-Form* (Spring 1995): 12–15.

Williams, John. "Re-Creating Their Media Image: Two Generations of Black Women Filmmakers." *Cineaste* 20: 3 (April 1994): 38–41.

"Woman with a Mission: Zeinabu irene Davis on Filmmaking." *Hotwire* (January 1991): 18, 19, 56.

"Women in the Director's Chair African American Films and Videos." *Chicago Defender*, March 6, 1991, 17.

index

A

A Different World, 14
Aaron, Jane, 101
Abbott, Berenice, 28
Abdulhafiz, Abdosh, 21
Abernathy, Ralph David, 15
abolitionists, 110, 118, 119, 122
abortion, 61, 68, 195
Academy Award, 14, 109, 112, 178
activism, xii, xviii, 9, 196
Adams, Alice: *Thinking of Billie,* 197
Adams, Ansel, 28
Afram Associates, 100
Africa, xii, 29, 32, 147–8, 200
African: art, 29–30; cinema, 53–6; history, 39, 50
African American: community, 99, 183; culture, 29, 36, 103, 145; filmmakers, 102, 139; folklore, 51, 103; history, 36, 39, 50, 109–24; musical traditions, 27, 145; photography, 26–8; women. See Black women
Africanism, xii, 23, 26, 65n 20; Morrisonian, 25, 29, 31, 37
Afrocentrism, 22–3, 36, 39
AIDS, 186

Ajalon, Jamika, 217
Alston, Morris, 96
American Experience, The. See Public Broadcasting Service
American Film Institute, 38, 102, 179
Anderson, Madeline, xii, xv, 97, 208, 209, 217; *I Am Somebody,* 8, 14, 209
Angelou, Maya, 57, 59
apartheid, 17, 126, 168, 202
Arinze, Emmanuel, 29–30
Armstrong, Nancy, and Tennenhouse, Leonard: *The Violence of Representation,* 71–2
Arriflex, 154, 159, 172n 3
Art Ensemble of Chicago, 203
Asante, Molefi Kete, 22, 23
autobiography, 68, 186

B

Babu, Ayuko, 41n 18
Bagwell, Orlando, 104
Baker, Ella, 9, 14–18. *See also* Grant, Joanne; "Developing Community Leadership," 210
Baker, Houston A., 36, 39, 39n 2, 40n 2
Baker, Josephine, 204

Baldwin, James, 118, 133
Ballenger, Melvonna, 21, 33, 41n 18, 217; *Nappy-Headed Lady,* 41n 18; *Rain,* 41n 18
Bambara, Toni Cade, 4, 36; *Gorilla, My Love,* 24
Banks, Larry, 161
Bar, Eugene: "Things Are Stories: A Manifesto for a Reflexive Semiotics," 51–2
Baraka, Amiri, 32; *The Autobiography of Leroi Jones,* 22
Barnette, Mary Neema, 14, 180, 217
Bean, Denise, 136
Bearden, Romare, 27, 38
bebop, 27, 164
Belafonte, Harry, 165
Benson, Lillian, 122n 3
Berger, Mark, 105
Bernstein, Steven, 157; *The Professional Cameraman's Handbook,* 157
Billops, Camille, 67–90, 218. *See also* Hatch and Billops; Hatch, James; *Finding Christa,* xiii–xiv, 68–9, 72–5, 77–8, 80, 83, 84, 213; *Older Women and Love,* 68, 81, 82; *Suzanne, Suzanne,* xiii, 68, 69–72, 77–8, 81, 213; *The KKK Boutique Ain't Just Rednecks,* xiii, 68, 82, 84–5, 87, 213
Birmingham Black Barons, 103
Black: abolitionists, xv, 110; aesthetic, 27, 32, 160, 167–8; Amazon science fiction, 179, 180; Arts Movement, 21, 31, 39n 2; British filmmakers, 57, 65n 34; Canadian filmmakers, 60; community, 134, 139, 188; culture, xvi, 10; exploitation, 94, 168; feminists. See feminism, Black; filmmakers and videographers, 3–19, 21–41, 63n 2, 107, 136, 158, 162, 168, 177–88, 207–16; history, 114, 117; lesbian filmmaking, 177–88; life, xvii, 9–12; literature, 182, 189; men, xv, 118–20, 126, 129, 168; people, 94, 106, 129, 134, 139, 205; womanhood, 57–9, 62, 63, 83; women. See Black women
Black Film Review, 4
Black Film/Video Association, 137
Black Girl, 134, 136
Black History Month, 115, 180
Black Journal, 95, 96
Black Liberation Movement, the, 24
Black Panther Party, 22, 32, 40n 4, 127
Black Popular Culture Conference, 4
Black Power Movement, 195
Black Scholar, 23
Black soldiers: and the Civil War, 109–24. *See also* Shearer, Jacqueline; and World War One, 7; Union, 109–24
Black West, the, 103, 105

Black women, xvi, xviii, 31, 133, 136, 146, 154, 162, 180, 182; and love, 139–52; biographies, 9–12; empowerment of, 43, 75, 118, 144; film and video artists, xi–xviii, 3–19, 43–66, 115–17, 140, 166, 175–88, 207–16, 217–24; scholars, xiii, 6, 45–6, 185
Black women's: creative process, xviii, 47; cultural history, xviii, 8, 9, 48, 57, 61, 73; cultural identity, 45, 47–9, 195; narratives, 12–14, 139–52; sexuality, 35, 56–9
Blackside, Inc., xv, 94
Blake, Grace, 162, 163
Bloomberg, Bob, 101
Blue, Carroll Parrot, xii, xiv, 21, 22, 32, 106, 135, 218; *Conversations with Roy DeCarava,* 26–8, 34, 211; *Nigerian Art: Kindred Spirits,* 26, 28, 29–30, 211; *Varnett's World: A Study of a Young Artist,* 10, 26, 28, 211
blues, the, 27, 32, 35, 141, 143, 145, 197
Blythe, Arthur, 35
Boas, Franz, 7
Bobo, Jacqueline, 47, 64n 5, 209; *Black Women as Cultural Readers,* 4, 212; *Black Women Film and Video Artists,* 208
Bond, Julian, 15
Bonnet, Lisa: *Angel Heart,* 58
Boseman, Keith: "Ayoka Chenzira: Sharing the Empowerment of Women," 215
Boston Newsreel Collective, 5–6
Bourne, St. Clair, 31
Bowser, Pearl, xii, 3–4, 6–8, 218; "Sexual Imagery and the Black Women in American Cinema," 212; *In Color: Years of Images of Minority Women in the Media,* 4
Boyer, Horace, 123n 11
Boyz 'N the Hood, 110, 168
Brand, Dionne and Ginny Strikeman, 49, 218; *Sisters in the Struggle,* xiii, 44, 59–61, 63, 66n 39, 66n 43
Brando, Marlon, 75, 77
Braxton, Joanne, 73
Brecht, Bertolt: *Mother Courage and Her Children,* 190
Briseno, Theodore, 137
Broderick, Matthew, 109, 112
Brown, John, 109
Brown, Sterling, 179
Bullins, Ed, 190
Bunyan, Maureen, 97
Burch, Aarin, 5, 184, 218; *Spin Cycle,* 214
Burnett, Charles, 21, 31, 106, 135, 136; *America Becoming,* 26; *Killer of Sheep,* 24, 26; *To Sleep with Anger,* 34, 107, 158
Burns, Ken, 110, 117
Burroughs, Nanny Helen, 179

Bush, George, 132, 163
Butler, Rick, 104

C
Cabral, Amilcar, 32, 40n 7
Caldwell, Ben, 21, 31, 32, 136
California Afro-American Museum, xvi, 127, 130
Callahan, Harry, 28
Calloway, Cab, 103, 106
Camera Operator, 157, 163, 169
Camp, Sokari Douglas, 30
Campbell, Loretta, 18n 4
Campbell, Veda, 181
Carby, Hazel, 56
Carew, Topper, 100
Carpentier, 202−3
Carson, Verne and Sylvia: *The Professional Cameraman's Handbook,* 171n 1, 172n 5
Carter, Betty, 177
Carter, Bunchy, 22
Carter, John, 13
Caught Looking, 196
CBS, 14, 113, 134
Cesaire, Aime, 203
Charles, Ray, 165
Chavis, Reverend Ben, 17
Chenzira, Ayoka, xiv, 106, 184, 218; *Alma's Rainbow,* 11, 14, 215; *Hair Piece: A Film for Nappyheaded People,* 11; *Syvilla: They Dance to Her Drum,* 9
Cherry, Don, 35
Children's Home Society, xiii, 69, 73
Childrens' Television Workshop, 95
Chin, Michael, 104
Chinese Americans, 85, 179
Chinlund, Jennifer, 104
Chinosole, 46
Chisholm, Cheryl, 218
Choy, Christine, 4
Choy, Curtis, 104
Christian, Barbara: "The Race for Theory," 211
Chung, Reverend, 179
Ciccolini, Chic, 104
civil rights. See rights, civil
Civil War, the, xv, 109−24
Clark, Larry, 31, 106, 135, 136; *Passing Through,* 23
Clark, Mark, 127
Clark, Septima, 15
Clark, VeVe, 102
Clarke, Shirley, 136
classism, 54, 57, 60, 63, 157, 162
Clay-Alexander Productions, 107
clitorectomy, xviii, 199−20
Coachman, Alice, 103, 106
Cobb, Portia, 218
Cobo, Juan, 156, 173n 15

Coleman, Ornette, 35
Coleman, Wanda, 41n 18
Collins, Bud, 99
Collins, Kathleen, xii, 4, 8−9, 12−13, 102, 190, 219. *See also* Franklin, Oliver; *Losing Ground,* 9, 210; *The Cruz Brothers and Miss Malloy,* 8−9, 12−13, 210. *See also* Roth, Henry H.
Collins, Patricia Hill, 64n 5
colonialism, 24, 134, 148
color: people of, xv, 22, 87, 93, 161, 164, 166, 170, 182, 189, 201, 204; women of, 47, 67, 73, 113, 156, 166−7, 169, 182, 194−5; writers of, 201−3
Coltrane, John, 203
Committee of Black Writers, 107
Conwill, Kinshasha, 33
Coolidge, Martha, 180; *Fast Times at Ridgemont High,* 158
Cooper, Ruth, 132
Coppola, Francis Ford: *The Cotton Club,* 107
Corporation for Public Broadcasting (CPB), 102−4, 105; Television Program Fund, 104
Corrigan, Timothy, 208, 210, 211; *A Short Guide to Writing About Film,* 208
Cotton Club, 103, 106
Coustaut, Carmen, xiv, xvii, 4, 219; *Extra Change,* xvi, 14, 140, 144, 148−50, 214; *Harmonica Man,* xvi, 141−51; *Justifiable Homicide,* 139, 144; *Listen to the Wind,* xvi, 145−50; *Roundtable Discussion,* xvi, 147, 150
Craig, Margaret, 101
Creel, Margaret Washington, 51, 64n 20
Crenshaw, Michelle, xiv, 181
Crichton, Judy, 112
cultural: identity, 48, 50, 54, 63, 160; nationalism, 22; politics, xii, 22; scholarship, 159−60
cultural criticism, 170, 207; Black feminist, xi, 183
Cummins Engine Foundation, 101
Cuomo, Mario, 178−9
Cupit, Sandi, 104
Cutrufelli, Maria, 200

D
Daa'ood, Kamau, 33
Damas, Leon, 203
Dammond, Howard, 94
Dammond, Peggy, 102
Daniel, Margaret, 5
Dante: *Inferno,* 86−7
Dash, Julie, xii, 4, 21, 22, 23, 25, 40n 8, 41n 24, 49, 65n 20, 106, 127, 135, 186−7, 219; *Daughters of the Dust,* xiii, 4, 6, 9, 13, 14, 30, 34, 35, 36−9, 44, 47, 49−53, 56, 59, 61, 63, 66n 39, 66n 43, 123n 9, 167, 168,

184, 187, 212. *See also* Davis, Zeinabu irene; de Albuquerque Klaus; *Diary of An African Nun,* 22, 23, 24–5, 29; *Four Women,* 26, 30–1, 32–3, 35–6, 102, 212; *Illusions,* 212; *Praise House,* 32–3, 40n 10, 212; *The Legend of Carl Lee Duvall,* 22

Davis, Angela, 18, 40n 3, 156. *See also* Griffith; *An Autobiography,* 22

Davis, Bridgett: *Naked Acts,* 14

Davis, Miles, 164

Davis, Zeinabu irene, xiv, 4, 5, 18n 1, 21, 41n 18, 219. *See also* Filemyr, Ann; *"Daughters of the Dust,"* 212; "Daunting Inferno," 215; *A Powerful Thang,* 14, 184; *Cycles,* 214; *Mother of the River,* 14, 213

DC Humanities Council, 180

de Albuquerque, Klaus: "*Daughters of the Dust:* The Making of an American Classic," 36–9

De Larverie, Storme, 177, 178

DeCarava, Roy, xii, 41n 13

Dee, Ruby, 29; *Zora is My Name,* 14

DeFina, Marianna, 104

Delany, Martin, 111

Dent, Gina, 19n 7

Dessisso, Ed, 104

diaspora, 59, 60, 65n 43; African, 48, 63, 98, 182; matrilineal, 46, 63; the Black, 31, 32, 34, 37, 38, 44

Diawara, Manthia, 54, 160

Dill, Bill, 166

Directing Workshop for Women, 180

distributors, 225–28

Dixon, Willie, 103, 106

documentary film(s), xii, 9–12, 12, 14–18, 26, 53–7, 60, 68–9, 82, 111, 140, 165, 186, 208

Dolphy, Eric, 35

domestic violence, 68, 71

Douglass, Frederick, 111

DP, 156, 163, 169, 173n 14, 173n 15, 181

Dreyfuss, Joel: *Kuumba: Simon's New Sound,* 101

Du Bois, W.E.B., 23; *The Souls of Black Folk,* 37

Duke, Bill: *Deep Cover,* 158; *The Cemetery Club,* 158

Dunye, Cheryl, 184, 219; *She Don't Fade,* 214; *The Potluck and the Passion,* 214; *Watermelon Woman,* 14

E

East Coast Documentary Movement, the, 31–3

Edelman, Marian Wright, 127

Elliot, Dolores, 173n 15

Emecheta, Buchi, 58–9

Enwonwu, Ben, 30

Eurocentricity, 23, 25, 48

Evans, Paul, 104

Evers, Myrlie, 127

Eyes on the Prize I and II, xv, 95, 111, 115, 117, 120, 122n 3

F

Fabio-Bradford, Cheryl, 4, 5, 219

Fakeye, Lamidi, 30

Fanaka, Jamaa, 21, 135

Fanon, Frantz, 32

Faulkner, William, 103; *The Days When the Animals Talked,* 98

Faye, Safi, 53

Featherston, Elena, 219

feminism, xviii, 63n 1, 68, 69, 77, 79, 88, 121, 181, 185, 186, 189; Black, xi, 45–6, 62, 64n 5, 67, 72, 182–3, 190, 194–201; Eurocentric, 45, 195

Ferreira, Patricia: "The Triple Duty of a Black Woman Filmmaker: An Interview with Carmen Coustaut," 214

Fielder, A.J., 169

Fields, Barbara, 110, 117, 119–20, 123n 10

Filemyr, Ann: "Zeinabu irene Davis: Filmmaker, Teacher With a Powerful Mission," 215

film: analysis, 208–9; course design, 207–16; criticism, 160, 168, 208–9; distributors, 225–28; genre, 160, 178; industry, 161, 170; production, 158, 160, 170; studies, 207–16; technicians, 153–74; theory, 157, 160, 170–1

filmography, 217–24

First AC, 157–8, 163, 172n 6

Fishburne, Larry, 110, 111, 120

Foiles, Stanley, 104

folk narrative, 58, 65n 18, 98, 115

Forten, Charlotte, 119

Frank's Place, 14

Franklin, Oliver: "An Interview: Kathleen Collins," 210

Frazier, Jacqueline, 220

freedom, 116–18, 121, 126

Freeman, Bee, 103

Freeman, Monica, xii, 11, 106, 220; *A Sense of Pride: Hamilton Heights in Harlem,* 10, 209; *Learning Through the Arts: The Children's Art Carnival,* 10, 11, 209; *Valerie: A Woman, an Artist, a Philosophy of Life,* 8, 9, 10, 209

Freeman, Morgan, 109, 110, 111, 112, 120

Frilot, Shari, 220

Fugitive Slave Act, 118, 123n 8

funding, 4, 146, 187, 189

fundraising, 112, 150, 191

Fusco, Coco, 41n 18

G

Gardner, Erroll, 35

Garner, Margaret, 73–5
Gates, Henry Louis Jr., 23, 40n 2, 64n 5
gay: Black men, 184–6
gay and lesbian: communities, xvii, 183
gaze: filmic, 50, 153–173; male, 166–8
gender, xiv, 69, 77, 80, 119, 158, 162, 166, 167, 177
General Camera Corporation, 161, 163–4
George, Lynell, 41n 18
Gerima, Haile, 21, 103, 135, 163; *After Winter: Sterling Brown,* 26; *Bush Mama,* 23, 26, 61; *Sankofa,* 22–3, 26, 41n 18; *The Wilmington Ten—U.S.A. Ten Thousand,* 17, 26
Gerima, Shirikiana, 220
Gibson, Gloria, 3, 4, 18n 1, 213
Gibson, Linda, xvii, 4, 5
Gibson, Ray, 40n 11
Gibson-Hudson, Gloria J., xii, xiii, 7, 64n 5, 66n 40, 211; "African American Literary Criticism as a Model for the Analysis of Films by African American Women," 212; "Aspects of Black Feminist Cultural Ideology in Films by Black Women Independent Artists," 210
Giddings, Paula, 64n 15
Gillespie, Dizzy, 164–5
Gilliam, Leah, 220
Giovanni, Nikki, 182
Gist, Eloyce, 7
Glatthaar, Joseph, 110
Glory, 109–110, 112, 120
Glover, Danny, 105
Goldberg, Whoopi, 14
Gomez, Jewelle, 96
Gordon, Dexter, 35
Grant, Joanne, xii, 220; *Fundi: The Story of Ella Baker,* 9, 14–16, 18, 209
Grayson, Brenda, 104
Greaves, William, 31
Greenway, Frank, 103
Griffin, Ada Gay, 4, 162, 178, 181; Griffin, Ada Gay and Michelle Parkerson: *A Litany for Survival: The Life and Work of Audre Lorde,* xvii, 10, 169–70, 178, 181, 213. *See also* Lorde, Audrey
Griffith, C.A., xiv, xvii, 214, 220; *The Angela Davis Project,* 156
Griffith, Crystal, 5
Guillory, Monique, xiii–xiv; "The Functional Family of Camille Billops," 213
Gullah, the, 38, 49–51, 65n 18, 65n 20
Gumbs, Mignonne, 96

H
hagiography, 121–22
Haines, Randa, 180

Hall, Stuart, 43, 47–8, 63
Hamer, Fannie Lou, 18
Hamilton, Sylvia, and Prieto, Claire: *Black Mother, Black Daughter,* 60
Hammons, David, 33–4
Hampton, Fred, 127
Hampton, Henry, 94–5, 120; *Eyes on the Prize,* 95. *See also Eyes on the Prize*
Hansberry, Lorraine, 190
Harding, Vincent, 15
Harlem, 10, 11, 27, 146; Renaissance, 21, 26, 39n 2, 103
Harlins, Latisha, 126, 137n 1
Harris, Alston, 10–11
Harris, Evelyn, 17
Harris, Kwasi, 40n 9; "New Images: An Interview with Julie Dash and Alile Sharon Larkin," 212
Harris, Leslie: *Just Another Girl on the IRT,* 13, 14, 158
Harris, Monika: *The Promised Land,* 14
Harris, Thomas, 184
Hartman, S.V., and Farah Jasmine Griffin: "Are You as Colored as That Negro?: The Politics of Being Seen in Julie Dash's *Illusions*," 212
Hatch and Billops, 82–8; *String of Pearls,* 68
Hatch, James, 67, 77
Haynes, Charlene, 97
Hayward, Ann, 104
Head, Helaine: *My Past is My Own,* 14
Helfinch, Ruth, 86
Heresies, 4
Higgins, Billy, 35
Hill, Anita, 127
Hilliard, Tricia, 220
Hillstein, Mel, 84
Hines, Earl, 35
Hite, Shere, 199
Holiday, Billie, 165, 197
homoerotic cinematic aesthetic, xvii, 178, 184–5
homophobia, 60, 130, 161; in Black communities, xvii, 176, 187
Honeywood, Varnette, xii, 28–9
hooks, bell, 36, 39, 185
Horton, James, 123n 10
Houston, Dianne: *Tuesday Morning Ride,* 14
Howard University Choir, 123n 11
Hudlin, Warrington, 106
Huggins, John, 22
Hughes, Langston, 41n 13; *Anthology of New Black Poets,* 182; *New Black Voices,* 182; *The Sweet Flypaper of Life,* 27
Hurston, Zora Neale, 7, 65n 18

I
IATSE, 161, 172n 13
identity formation, 49–51, 54, 56, 58,

59—60
imperialism, 24, 201
In Living Color, 184
Independent: Documentary Association, 107; Feature Project, 107; Television Service (ITS), xiv
Intermedia Arts Galleria, 179
International Black Book Conference, 202
Irigaray, Luce, 80
Irving, Kathy, 104

J
Jackson, Billy: *Didn't We Ramble On: The Roots of Black Marching Bands*, 164
Jackson, Jesse, 203
Jafa, Arthur, 38, 123n 9, 167
James Irvine Foundation, 101, 102
James, C.L.R., 23
James, Lily, 159
Jansco, Miklos, 38
jazz, 27, 30, 32, 34—5, 143, 145, 165, 175, 197, 201
Jeffers, Lance, 182
Jegede, Dele, 30
Jegede, Emmanuel Taiwo, 30
Jennings, Pamela, 220
Jewel Box Revue, 177
Johnson, Henry, 96
Johnson, Noble and George, 7
Johnson, William H., 29
Johnson-Odim, Cheryl: "Common Themes, Different Contexts," 55—6
Jones, Grace: *Vamp*, 58
Jordan, Barbara, 127, 132
Jordan, Dr. Joseph, 180
Jordan, June: "Many Rivers to Cross," 213
Joseph, Gloria: SISA (Sisters in Solidarity with Sisters in South Africa), 181, 182—3
Journal of American History, the, 110
Juice, xvii, 161, 168
Julien, Isaac, 156, 184, 185—6
Jump Cut, 4

K
Kamoinge Workshop, 27
Karenga, Ron, 97
Karenina, Anna, 76
Kay, Kent, 104
Kennedy, Adrienne, 76—7; *A Movie Star Has to Star in Black and White*, 75; *Funny House of a Negro*, 75; *People Who Led to My Plays*, 76; *The Owl Answers*, 75
King, Martin Luther Jr., 8, 95
King, Rodney, xvi, 125, 127—30, 137n 2; trial of, 126—27
Kintz, Linda, 76
Kitchen Table: Women of Color Press, 67, 169, 182, 196. *See also* Billops,

Camille
Klotman, Phyllis R., and Cutler, Janet K.: "Keys to the Kingdom: A Final Interview with Jaqueline Shearer," 213
Kochiyama, Yuri, 156
Koon, Sergeant Stacey, 137n 2
Krepela, Neil, 105
Kyi, Daresha, 220; *Land Where My Fathers Died*, 14, 214

L
LA Rebellion, xvi, 127—34
Lacy, Madison Davis, 104
Ladd, Florence, 54
Ladysmith Black Mambazo, 190
Lark, Tony, 96
Larkin, Alile Sharon, xii, 21, 22, 23, 25, 33, 64n 5, 135—6, 221; "Black Women Filmmakers Defining Ourselves: Feminism in Our Own Voice," 212; *A Different Image*, 14, 22, 23, 25, 29, 211; *Dreadlocks and the Three Bears*, 34, 35, 211; *Miss Fluci Moses: A Video Documentary*, 10, 34; *Your Children Come Back to You*, 14, 211
Lathan, Stan, xv, 104
Lawrence, Carol Munday, xiv, 93—108, 211, 221; *Adventures of a Well-Traveled Colored Girl*, 108; *Sports Profiles*, 211; *The Days When the Animals Talked*, 211; *Umoja: Tiger and the Big Wind*, 98—100
Lawrence, Henry Johnson, xv
Lawrence, Jacob, 29, 103
Lee, Don L., 182
Lee, Leslie, 123
Lee, Spike, 164; *Joe's Bed-Stuy Barber Shop*, 106—7; *School Daze*, 173n 14; *She's Gotta Have It*, 107, 184
Lee-Smith, Hughie, 93, 103
lesbian: Black, 66n 39, 175—88; identity, 66n 39
Lekatsas, Barbara, 72, 81
Levesque, George, 123n 10
Levine, Lawrence, 51
Lewis, Bill, 104
Lewis, Don, 101, 105
Liebig, Margaret, 77, 80
Litwack, Leon, 123n 10
Lomax, Melanie, 132
Long, Avon, 103
Lorde, Audre, 169—70, 178, 181—2, 185, 187. See also Griffin, Ada Gay and Michelle Parkerson; *Sister Outsider: Essays and Speeches*, 178; *The Cancer Journals*, 178; *The Uses of the Erotic: The Erotic as Power*, 178, 213; *Zami: A New Spelling of My Name*, 178
Lorraine, Tamsin E.: *Gender, Identity, and the Production of Meaning*, 62
Los Angeles: International Gay and Les-

bian Film Festival, 170; Pan African Film Festival, 41n 18; Police Department, xvi, 130, 132, 134, 137n 2; School, the: women directors of, 21–41
Lott, Tommy, 160, 168
Louis Arnold Steel Band, 101
love, 139–52
Lukas, Kit, 104
Lumbly, Carl, 110, 111, 120

M
MacCallum, Bruce, 161
Mahabuti, Haki, 182
Majal, Taj, 101
Makarah, O.Funmilayo, xiv, xv–xvi, 4, 5, 21, 221; *Apple Pie,* 136; *Black Girl,* 134, 137; *Dialogue,* 136; *Feet,* 136; *Fired Up!,* xvi, 128–34, 214; *Naches,* 136; *Rummage Sale,* 136; *Survival–The Black South African Theater '77 Project,* 136; *Together,* 136
Malcolm X, 40n 4, 40n 8
Maldoror, Sarah, 53
Maple, Jessie, xiv, 222; *How to Become a Union Camerawoman: Film-Videotape,* xiv; *Twice As Nice,* 14; *Will,* 14
Mapp, Edward: "Black Women in Films: A Mixed Bag of Tricks," 212
Marable, Manning, 23
Marbury, Don, 104
marginalization, 54, 56, 63
Marquez, Linda, 104
Marsalis, Branford, 169
Martin, Darnelle: *I Like it Like That,* 13, 14
Masilela, Ntongela, xii, 211
Mason, Julie Ann, 190; *I'll Fly Away,* 190
Materre, Michelle, 4, 222
Maynard, Valerie, 8, 10
McCullough, Barbara, xii, 21, 22, 25, 31–5, 135, 221; *Horace Tapscott: Musical Griot,* 26, 30, 34–5. *See also* Tapscott, Horace; *Shopping Bag Spirits and Freeway Fetishes: Reflections on Ritual Space,* 26, 30, 33–4; *The World of Saxophone Quintet,* 26; *Water Ritual #1: An Urban Rite of Purification,* 35–6
McCullough, David, 109
McIntosh County Shouters, 123n 11
Mekuria, Salem, 49, 222; *Sidet: Forced Exile,* xiii, 44, 53–6, 61, 63, 66n 43
memory, 54–5, 57, 59; cultural, 49, 55–6, 59–61, 63; of Black women, 61, 63
MGMM, 162
Micheaux, Oscar, 7, 103, 105, 106
Michos, Anastas, 154
Middle Passage, the, 31, 37, 38
Million Man March, 168
Mingus, Charles, 35
Minh-ha, Trinh T., 43, 45–6, 48, 49–50, 63

Moon, Spencer: "Behind the Scenes: A Pioneer in Public Televsion," 210
Moore, Amzie, 15
Morrison, Toni, 49, 64n 16; *Beloved,* 73–4; *Playing in the Dark: Whiteness and the Literary Imagination,* xii, 23; *The Bluest Eye,* 25
Morse, Estrellita, 106
Moses, Bob, 15
Moses, Gilbert, 104
mother/daughter bond, xiii, 69–72
motherhood, 77; rites of, 72–5
Mueller, Carol: "Ella Baker and the Origins of 'Participatory Democracy'", 210; and the Student Nonviolent Coordinating Comittee, 15
Murphy, Eddie, 184
Murray, Albert, 27
Muse, Daphne, 101
N
NAACP, 14–16
narrative(s): Black women's, 12–14; cinematic, xii, xiii, 9, 13, 14, 49, 52, 58, 156, 186, 208
National: Commission for Museums and Monuments, 30; Endowment for the Arts, 11, 101; Endowment for the Arts' Expansion Arts Program, 102; Endowment for the Arts-sponsored American Film Institute, xiv; Endowment for the Humanities Grant, xiv
nationalism, 22, 32
Neal, Larry, 32; *Visions of a Liberated Future: Black Arts Movement Writings,* 32
Negro Baseball League, 103, 106
Negundi, N'senga, 33
Neruda, Pablo, 202–3
New York Times, the, 28
Nguzo Saba, 98, 100
Nguzo Saba Films, Inc., xv, 101–4, 106–7
Nguzo Saba Folklore Series of Animated Films, xv
Nicholas Brothers, 103, 106
Nichols, Bill, 55, 82
Nicholson, David: "A Committment to Writing: A Conversation with Kathleen Collins Prettyman," 210
Nicolas, Bernard, 21
Nike, 30
Nixon, E.D., 15
Njeri, Itabari, 41n 18
Noble, Will, 101, 105
Norris, Eunice, 103
Norton, Eleanor Holmes, 11
Nyerere, Julius, xv, 98
O
O'Dell, John: "Charleston's Legacy to the Poor People's Campaign," 210

Obsatz, Victor, 28
Odetta, 98, 101
Ogun, 197
Ojenke, Raspoeter, 33
Okeke, Simon, 30
Okeke, Uche, 30
Olatunji, Babatunde, 101
Oliver, Ruby: *Love Your Mama*, 14
Omori, Emiko, 104
Onabula, Aina, 30
Onwurah, Ngozi, 49, 65n 34, 222; *And Still I Rise*, xiii, 44, 56–9, 61, 63
oppression, 14, 27, 31, 46, 47, 58, 167–8, 187, 198, 200; resistance to, xiii, 14, 17, 45, 60, 159, 167, 196
Other, the, 36, 43, 60, 162

P
Painter, Nell Irvin: "Soul Murder and Slavery: Toward a Fully Loaded Cost Accounting," 213
Pajan, Ilka, 81–2
Palmer, Opal, 101
pan-Africanism, xii, 23, 34, 182
Parkerson, Michelle, xii, xvii, 4, 106, 162, 177–88, 222. *See also* Griffin, Ada Gay; *... But Then, She's Betty Carter*, 9–10, 178, 184; *Gotta Make This Journey: Sweet Honey in the Rock*, 9, 14, 16, 17, 178, 184, 210. *See Also* Reagon, Bernice; Sweet Honey and the Rock; *Odds and Ends*, 179, 180; *Storme: The Lady of the Jewel Box*, xvii, 10, 178, 179, 184; *The Amazon Papers*, 179; *Urban Odyssey*, 179; *Waiting Room*, 179
Parkerson, Michelle, and Jimi Lyons Jr.: *Soujourn*, 178
Parmar, Pratibha, 185
patriarchy, 25, 43, 59, 62, 77, 81, 196–8
Pellington, Mark: MTV, 162
Pennebaker, D.A., 169
Petino, Barbie Fujimoto, 104
Petty, Sheila, 64n 5
Pfaff, Francoise, 53–4
Phipps, Cyrille, 222
Pickett, Bill, 103
Pietre, Pedro, 191
Point of View, 77
Pollard, Tommy, 135
poverty, 54, 61, 63, 168
Powell, Officer Laurence, 137n 2
Prieto, Claire, and Brand, Dionne: *Older Stronger Wiser*, 60
Public Broadcasting Service (PBS), xii, 14, 77, 103–6; *The American Experience*, 109, 111, 112, 113, 114
Purpose, Nia, 101
Q
Quan, H.T.L., 156

R
race, 127, 157, 166–8, 177, 190; films, 6–7
racism, xiii, 25, 28, 37, 57, 60–3, 68, 86–8, 130, 133, 140, 158, 161–2, 187–8, 199
Raciti, Salvadore, 98, 101
Ramirez, Trudy, 104
Randall, Dudley, 182
Reagen, Ronald, 163
Reagon, Bernice Johnson, 15–18, 178. *See also* Sweet Honey and the Rock; Parkerson, Michelle; "Let Your Light Shine: Historical Notes," 210; "We Who Believe in Freedom," 16; *We Who Believe in Freedom: Sweet Honey and the Rock ... Still On the Journey*, 16
Reconstruction, 36
Reed, Ishmael, 201
Reid, Mark, 64n 5
resistance to oppression, xiii, 14, 17, 45, 60, 159, 167, 196. *See also* oppression
Reyes, Gilberto, 81–2
Rhines, Jesse: "Stimulating a Dialogue Among African-American Viewers: An Interview with Daresha Kyi," 214
Rhue, Sylvia, 184
Rich, Adrienne, 197
Richardson, Ray: *Say Brother*, 95–6
Riggs, Marlon, 184, 186
right(s): civil, 9, 14–16, 24, 61, 137n 2, 159, 203; human, 17, 200; to vote, 16, 126
Rivero, Marita, 97, 100, 102
Robeson, Eslanda Goode, 7
Robeson, Paul, 7; *The Emperor Jones*, 183
Robinson, Cedric, 156, 168–9, 173n 19
Robinson, Debra, 223; *I Been Done Was Is*, 11; *Kiss Grandma Goodbye*, 11
Rollins, Elizabeth Lorde, 181
Rollins, Jonathan Lorde, 181
Ross, John, 123n 11
Ross, Monty, 164
Roth, Henry H.: *The Cruz Chronicle: A Novel of Adventure and Close Calls*, 12. *See also* Collins, Kathleen
Royals, Demetria and Louise Diamond, 223
Rushing, Byron, 110
Russell, Alice B., 7
Ryskamp, Judge Kenneth L., 132

S
Saar, Bettye, 25, 33
Sanchez, Sonia, 21, 24, 40n 8, 182; *Homecoming*, 24
Sandler, Kathe, 162, 223; "Finding a Space for Myself in My Film About Color Consciousness," 214; *A Question of Color*, 214; *Remembering Thelma*, 10
Saraf, Irving, 104

Say Brother, 95–6, 99–100
Sayles, John: *Brother From Another Planet,* 158
Schmidt, Nancy, 53
Scott, Dred, 132
Scott, Oz, xvii
Seiter, Ellen, 47, 64n 5
self-esteem, 59–60, 70
Sembene, Ousmane, 134
Senghor, Leopold Sedar, 29
Sesame Street, 95, 96. *See also* Public Broadcasting Service
Seven Principles, 97, 100, 102
sexism, 25, 54, 57, 60, 61–2, 87, 140, 158, 161–2, 187, 196
sexual harassment, 166, 173n 14
sexuality, xii, 56, 157, 167
Shange, Ntozake, 189–206; A Photograph, Spell #7, 189; *Betsy Brown,* 189, 194; *Boogie Woogie Landscape,* 189; *for colored girls who have considered suicide/when the rainbow is enuf,* xvii–xviii; *Liliane: Resurrection of the Daughter,* 189, 190; *nappy edges,* 189; *Ridin' the Moon in Texas,* 189, 192; *Sassafrass, Cypress & Indigo,* 189, 195, 196; *The Love Space Demands,* 189, 190
Shange, Ntozake, and Ladysmith Black Mambazo: *Nomathemba,* 190
Sharp, Saundra, 223
Shaw, Robert Gould, 109, 112
Shaw, Sara-Ann, 96
Shearer, Jacqueline, xiv, 4, 5–6, 209, 223; *A Minor Altercation,* 5–6, 8, 14, 110, 122n 6, 209; *The Massachusetts's 54th Colored Infantry,* xv, 5, 109–24, 213
Shen, Ted: "Reel Life: New Lessons From African Folklore," 213
Shepard, Bobby, 161, 164, 169
Shoup, Bob, 104
Simmonds, Felly Nkweto: *"She's Gotta Have It:* The Representation of Black Female Sexuality in Film," 212
Simmons, Aishah Shahidah, 223
Simone, Nina, 30–1
Simpson, Coreen, 79
slavery, xv, 10, 31, 37–8, 53, 56–8, 60, 62, 73–4, 75, 118, 126, 192, 196; shame about, 113–14, 117–18
Sly and the Family Stone, 96
Smith, Barbara, 67, 169, 182; "The Truth That Never Hurts: Black Lesbians in Fiction in the 1980s," 214
Smith, Cauleen, 5
Smith, Llew, 111
Smith, Valerie, 4, 69, 72; "Julie Dash: Filmmaker," 212; "Telling Family Secrets: Narrative and Ideology in *Suzanne, Suzanne,*" 213
Smith, Vejan Lee, 223

SNCC Freedom Singers, 16
social and cultural movements, 14–18
social realist cinema, 54–5, 57, 62
Solomons, Gus, 96
Soon Ja Du, 137n 1
Soul!, 95
South Africa, 17, 126
Southern Christian Leadership Conference (SCLC), 8, 16
Spillers, Hortense: "Mama's Baby, Papa's Maybe," 75
Splawn, P. Jane, xvii–xviii; "An Intimate Talk with Ntozake Shange: An Interview," 215
Springer, Christina, 223; "Waiting and Dreaming, Praying and Cleaning," 215
Springer, Claudia, 18n 4
Spruill, Jim, 96
Steichen, Edward, 28, 41n 12
stereotypes, 125, 140, 149, 183, 184; racist, 139, 184
Stone, Karen: *Medipaid Queens,* 14
storytelling, 120–21
Styron, William, 196–7
Suggs, Dawn, 170, 184, 224; *I Never Danced the Way Girls Were Supposed To,* 214
Sumter, Ellen, 224; *Rags and Old Love,* 14
Sundance Film Festival, xiii, 68, 123n 9, 146, 156
surrealism, 82–8, 93
Sweet Honey and the Rock, 16, 17, 19n 21, 178. *See also* Reagon, Bernice; Parkerson, Michelle

T
Tajima, Renee, 4
Tapscott, Horace, 35. *See also* McCullough, Barbara
Tarkovsky, Andrei, 38
Tate, Greg, 36
Tatum, Art, 35
Taylor, Betty Blayton, 11
Taylor, Jocelyn, 184, 224
Teshome, Gabriel, 21
The Cosby Show, 14
The Green Pastures, 134
Thigpen, Dorothy: "A Conversation with Ayoka Chenzira," 215
Thiong'o, Ngugi wa, 25
Third World Newsreel, 4, 178
Third World, the, 39n 1, 136, 191, 201–5
Thomas, Roy, 10
Tillman, Russell, 96
Tucker, Lorenzo, 103
Turner, Nat, 196–7
U
UCLA: The Los Angeles School, 21–41
UCLA Film and Television Archives, 137

Udechukwu, Obiora, 30
Udongo, Ayanna, 224
Underwood, Blair, 110, 111, 120

V
Van der Zee, James, 26, 38
Van Peebles, Mario: *New Jack City,* 158
Vaughan, Sarah, 165
Victoria, Christa, 68
Vidato, Yolanda, 35
video installations, xvi, 130–4, 167
Vietnam, 95, 114
Visual Communications (VC), 136
Vorkapich, Slavko, 38
voter registration project, 15, 16

W
Walker, Alice, 23–4, 40n 8, 65n 37, 101, 197; "Finding the Green Stone," 40; *The Color Purple,* xviii
Walker, Madame C.J., 7; and the Walker Theatre, 7
Wallace, Michelle: "Negative Images: Towards a Black Feminist Cultural Criticsim," 211
Washington, Booker T., 7
Washington, Denzel, 109, 112
Washington, Dinah, 165
Waters, Jack, 184
Waters, Maxine, 127
Watkins, Claire Andrade, 4
Watts, 139; Rebellion, the, 22, 23. *See also* L.A. Rebellion
Weber, Alicia, 161
Weems, Carrie May, 26
Welbon, Yvonne, 5, 224; "Black Lesbian Film and Video Art: Feminism Studies, Performance Studies," 214; *Cinematic Jazz of Julie Dash,* 212; *Remembering Wei Yi-Fang, Remembering Myself,* 214; *Sisters in the Life: First Love,* 214
Welcome, Madame Toussaint, 7
welfare, 61, 75
Wells, Ida B., 126
Were You There, xv, 102, 104–7
West, Carmen Langford, 104
West, Cornell, 44

WGBH-TV, xv, 95–9, 112, 113
White, Charles, 27
White, Minor, 28
Whitfield, Lynn, xvii
Whitfield, Vantile, 78–9, 102
Wilcox, Preston, 100
Wilentz, Gay, 46; *Binding Cultures: Black Women Writers in Africa and the Diaspora,* 44
Williams, Patricia, 75
Wills, Dorothy, 60
Wilmington Ten, the, 17
Wilson, Artie, 103
Wilson, August, 114; *Joe Turner's Come and Gone,* 114
Wind, Timothy, 137
Winters, Shelley, 75
WNET-NY, 13, 95
Wolfe, George C., 79, 84, 86
Wolof, 132, 148
Women: Against Pornography, 196; Against Violence Against Women and Children, 196; Make Movies, 4, 6
Wonder, Stevie, 95
Wong, Eddie, 136
Woodard, Alfred, xvii
Woodberry, Billy, 21, 106, 136
Woods, Fronza, 224
Woodson, Jacqueline and Catherine Saalfield, 224
Wright, Josephine, 123n 11
Wright, Richard: *The Outsider,* 173n 14; *Twelve Million Black Votes,* 28

Y
Year of the Jubilee Choir, 123n 11
Yoruba, the, 30, 38
Young, Jean, xiv
Young, Linda, 31

Z
Zaentz, Saul: Fantasy Films, 105
Zagone, Bob, 104
Zollar, Jawole Willa Jo, 32